Using Wordless Picture Books
Authors and Activities

Katharyn Tuten-Puckett
Virginia H. Richey

1993
TEACHER IDEAS PRESS
A Division of
Libraries Unlimited, Inc.
Englewood, Colorado

TEACHER IDEAS PRESS
A Division of
Libraries Unlimited, Inc.
P.O. Box 6633
Englewood, CO 80155-6633

Library of Congress Cataloging-in-Publication Data

Tuten-Puckett, Katharyn E.
    Using wordless picture books : authors and activities / Katharyn
Tuten-Puckett, Virginia H. Richey.
    xxi, 233 p. 22x28 cm.
    Includes bibliographical references and index.
    ISBN 0-87287-877-5
    1. Picture books for children--United States--Educational aspects-
-Handbooks, manuals, etc. 2. Language arts--United States-
-Handbooks, manuals, etc. 3. Children's literature--United States-
-Bibliography. 4. Picture books for children--United States-
-Bibliography. I. Richey, Virginia H. II. Title.
LB1044.9.P49T88 1993
372.64--dc20   93-10792
                                   CIP

minster
OX2
5)
5)

Using W   ill   oks

Contents

Foreword

One of my favorite artifacts of literacy comes from a kindergarten classroom. Emily's picture says it all. "I'm into books! Once I get into them I can't get out!"

In this book, Katharyn Tuten-Puckett and Virginia Richey suggest that one easy way to get children into books is by using wordless ones. They argue that because wordless picture books demand that the reader be an active composer, they are an ideal medium that teachers can use to initiate literacy instruction in the classroom.

Wordless picture books hold a unique place in the history of children's literature as well as in the history of picture books and illustration. Wordless picture books focus attention on the act of interpretation and pose literacy as an act of composition. Wordless picture books call for careful observation and invite children, such as Emily, to really "get into books." You—like me, Emily, Emily's teacher, and the authors of *Using Wordless Picture Books: Authors and Activities*—will find that "once you are into them, you can't get out!"

Preschool teachers, special education teachers, teachers of children whose primary language is something other than English, and persons working with adults new to literacy will find this resource invaluable. Whole language teachers and media specialists will find this a resource they cannot live without.

Jerome C. Harste, Ph.D.
Indiana University
President, Whole Language Umbrella, 1993-1995
Board member of the International Reading Association,
    1989-1992

Acknowledgments

We wish to thank all the artists/authors for their wordless picture books; these books have provided us with so much reading pleasure and have stimulated numerous discussions and ideas. We also want to thank their editors and publishers for seeing the value of this genre of books. We appreciate the prompt replies that authors and editors have given to our written requests for information and photographs.

Special thanks to our editors, Dr. David Loertscher, for his continued support and his great patience, and Dr. Suzanne Barchers for her suggestions; to William Hamlin for his knowledge of computers and his willingness to share that knowledge; and to Elizabeth Richey for her editing skills and advice.

This book would not have been possible without the assistance and support of many people, and we are most grateful to each of them.

Our families—Marliece and James Puckett, Thayr and Will Richey—have encouraged us and been understanding about the time we have devoted to this project.

We thank the staff members of the children's department at Monroe County Public Library, who are always there when we need them; so are Nola Hartman and Susan Jackson in the reference department. Judith Dye, Indiana University School of Library and Information Science, has provided encouragement and resources. Linda Cornwell, Learning Resources Unit, Indiana Department of Education, is consistently supportive and enthusiastic about the use of children's literature for learning and enjoyment.

Sandi Ali, Lyons Elementary School; Denise Ogren, Stinesville Elementary School; Margaret Lieberman and Mollie Dudgeon, West Vigo Elementary School; and others have reviewed sections of the manuscript and provided useful comments.

Introduction

A wordless picture book is a unique form of literature in which the meaning and content of the work is conveyed entirely in illustration.

The inclusion of these works in library and media center activities and in classrooms has many benefits. The wordless picture book

- stimulates creative writing and other active responses to literature;

- establishes skills used in reading for the prereader;

- reinforces skills used in reading for the weak reader;

- liberates the reader to use personal vocabulary;

- offers successful, peer-level experiences for those for whom print poses difficulty;

- allows gifted students to respond to their potential levels;

- gives each student the opportunity to participate in creating meaning along with the artist/author of the book;

- enables the non-English speaking or nonliterate adult to share literature with a child;

- encourages the appreciation of illustration and narrative art forms;

- develops sophistication in story making;

- enhances visual competence;

- increases visual literacy;

- furthers language skills.

Many educational techniques used with other forms of literature can also be used with wordless picture books. Librarians can use them in booktalks; students can use them for book reports; teachers can incorporate them into curriculum units and lesson plans. This book is designed as a starting point for those who want to go further in incorporating wordless picture books into their literature explorations.

Using Wordless Picture Books is intended to be a project starter and an idea sparker. Please don't feel tied to the specifics of our suggestions. For example, if a title listed under "Related Materials" is not available, look for substitute titles.

When references are made to a type of material or activity and directions are not given, it is because specific ones are not needed. For example, many different science projects might be used to illustrate a principle such as condensation, with different projects selected for a kindergarten class, an older elementary gifted and talented class, and a public library. Each of these projects would serve equally as a related experience for the wordless picture book. Use local resources to select appropriate projects.

What about age or grade level? We recommend wordless picture books for an extremely wide range of ages, including adult learners. Occasionally we have said older or younger, but in general we have not specified a level for several reasons. Librarians often work with many ages at once, or present the same activity at various levels. Many school systems are grouping students in multiage and multilevel classrooms. Traditional categories may not apply to a user's situation. We often find that the same book or activity can be presented to both older and younger readers with differing outcomes due to the developmental stages of the audience, but with equally satisfying results. A wordless picture book will have different levels of meaning depending on the age and experience of the reader.

You will notice some activites under the headings "In the Library (or In the Classroom)" and "In the Classroom (or In the Library)." We hope to facilitate cooperative ventures in which librarians and teachers focus together on authors or titles. Many teachers will want to use library activities, and many librarians will want to use classroom activities. Use any idea that appeals to you, regardless of the designation.

Be creative, adapt these ideas and add your own to them. Find additional resources to use with each activity. Use this book as a starting place for you and the children and students you work with to begin an enjoyable exploration of this rich and marvelous genre of literature.

BOOK ORGANIZATION

Section 1—Individual Author Studies

We have selected artists/authors with a variety of illustrative styles and storytelling techniques. In considering authors we looked for an international representation, for establishd artists with a body of wordless works, and for a variety in genre and type of book. Section 1 includes:

- Portraits of the authors, along with a personal quote about wordless picture books from each of them.

- Brief biographies of the authors taken from information they and their publishers provided, and from published sources such as *Something About the Author* (additional information may be found in biographical references to supplement what we have provided).

- Selected bibliographies of the authors' works, including books with text and books written by someone else, but illustrated by the featured artist. In the bibliography of each person's wordless books we have attempted to be complete. When possible, we have included some of the various nonprint formats in which his or her work appears.

- An overview of the wordless titles by each artist/author.

- Activities for incorporating these artists/authors and their wordless picture books in classrooms, library media centers, and public libraries. The activities under each artist/author are numbered beginning with 1. The section "Ways to Use Activities" lists the activities that can be used with each of the specific titles, plus the activities to use to promote the study of the author. Activities are grouped by curriculum area to promote the inclusion of wordless picture books in literature studies across the curriculum.

Section 2—Individual Title Studies

In section 2, individual wordless picture books are used as a basis for activities in the classroom, the library media center, and the public library. Titles were selected to represent a variety of illustrative styles and storytelling techniques, fiction and nonfiction, and both established and beginning authors. An attempt was made to include books in print. This section includes the following:

- Brief information is given about each artist/author. Limited information was found for several of the newer authors or those with fewer publications.

- A selected list of books the artist has written or illustrated is included, followed by a list of his or her wordless picture books.

- A brief description of the title is given.

- Five activities that might be used in the library (or classroom), and five activities that might be used in the classroom (or library) are suggested. Lists of possible resources are included for those activities that require them. These lists are divided into fiction and nonfiction works and into print and nonprint works. A listing of distributors for the nonprint materials appears in appendix C.

Appendix A — Author Birthdates

A list of known birthdays for artists/authors from both sections 1 and 2 are organized month by month. This list can be used to celebrate authors' birthdays (by featuring their works) or to focus on an author each month.

Appendix B — Author Geography

Wordless picture books are an international genre and the artists/authors come from many different countries. The original birthplace and the current home of the author is included, depending on the availability of the information.

Appendix C — Addresses for Nonprint Resources

Section 1

Individual Author Studies

Mitsumasa Anno

I believe that the world created by words and the world created by images are different. Very often I hear that because some of my books do not have any text, they are difficult to understand. I really do not know how to respond to such a comment. Look at the paintings at museums. They hardly have any words. I hope this will tell you why I make the wordless picture books.

—Mitsumasa Anno

ABOUT THE AUTHOR

Mitsumasa Anno was born on March 20, 1926, in the small town of Tsuwano in western Japan, where his parents owned an inn. Tsuwano is in a valley surrounded by mountains, and as a child Anno wondered what was on the other side. As he grew and saw the rice fields on the other side of the mountains, and the ocean beyond, he wanted to continue traveling and seeing more. His desire to be an artist started in his childhood, when he liked to draw favorite scenes from historical stories.

After high school, Anno was drafted into the army, and later he was an elementary school art teacher. He believes that children see things differently than adults, that they have a different sense of perspective—partly because of their small faces with close-set eyes, and partly because of their limited life experiences.

Anno is recognized internationally as an innovative illustrator because of his artistic vision, his use of a variety of techniques, and his unique ability to translate abstractions into illustrations.

Anno has received numerous awards and honors in Japan and internationally. *Anno's Alphabet* received a 1974 Kate Greenaway Medal commendation, the 1975 Boston Globe-Horn Book Award, the 1976 Christopher Award, and the 1977 Golden Apple Award. He also received the Boston Globe-Horn Book Award in 1978 for *Anno's Journey*. He has twice received the prestigious Bologna Children's Book Fair First Prize for Graphic Excellence in Books for Youth, in 1978 for *The Unique World of Mitsumasa Anno* and in 1980 for *Anno's Song Book*. He was awarded the 1984 Hans Christian Andersen Medal for his body of work.

Anno is married and has two grown children, a son and a daughter. He lives in Tokyo, Japan.

ANNO'S BOOKLIST

Selected Books by the Author

Anno's Aesop: A Book of Fables by Aesop and Mr. Fox Retold by Mitsumasa Anno. Orchard, 1989.

Anno's Magical ABC: An Anamorphic Alphabet. Philomel, 1981.

Anno's Math Games. Philomel, 1987.

Anno's Math Games II. Philomel, 1989.

Anno's Math Games III. Philomel, 1991.

Anno's Medieval World. Philomel, 1990.

Anno's Mysterious Multiplying Jar. Philomel, 1983.

Anno's Sundial. Philomel, 1987.

In Shadowland. Orchard, 1988.

The King's Flower. Philomel, 1979.

The Unique World of Mitsumasa Anno: Selected Works 1968-1977. Philomel, 1980.

Upside-Downers: More Pictures to Stretch the Imagination. Weatherhill, 1971.

Selected Books Illustrated by the Author

All in a Day. Philomel, 1990.

Anno's Hat Tricks by Akihiro Nozaki. Philomel, 1985.

Socrates and the Three Little Pigs by Tuyosi Mori. Putnam, 1986.

Wordless Books by the Author

Anno's Alphabet: An Adventure in Imagination. Crowell, 1975.

Anno's Animals. Philomel, 1979.

Anno's Britain. Philomel, 1982.

Anno's Counting Book. Crowell, 1977.

Anno's Counting House. Philomel, 1982.

Anno's Faces. Philomel, 1989.

Anno's Flea Market. Philomel, 1984.

Anno's Italy. Philomel, 1980.

Anno's Journey. Philomel, 1981.

Anno's Masks. Philomel, 1990.

Anno's Peekaboo. Philomel, 1988.

Anno's U.S.A. Philomel, 1983.

Dr. Anno's Magical Midnight Circus. Weatherhill, 1972.

Topsy-Turvies: Pictures to Stretch the Imagination. Weatherhill, 1970.

ABOUT ANNO'S WORDLESS BOOKS

The depth of thought behind each of these works makes them approachable on many different levels. A cool, intellectual style with a whimsical sense of humor marks Anno's artwork. His careful line is enlivened with a subtle and effective use of color.

Three concept books, *Anno's Alphabet, Anno's Counting Book*, and *Anno's Counting House*, take genres often restricted to the youngest reader and create an interest and challenge for all ages. The alphabet letters are apparently crafted from wood, yet each has a peculiar twist to tease the eye and confuse the mind. The two counting books go beyond the presentation of numbers. Concepts include sets, manipulations of amounts, numerical relationships and properties, and other mathematical ideas.

Anno's Journey books follow a lone traveler through Europe, Britain, Italy, and the United States. In each title, the landscape is spread out like a map unrolling, with the small figure on horseback proceeding through a montage of significant details. The reader can find characters from history, religion, and literature; famous landmarks and typical architecture; scenes from fine art and folklore; curious visual jokes; snatches of music; and activities typical of each region and its past. The more culturally literate reader will identify more of the items pictured, but even a young child can enjoy finding the man and his horse in each busy scene.

Anno's Flea Market takes the fascination with artifacts of cultural significance even further. Here, in an open air market, wares of all sorts are spread before the viewer, encapsulating history and detailing the development of such diverse areas as dentistry and music.

Another type of visual game is found in *Anno's Animals*. Here approximately 100 outline animals have been hidden in dull green spreads of a woods, with trees and leaves drawn in a broken line, which makes finding the hidden pictures a difficult challenge.

Dr. Anno's Magical Midnight Circus and *Topsy-Turvies* are intricately detailed visual puzzles in which the impossible becomes visible. Inspired inventiveness shows tiny people busy in situations that defy logic and gravity. In the manner of Escher, up becomes down and inside becomes outside, while transformations of one thing into another trick the eye. These illusions are drawn with sharply detailed lines and watercolors in vibrant hues.

In contrast to these visually sophisticated and symbolically complex works, Anno has also created several very simple books for the youngest reader, who will enjoy playing peekaboo with *Anno's Peekaboo* and will laugh at the vegetables with funny faces in *Anno's Faces*.

ACTIVITIES

Arts/Crafts

1. Anno has commented that the works of Escher affected his style, and he has been called the "nursery Escher." Share pictures of works by artists from the surrealistic school of art, such as Escher, Dali, and Magritte, and have students compare elements of their art to Anno's illustrations.

2. Anno uses details, or "quotes," from many famous artworks. Bring in pictures of the original works by Courbet, Renoir, Millet, and Seurat. Locate the "quote" that Anno has used and compare it to the original.

3. Have students pay close attention to the deceptive use of perspective in *Topsy-Turvies* before drawing their own box, staircase, wall, or house showing perspective.

4. Enlarge and reproduce the empty room from *Anno's Counting House* so that each student has her or his own copy to furnish to scale with original drawings.

5. Share *Anno's Alphabet* with the class, having students note the unusual three-dimensional letters, the visuals representing those letters, and in page borders the hidden objects that begin with each letter. Have each student design a two-page spread using one letter of the alphabet to make a class alphabet book. Include mirror borders with hidden objects beginning with that letter.

Bulletin Board/Display

6. Make a display of books written and/or illustrated by Mitsumasa Anno. Use a photocopier to enlarge his photograph and use as the center of the display.

7. After sharing *Anno's Flea Market*, have students design a flea market mural. Students select individual "booths" for their wares and then use magazines, mail order catalogs, and newspapers to cut out pictures of goods for their booths.

8. After sharing Anno's Journey books, have students, through research, design a mural to guide Anno's traveler through their state. Students can incorporate state literature, folklore, historical events, famous people, landmarks, and activities as the traveler goes from area to area. Anno's traveler is available as a rubber stamp from Kidstamps.

9. In *Dr. Anno's Magical Midnight Circus*, the various scenes appear to come out of the pages of the illustrated book, which is open and acts as a backdrop to the action, creating a three-dimensional effect. Design a bulletin board for student book reports using a similar technique. A white paper cutout of an opened book can be used in the background, and students can design a scene from the book to place in front to simulate the scene coming from the pages. The book title and author and the student's name can be placed on a label to go above or below the book.

Geography

10. Mitsumasa Anno was born in the small village of Tsuwano in western Japan. He currently lives in Tokyo. Locate these two places on a map of Japan. Students can use library resources to learn about Japan and the culture of that country. What is the geography and climate? What is the language and how is it written? What foods do the Japanese eat and how do they eat them? What are some of the famous landmarks? Students can create a book or mural of their findings similar to Anno's Journey books.

Language Arts

11. As you share one of the Journey books with a small group, have students keep a list of the discoveries they make as they carefully view the picture. Discuss what each object represents and why it might have been included by the author.

12. When the reader opens *Topsy-Turvies* or *Dr. Anno's Magical Midnight Circus*, the little people appear to be mysteriously occupied and to have been engaged in their activities for some time. Have students create the story of what was happening before the book was opened, or what might happen after it is closed.

13. Many of the illustrations in these books appear to be nonsensical. Before having students write their own nonsensical poems, share with them nonsensical writing from authors such as Lewis Carroll and Edward Lear.

14. As Anno's lone traveler goes through the Journey books, there are many things the reader views that the traveler wouldn't be able to see. Have students imagine themselves as the lone traveler as he goes through one of the books and write a travel journal of what the traveler might see and think as he goes on one of his journeys.

15. Although these books are told in visual narrative form, Anno's traveler would encounter many languages as he travels through these countries. Develop a class list of languages that the traveler might hear on his journeys. Provide examples of each of these languages and discuss language development and acquisition. Discuss the language of visual narrative and how it can be understood by people in many countries. Is visual narrative a universal language, or does the viewer have to be visually literate?

16. Use *Anno's Counting House* to begin a discussion on moving into a new house. Have students describe, orally or in writing, the room of their dreams and how they would furnish it.

Library Research

17. Have students use the author catalog to locate other books written and/or illustrated by Mitsumasa Anno. Develop a set of books by this author for use in the library or classroom.

18. As students read the Journey books, have them select individual topics they would like to know more about and use library resources to research those topics. Example: Fox hunting in England; the significance of storks nesting on roofs in northern Europe; the Brunelleschi Dome in Florence, Italy.

19. Have students use the subject catalog to locate other alphabet or counting books to compare and contrast with the ones by Anno.

20. Use the library to locate tourist travel guides to Italy (such as Frommer's). Compare tourist guides to *Anno's Italy*.

21. Have students use *Anno's Italy, Anno's Britain*, or *Anno's U.S.A.* as a resource to develop a text set about one of those countries. As students find historical events, landmarks, architecture, and so forth in Anno's book, they can look for other library resources on those topics.

Math

22. Discuss the conservation of numbers using *Anno's Counting House*. Use a felt board with felt outlines of the two houses and felt pieces to represent the children as they move from one house to the other. Help younger students understand that there is always the same number of figures, whether they are in one house or split between the two houses.

23. *Anno's Counting Book* begins with a blank page, and as the pages are turned, objects on the pages accumulate to represent numbers from 0 to 12. Have students use markers in different colors to match the number of things as they accumulate. Do cumulative problems.

24. *Topsy-Turvies* can be used to begin a discussion of the principles of topological geometry.

25. Many of Anno's drawings appear to have only one surface, causing the reader to wonder if such a structure could actually exist. Construct Möbius strips and demonstrate that each one has only one surface by drawing a continuous center line that covers the entire strip.

Music

26. The characters in *Dr. Anno's Magical Midnight Circus* play music on instruments made from common household objects such as a glass, a comb, spoons, and so forth. Discuss homemade musical instruments and have students find things with which to create their own band.

27. Most of Anno's books include a picture of a parade. Look for the parade scenes in these books to share with students. Discuss instruments used in parades and why music is part of most parades. Play parade music and have a parade around the school.

28. Many famous musicians appear in the Journey books. Search through the books and make a list of the musicians. Play selections from their music and discuss why Anno included them.

29. Invite students to make a list of the countries that the lone traveler goes through on his journeys. Locate selections of music from each of the countries listed. Play the music and discuss how music differs from region to region.

Science

30. Begin a discussion on optical illusions by locating and examining examples in Anno's books. Study how the eye can be tricked by optical illusions.

31. As students work individually or in pairs, have them locate as many animals as they can in *Anno's Animals*. Compile a class list of the animals that are hidden in this book. Discuss animal camouflage and the ways different animals use natural camouflage to protect themselves in the natural environment.

32. The little men in *Topsy-Turvies* are busily building a variety of unusual objects. Rube Goldberg inventions are also unusual objects. Discuss these inventions and have students design their own Rube Goldberg invention that the little men could work on.

Social Studies

33. As students look through the Journey books, have them pay special attention to the variety of architecture represented. What historical periods can be identified by the architecture? What accounts for the differences in styles, materials used, and so forth?

34. The Journey books include pictures of many traditional games such as hopscotch and Maypole dances. Have students go through the books, locating games that children are playing, and make a list of traditional games. Research these games to learn about their background and how to play them.

35. Discuss the term *popular culture*. As students read *Anno's U.S.A.*, have them look for examples of popular culture and make a list of their findings. Have the class review the list and determine what has been left off. What other things might be included?

36. As students read *Anno's Journey* and *Anno's Britain*, have them look for examples of craftspeople and traditional crafts such as shearing, spinning, working a cider press, basket weaving, and so forth. Make a class list of these crafts, then invite students to each choose one craft to learn more about.

37. The Journey books portray numerous people involved in diverse activities. Develop a class list of activities that appear in one of the books and begin a discussion on which of the activities still exist and which ones have changed through the use of machinery and technology.

Group Activities

38. Take a class walking field trip with each student pretending to be Anno's lone traveler. Have students make careful observations of the details they see and keep a written journal or artist's sketchbook. Use these travel notes to create a classroom mural of the walk.

Other

39. List the titles of books referred to in the Journey books through visual references of characters in the illustrations. Locate the books and make a display of them. Discuss with the students why Anno might have included those titles.

40. Invite a librarian to present a booktalk or storyhour on other books illustrated by Japanese illustrators, or to do a presentation of Japanese folktales.

Ways to Use Activities

For an author study. *See* 1, 6, 10, 17

For *Anno's Alphabet*. *See* 5, 19, 25

For *Anno's Animals*. *See* 31

For *Anno's Britain*. *See* 2, 8, 11, 14, 15, 18, 21, 28, 29, 33, 34, 36, 37, 38, 39

For *Anno's Counting Book*. *See* 19, 23

For *Anno's Counting House*. *See* 4, 16, 19, 22

For *Anno's Flea Market*. *See* 2, 7, 18, 28, 33, 34, 37

For *Anno's Italy*. *See* 2, 8, 11, 14, 15, 18, 20, 21, 28, 29, 33, 34, 37, 38, 39

For *Anno's Journey*. *See* 2, 8, 11, 14, 15, 18, 28, 29, 33, 34, 36, 37, 38, 39

For *Anno's U.S.A*. *See* 2, 8, 11, 14, 15, 18, 21, 28, 29, 33, 34, 35, 37, 38, 39

For *Dr. Anno's Magical Midnight Circus*. *See* 9, 12, 13, 26

For *Topsy-Turvies*. *See* 3, 12, 13, 24, 25, 32

For all titles by Anno. *See* 13, 25, 27, 30, 38, 39, 40

Alexandra Day

The nearly wordless "format" of the "Carl" books was not so much a choice against using words to tell the story as a choice to identify with Carl and the baby in their activities, and dogs and babies don't talk. Even this is something which happened naturally, and I didn't even think about why I had not chosen to narrate it until much later. The silence—as the great silent comedians discovered—also has advantages in that the attention is kept focused on the visual, and little details, visual jokes, etc. are easier and more natural in the atmosphere of no words. I am primarily an illustrator—I grew up wanting to be a painter and still paint for my own pleasure when I can squeeze in the time—so the visual is my natural medium.

—Alexandra Day

ABOUT THE AUTHOR

Alexandra Day is the pseudonym used by Sandra Darling. She was born into a family of artists on September 7, 1941. She grew up wanting to be a painter and was trained as an artist from an early age. She has gained recognition for her lifelike, detailed illustrations and creative animal stories. She has designed stationery and note cards and, in addition to writing and illustrating her own works, has illustrated books for other writers. Sandra Darling was married from 1970 to 1986 and has four children. The Darlings founded the Blue Lantern Studio in San Diego.

Alexandra Day has received several honors for her works, including the 1984 Children's Choice Award from the International Reading Association and Children's Book Council for *Teddy Bears' Picnic* and the 1984 Parents' Choice Award for Illustration for *The Blue Faience Hippopotamus*.

DAY'S BOOKLIST

Selected Books by the Author

Frank and Ernest. Scholastic, 1988.

Frank and Ernest Drive a Truck. Scholastic, due fall 1993.

Frank and Ernest Play Ball. Scholastic, 1990.

Paddy's Payday. Viking, 1989.

River Parade. Viking, 1990.

Selected Books Illustrated by the Author

The Blue Faience Hippopotamus by Jean Marshall Grant. Green Tiger, 1984.

Children of Wonder, 4 vols., by Cooper Edens. Vol. 1, *Helping the Sun*; vol. 2, *Helping the Animals*; vol. 3, *Helping the Flowers*; vol. 4, *Helping the Night*. Green Tiger, 1987.

Teddy Bears' Picnic by Jimmy Kennedy. Green Tiger, 1983.

Teddy Bears' Picnic Cookbook with Abigail Darling. Penguin, 1991.

When You Wish Upon a Star by Ned Washington. Green Tiger, 1987.

Wordless Books by the Author

Carl Goes Shopping. Farrar, Straus & Giroux, 1989.

Carl's Afternoon in the Park. Farrar, Straus & Giroux, 1991.

Carl's Christmas. Farrar, Straus & Giroux, 1990.

Carl's Masquerade. Farrar, Straus & Giroux, 1992.

Good Dog, Carl. Farrar, Straus & Giroux, 1985.

ABOUT DAY'S WORDLESS BOOKS

The premise of this series of books is that a mother leaves Carl, a large cheerful rottweiler dog, as a babysitter. In each book, Carl and the baby are left in different surroundings or circumstances, which they explore together (often creating messes as they do so), and each time Carl manages to have the baby back where it was left by the time the parent returns. The unaware mother inevitably praises Carl, leaving the reader as the only witness to the way in which Carl has entertained the baby. The good dog who supposedly hasn't moved from his post by the baby's side is shown to have a secret life, which he shares affectionately with his small charge.

Carl is portrayed as a cheerful participant in the baby's escapades, a mischievous instigator of romps, as well as a thoughtful caretaker. In *Good Dog, Carl*, the action takes place in the home as Carl helps the baby climb out of the crib, bounce on the mother's bed and explore her dresser, slide down the laundry chute, dance, fix a snack, and clean up afterward. There seems to be a familiarity about their actions, as if these events take place regularly when the parent leaves.

In *Carl Goes Shopping*, the duo is left at the bottom of an escalator in a large department store. While mother goes off to shop, Carl and the baby visit various departments—snacking in the food department, letting out the pets in the pet department, and trying on hats in front of the television sets. Carl races the baby back to the carriage just in time and is sitting patiently by the carriage when the mother returns.

The parents leave Carl in charge as they leave the house after trimming the tree in *Carl's Christmas*. Carl dresses the baby warmly and they go outside on the snowy Christmas eve. The two visit a toy store, give to the poor, join a group of carolers, and take a stray dog home with them to await Santa. Carl helps Santa Claus distribute the presents before taking his place by the slumbering baby.

Carl's Afternoon in the Park is full of the sun-drenched ambience of a big city park. Here Carl and the baby are joined by a rambunctious rottweiler puppy. While the mother and her friend go off to have tea, the puppy and the baby are left in Carl's care. The trio enjoys the flowers, petting zoo, ice cream, and other pleasures of the park until Carl spies the adults preparing to return and gets everyone back to the spot where they were left.

The parents leave Carl in charge of the baby once again as they leave for a masquerade party in *Carl's Masquerade*. With the baby on his back, Carl goes to the party, where they eat ice cream bars and see a guest costumed as a rottweiler with a baby on its back, among the other original and creative costumes. The pair sees the baby's parents and carefully avoids them. They enjoy the revelry and have their photograph taken. Carl and the baby race home when the parents leave the party, and when the mother returns home, the baby is carefully tucked in her crib with Carl on the floor beside it.

Sumptuous paintings, rich with color and texture, lift this series above others. The beautifully realized illustration has an old-fashioned flavor and gives a feel of the 1940s. Careful attention to detail rewards the observant reader with the thrill of being in on a very special secret. Each escapade is good-humored and funny to small children. The fantasy idea of the dog as caretaker and the overall warmth and pleasant nature of the books create great appeal. The "don't let mother know" nature of the endings provides a satisfying conclusion for young readers.

ACTIVITIES

Arts/Crafts

1. The author uses egg tempera for some of her illustrations. Discuss the technique and then invite students to use tempera paints to create their own pictures of Carl and the baby.

2. Carl's paw print can be seen on the last page of both *Carl Goes Shopping* and *Carl's Christmas*. Have students make paw prints on paper using a carved potato or other print-making technique.

3. In *Carl's Afternoon in the Park*, an outdoor painter paints a picture on his easel of Carl and the baby. Discuss the different styles and paints the artist might use for his painting. Take students outdoors to sketch something they see.

4. Teach students to twist long, thin balloons into dog shapes, such as the ones Carl and the baby see in *Carl's Afternoon in the Park*.

5. Have students design costumes they might wear to a masquerade. Designs can be drawn or painted on paper; or students could make costumes to wear to a classroom masquerade.

Bulletin Board/Display

6. Make a display of books written and/or illustrated by Alexandra Day. Use a photocopier to enlarge her photo and use as the center of the display.

7. Divide students into groups and have each group make a mural for the setting of one of the Carl books (the house, the store, the park, the neighborhood, the party).

8. Use the overhead projector to make large pictures of Carl, the baby, the puppy, and the mother. Color or paint each character, and laminate and display the pictures with multiple copies of the books.

Geography

9. The author lives in San Diego, California. Use library resources to learn about San Diego. Where is it located? What is the climate? How big is the city? What are some San Diego landmarks? *Carl's Afternoon in the Park* is set in Balboa Park. What can you learn about Balboa Park? What other San Diego settings might be used for books about Carl and the baby?

Language Arts

10. Have students take one of the books and relate the story to a personal experience by telling about a time they have been shopping, gone to the park, had a babysitter, been to a party, and so forth.

11. Have students write journal entries, from the mother's point of view, about a day featured in one of the books.

12. Have students, working in pairs, select a scene from one of the books and create dialogue for the characters in that scene to present to the rest of the class.

13. After a discussion of verbs, have students go through one of the Carl books and use verbs to describe all of the things happening on a page. You may want to make a class list of the verbs to use in writing other sentences or paragraphs about Carl.

14. In storytelling form, narrate *Carl's Afternoon in the Park* as you share it with the class. Stop as the puppy takes hold of the balloon and begins to become airborne (cover the following page so it doesn't show). From that point, have students develop a class story. The teacher can stop and point to a student to continue the adventure. After 30-45 seconds, the student stops and points to another student to continue the story, and so forth.

Library Research

15. Have students use the subject catalog or booklists to develop a collection of fiction and picture books that have dogs as main characters, or books that portray a special relationship between a dog and a child. Each student can read one of these books and tell how the characters are the same or different from Carl and the baby.

16. Have students use library resources to learn about the breed and care of dogs known as rottweilers.

Math

17. Make a movable elevator dial, such as the one seen in *Carl Goes Shopping*, to be used for number recognition with young students. Working in small groups, children can take turns calling out the number of the floor they want to go to and setting the elevator dial.

18. In both *Carl's Christmas* and *Carl Goes Shopping*, there are many things that shoppers could purchase. Use these pictures to introduce spending money and making shopping lists. Have students look through the books, find things they would like to purchase, and write those items on their shopping lists. Use mail order catalogs for prices, or make them up. Discuss how much it would cost students to buy all the things on their individual lists. Talk about taxes and add the amount of tax to the purchase price.

Music

19. Make a class list of the songs the carolers might sing in *Carl's Christmas*. Choose one song and have the class "bark along" as Carl might do.

20. In *Good Dog, Carl*, the radio is turned on and Carl and the baby dance; in *Carl's Masquerade*, the costumed guests dance. What type of music might they be dancing to? Have students bring in music they like to dance to and have a class dance.

21. There is a merry-go-round in *Carl's Afternoon in the Park*. Discuss merry-go-rounds and the type of music they play. Play a recording of merry-go-round or calliope music.

Science

22. The illustrations in *Carl's Afternoon in the Park* show the beautiful flora found in the park. Use these illustrations to begin a discussion on local flora. Take a walking field trip around the neighborhood to look for flora, and use field guides to identify them.

23. Carl is a rottweiler. Discuss different breeds of dogs and their characteristics. How have different breeds developed?

24. While Carl, the baby, and the puppy are going through the park, they meet a man who has binoculars and they each look through a pair. What do they see? Have students look through binoculars, telescopes, and microscopes. What do they see? How are these scientific instruments different? Discuss their uses and how they are made. Include information about the lenses and how they are made.

Social Studies

25. As each of the Carl books is shared, have students notice the artifacts in each (escalators, radios, refrigerators, television sets, and so forth). Make a class list of artifacts for each book. What do these lists tell about the society in which the books are set? Would these artifacts be found in all societies of the world? Have a class discussion on these items. Are any of them universal? Are any of them European in origin? In what other countries might they have originated? Are any of them found only in the United States? What do these artifacts tell about socioeconomic conditions?

26. Use *Carl Goes Shopping* to begin a study on the rise and fall of the American department store. How many students have been to a department store that has an escalator or an elevator? Have students talk with their parents and grandparents about department stores and downtown locations, then compare them to malls. Where is most of the shopping done in your area?

27. As you share the Carl books, introduce a unit on child care, since many students have younger siblings or will be babysitting for others. What care do babies need? Who provides care for babies and small children? What do caretakers of young children need to know? Would you really leave a baby or toddler in the care of a dog?

Group Activities

28. Carl is left in charge of the baby and the puppy when his owner goes to have tea with her friend in *Carl's Afternoon in the Park*. Afternoon tea is a tradition in Great Britain. As a class, plan to have an afternoon tea and invite parents, grandparents, or other special guests. Students can plan and make tea sandwiches and sweets. Serve herb teas and juice drinks.

29. Take a class field trip to a park, a department store, or a petting zoo. When you return have students compare the sights on their trip to the illustrations in the Carl book that corresponds to that trip.

30. As students read these books, have them observe the variety of snacks Carl and the baby have. Discuss the snacks in the books and healthy snacks students might have at home or when they are out on adventures. Decide on a snack for the class to prepare and eat.

Other

31. When Carl is left to watch the baby and the puppy, the three of them have a lively time in the park together. They exhibit both responsible and irresponsible behavior as they go through the park. Have children decide which actions are responsible and which ones are irresponsible. Share other books where characters exhibit either or both of these types of behavior. Discuss responsible and irresponsible actions in the class, in the neighborhood, and at home.

32. Use the Carl books to begin discussions and study on health and safety in the home, while shopping, at the park, and during the Christmas holidays. The class can be divided into groups, and each group can take one of the Carl books to determine which things might not be safe in real life.

33. When Carl is left to care for the baby, he is acting in the role of a nanny. Discuss the term *nanny*, and what nannies do. Share several books with unusual nannies, such as *Mary Poppins* and *Peter Pan*.

Ways to Use Activities

For an author study. *See* 6, 9

For *Carl Goes Shopping*. *See* 2, 17, 18, 26, 32

For *Carl's Afternoon in the Park*. *See* 3, 4, 9, 14, 21, 22, 24, 28, 31, 32

For *Carl's Christmas*. *See* 2, 18, 19, 32

For *Carl's Masquerade*. *See* 5, 20

For *Good Dog, Carl*. *See* 20, 32

For all Carl books. *See* 1, 7, 8, 10, 11, 12, 13, 15, 16, 23, 25, 27, 29, 30, 31, 32, 33

Tomie dePaola

    Naturally it is a big temptation to let the pictures dictate the book and, of course, I feel this would be a mistake. Even in wordless-picture books, I write a type of "film-script." I do believe that even a book with minimal text does rely on the STORY.

    My personal definition for picture-book (as opposed to an illustrated story-book) is that the very young child who may not even know how to decipher words can indeed read the book by actually "reading the pictures." Reading the pictures, that's an interesting phrase. I find, that quite often, adults will read the text only, flipping the pages as soon as the words are finished instead of lingering over the pictures.

—Tomie dePaola

ABOUT THE AUTHOR

Tomie dePaola was born on September 15, 1934, in Meriden, Connecticut. He was given the name Thomas Anthony by his parents, who were Irish and Italian. He grew up with a brother and two sisters. His childhood experiences with his Italian grandmother provided stories for two of his books, *Watch Out for the Chicken Feet in Your Soup* and *Nana Upstairs and Nana Downstairs*. He learned to share his mother's love of books as she read aloud, and he decided by the time he was in first grade that he wanted to make picture books when he grew up. He credits his vivid imagination to listening to his mother's stories and listening to a radio program called "Let's Pretend." Using common experiences, he still asks himself, what if? and lets his imagination take over.

Tomie dePaola enjoyed drawing all through his school years. He received his B.F.A. from the Pratt Institute in Brooklyn, New York, in 1956; an M.F.A. from California College of Arts and Crafts in Oakland in 1969; and a doctoral equivalency from Lone Mountain College in San Francisco in 1970. Since 1956, his career has been as a professional artist and designer, a teacher of art, a painter and muralist, and an illustrator and author of books for children. He has illustrated over 200 books and has written the stories for one-third of those books.

His works have been exhibited in many one-man and group shows at art museums, including those in Houston (Texas), Cedar Rapids (Iowa), and Dayton (Ohio). He has created many paintings and murals for churches and monasteries in New England.

Tomie dePaola has written and illustrated books for children in three areas: informational books, folktales, and fiction that blends realism and fantasy. His books have been published in 15 different countries. He has won many awards, including the 1976 Caldecott Honor Book Award for *Strega Nona*, which was also an American Library Association Notable Book. In 1990, Tomie dePaola was the only U.S. nominee for the prestigious international award, the Hans Christian Andersen Medal. In the same year, the Smithsonian Institution awarded him the Smithson Medal. He has been honored with the Catholic Library Association's Regina Medal and the Kerlan Award from the University of Minnesota for his contributions to children's literature. His favorite honor is having a book on the International Reading Association Children's Choices list, since the titles are selected each year by children.

Redwing Farm in New London, New Hampshire, is Tomie dePaola's home, where he lives and works. Single with no children, he shares his house with three dogs and three cats. A room named for him in the Tracy Memorial Library in New London houses one-half of his personal archives.

DEPAOLA'S BOOKLIST
Selected Books by the Author

The Art Lesson. Putnam, 1989.

Bill and Pete Go Down the Nile. Putnam, 1987.

Charlie Needs a Cloak. Prentice-Hall, 1973.

The Cloud Book. Holiday House, 1975.

The Clown of God. Harcourt Brace Jovanovich, 1978.

Four Stories for Four Seasons. Prentice-Hall, 1977.

Helga's Dowry. Harcourt Brace Jovanovich, 1977.

Jamie O'Rourke and the Big Potato. Whitebird/ Putnam, 1992.

The Knight and the Dragon. Putnam, 1980.

The Legend of the Indian Paintbrush. Putnam, 1988.

Michael Bird Boy. Prentice-Hall, 1975.

Nana Upstairs and Nana Downstairs. Putnam, 1973.

Patrick: Patron Saint of Ireland. Holiday House, 1992.

The Popcorn Book. Holiday House, 1978.

Strega Nona. Prentice-Hall, 1975.

Watch Out for the Chicken Feet in Your Soup. Prentice-Hall, 1974.

Selected Media from Books by the Author

The Art Lesson. Book and cassette. Listening Library.

Charlie Needs a Cloak. Directed by Gene Deitch. 16mm film/video. Weston Woods.

The Clown of God. Directed by Gary McGivney. 16mm film/video. Weston Woods.

The Legend of the Bluebonnet. Live action. 16mm film/video. Barr Films.

The Legend of the Indian Paintbrush. Sound filmstrip. American School Publishers.

Merry Christmas Strega Nona. Sound filmstrip. SVE.

Selected Books Illustrated by the Author

The Carsick Zebra and Other Animal Riddles by David A. Adler. Holiday House, 1983.

Cookie's Week by Cindy Ward. Putnam, 1988.

The Ghost with the Halloween Hiccups by Stephen Mooser. Watts, 1977.

The Good Giants and the Bad Pukwudgies by Jean Fritz. Putnam, 1982.

The Great Adventure of Christopher Columbus by Jean Fritz. Putnam, 1992.

Hark! A Christmas Sampler by Jane Yolen. Putnam, 1991.

I Love You Mouse by John Graham. Harcourt Brace Jovanovich, 1976.

Maggie and the Monster by Elizabeth Winthrop. Holiday House, 1987.

The Mountains of Quilt by Nancy Willard. Harcourt Brace Jovanovich, 1987.

Teeny Tiny by Jill Bennett. Putnam, 1986.

The Vanishing Pumpkin by Tony Johnston. Putnam, 1983.

Wordless Books by the Author

Flicks. Harcourt Brace Jovanovich, 1979.

The Hunter and the Animals. Holiday House, 1981.

Pancakes for Breakfast. Harcourt Brace Jovanovich, 1978.

Sing, Pierrot, Sing: A Picture Book in Mime. Harcourt Brace Jovanovich, 1983.

ABOUT DEPAOLA'S WORDLESS BOOKS

Each of these very different stories contains a simple plot that can be easily read and a symbolic content that will have meaning for the more sophisticated reader. The familiar rounded forms and outlined drawing style of Tomie dePaola receive a different treatment in each book.

Flicks uses only charcoal gray and pink to present five short wordless vignettes as if they were silent films being watched in a movie theater. Each short story is a humorous look at a situation young children can recognize: losing a tooth, mastering roller skates, confronting a birthday cake with candles that won't blow out, anticipating a new baby that turns out to be a kitten, and finally, going to bed. The nostalgic setting of the movie theater, with its dedication to "Mae, Shirley, Mickey, and Minnie," will be more recognizable to adults or older children.

Pancakes for Breakfast details a frustrating morning for a hungry older woman and her pets. She rises thinking of pancakes, and the pets look on expectantly while she checks the recipe and begins to assemble the ingredients. The dog follows her to the chicken coop and looks longingly at the eggs. The cat follows her to the barn to milk the cow, and both pets watch the long process of churning butter. When the woman goes out to buy one last ingredient—maple syrup—the pets can't wait, and they devour the raw ingredients left out on the kitchen table. Stymied for a moment, the woman follows the smell of pancakes to her neighbors' house and to a plate full of pancakes. Pastels and grays predominate the winter landscape setting. Here themes of persistence and self-sufficiency create depth for the simple story, and a subplot is provided by the pets.

Bright colors and a stylized design based on Hungarian folk art tell a moral tale of a hunter who cannot find the animals that have hidden in the forest in *The Hunter and the Animals*. As the hunter sleeps, the animals steal his gun. When he wakes, he is lost and confused until the animals return his possessions and show him the way home. The hunter then breaks his gun and becomes a friend to the animals.

The most complex of dePaola's four wordless books is *Sing, Pierrot, Sing*. The clown Pierrot, dressed as a traditional white-faced mime, dreams of the lovely Columbine and writes music for her. He is unaware that she is enjoying the company of Harlequin. One evening he attempts his long-planned serenade with lute, music, and a freshly picked rose. A crowd gathers and sees his humiliation when the rose he tosses to her balcony is caught by Harlequin. Pierrot retreats to the moon but is wooed back to earth by sympathetic children. In the moonlight, Pierrot and the children find happiness in song and dance. An Italian setting and the use of traditional commedia dell'arte characters combine with the dramatic use of color to create a mood piece. Carefully composed, flowing pictures give a musical feel to the illustration. Using colored inks and tempera with soft, sweet hues, the artist creates a wistful mood. The blue palate indicating sadness expands until a full page of blue offsets sad Pierrot sitting in the moon.

ACTIVITIES

Arts/Crafts

1. After sharing *The Hunter and the Animals*, discuss Hungarian folk art and share other pictures created with this technique. Have students use this style to make a picture.

2. Have students make tissue paper roses similar to the flower Pierrot gives Columbine on the balcony.

3. After sharing *Flicks*, demonstrate flip books and the way the illustrations appear to move as you flip through the book. Have students make their own small flip book of a simple character or situation.

4. Students can make their own theaters that show a silent filmstrip. Use shoeboxes for the theaters. Cut parallel 4½-inch slits on either side of the upper half of the box and cut out a 4-inch square for the "screen." Use lengths of paper that have been cut to a 4-inch width. Students can trace around a 4-inch square cardboard pattern leaving space between each square. When their "filmstrip" is prepared, they can draw their stories square by square. Before beginning, they need to think through their story and make a picture board film script so they will know how many squares they need and what they will put in each square. "Films" can be done in black-and-white or color. When the filmstrip is completed, it is placed through the slits on the sides of the box so that the picture shows in the screen area. The viewer can move the filmstrip through slowly. Have students leave approximately 6 inches of blank paper at each end to begin pulling through.

5. Students can make stick puppets of characters from one of these books to enact the story in front of the class.

Bulletin Board/Display

6. Make a display of books written and/or illustrated by Tomie dePaola. Use a photocopier to enlarge his photograph and use for the center of the display.

7. Rubber stamps of many of Tomie dePaola's characters can be ordered from the Kidstamps catalog. Students can use these with a stamp pad to make their own bookmarks on blank strips of medium-weight paper.

8. Use an overhead projector to enlarge the characters in these books. These characters can be painted or colored with markers, laminated, and used with displays of student work based on the relevant books.

9. Using the art in *Flicks* as an example, make silhouettes of students to put along the bottom of a bulletin board. Label the board "Now Showing..." and use the display to highlight student work about dePaola's four wordless titles.

10. Enlarge the cover illustration of Pierrot sitting on the moon and place it on a blue background on the bulletin board. Have students cut out stars and write the title of a favorite Tomie dePaola book on each star. Place the stars on the blue background surrounding Pierrot, and label the display "Books to Sing About."

11. Cut out hearts and acorns from folded paper to create a display border like the border in *Hunter*. Students can cut out trees and animals to make a mural.

Geography

12. The author was born in Meriden, Connecticut, and currently lives in New London, New Hampshire. Use a map of the United States to locate these two towns. Have students use library resources to learn about the two states—size, geographic features, population, landmarks, and so forth.

13. The author's father was Italian, and his mother was Irish. Locate Italy and Ireland on a world map. Use library resources to learn about the cultures of the two countries. The author has said that *Watch Out for the Chicken Feet in Your Soup* is based on the soup his Italian grandmother made when he was a child. As you look through other books dePaola has written and illustrated, what other things do you notice that might have come from his personal experiences?

Language Arts

14. After sharing these four books, have students choose a character from one of the books and create another story for that character.

15. Discuss main themes and how to develop themes in stories. Then have students help identify the main theme in each of these books and discuss why the themes are timeless and appear in many stories in many cultures (e.g., *Pancakes*—persistence pays off).

16. Discuss how recipes are written and why a list of ingredients and accurate measurements is needed. Make a class cookbook of real or imaginary pancake recipes for the old woman to try the next time she is hungry for a pancake breakfast.

17. After sharing *Hunter*, discuss other things people might go hunting for, such as mushrooms, antiques, comic books, or baseball cards.

18. As students read *Hunter*, have them use a first-person stream of consciousness narrative to tell or write the story from the hunter's point of view. What does he see? How does he feel?

19. Discuss the symbolism found in *Pierrot*. What might the rose, the moon, and the willow symbolize?

20. Compare the balcony scene in *Pierrot* with other famous balcony scenes, such as the one in *Romeo and Juliet* and the one in *Cyrano de Bergerac*.

Library Research

21. Have students use the author catalog to locate other books by Tomie dePaola. After students have gathered together many of his works, have them look through his books for wordless sequences (places where the illustration is used without any text). Invite students to discuss why they think he used the wordless sequences.

22. Use library resources to learn about Pierrot. Compare dePaola's version with other versions, including the original. Learn about the Italian commedia dell'arte in the history of theater and Pierrot's place in this drama form. Learn about the history of pantomime.

Math

23. Using the pancake recipe in *Pancakes*, show students how to double or triple the ingredients to make a larger batch and how to halve the ingredients to make a smaller batch. Practice enlarging and reducing recipes mathematically.

24. Use the pancake recipe as an introduction to measurements and their importance. Bring in teaspoons, tablespoons, cups, and other measurement containers and have students use water to measure the number of teaspoons in a tablespoon, in a cup, and so forth. Discuss the importance of standardized measurements and how they differ in various parts of the world. Discuss what it means to put a "pinch of something" into a recipe.

25. The hunter sleeps under a tree that has 25 leaves. Photocopy and enlarge the tree for a pattern and have children each make 25 leaves to put on their own tree. Count to 25 by ones. You can also use the leaves to practice multiplication by fives and for subtraction: If the tree lost three leaves, how many leaves would be left on the tree? You can make a tree for the flannel board and have students add and subtract felt leaves.

Music

26. Silent movies were shown while background music was played. Watch a video of a silent movie and listen to the music in the background; how does the music set the mood for each scene?

27. Divide the class into five groups and have each group select music to play for one of the features in *Flicks*.

28. Listen to sad, romantic lute or violin music that is wordless. What mood does it create? Play other lute or violin music with words. How is the mood created? Play songs Pierrot might have sung or music he might have played. Compare this music to current popular music.

29. In small groups, or as a class, compose music and words for Pierrot's serenade.

30. After reading *Hunter*, listen to Hungarian folk music and invite students to relate it to the folk art in this book.

Science

31. The old woman wants maple syrup for her pancakes. Learn where maple syrup comes from and how it is made. Bring in maple syrup for each student to taste.

32. Identify the many animals in *Hunter*. Discuss how realistically or unrealistically each is portrayed. (Foxes actually climb trees; beavers don't.)

33. The trees portrayed in *Hunter* are oak trees. Study oak trees and the way the small acorn grows into the mighty oak. Where do oak trees grow? What kind of animals are supported by oak forests?

34. Use a 16mm projector to discuss how a moving image is created. Have students observe the aperture, how the film moves, and how the lens works to project the film. Discuss the ability of the projector to fool the eye into thinking it is seeing a moving picture when it is actually viewing a series of still photos. Compare this with the flip books made in art and how they fool the eye into thinking that action is taking place as the book is flipped.

Social Studies

35. The old woman is very self-sufficient in *Pancakes*. Discuss what it means to be self-sufficient and ways that people are self-sufficient in a modern society.

36. Use *Flicks* as an introduction to the study of the history of film. Discuss silent movies, talkies, and modern filmmaking. Have students discuss their favorite films and the techniques used in those films.

37. After studying commedia dell'arte and silent films, view a silent film in which the main character saves the girl and she goes off with someone else (such as *Modern Times* with Charlie Chaplin). Discuss how the characters and situations are the same, yet different, in the way they reflect their times and cultures.

38. Neighbors play a role in all four of these books. The old woman goes to her neighbors when she wants pancakes. The children in *Flicks* watch a movie in the neighborhood theater. Pierrot has both human and animal neighbors, and the hunter becomes a good neighbor to the animals in the forest. Discuss the importance of neighbors and what it means to be a good neighbor.

Group Activities

39. Plan a multimedia Tomie dePaola Day and invite another class or parents to attend. Read dePaola's books aloud, show videos and filmstrips based on his books, and then have a pancake party where you make and eat stacks and stacks of pancakes.

40. Invite a local mime to come to the classroom and perform. Have students pay careful attention to the way the mime provides information without using speech or sounds. Have the mime teach the students basic miming.

Other

41. Use *Pancakes* to begin a discussion on the importance of eating a healthy breakfast. Have students tell about their favorite breakfasts. Make menus of healthy breakfasts that students can prepare by themselves.

42. Watch a video about the famous French mime Marcel Marceau, or other mimes. Students can develop a story in mime to present to the class, or they can mime one of Tomie dePaola's stories.

Ways to Use Activities

For an author study. *See* 6, 7, 12, 13, 21, 39

For *Flicks. See* 3, 4, 9, 26, 27, 34, 36, 37

For *The Hunter and the Animals. See* 1, 11, 17, 18, 25, 30, 32, 33

For *Pancakes for Breakfast. See* 16, 23, 24, 31, 35, 41

For *Sing, Pierrot, Sing. See* 2, 10, 19, 20, 22, 28, 29, 40, 42

For all four titles. *See* 5, 8, 14, 15, 38

John S. Goodall

    I am a painter and illustrator, not a writer, and therefore I prefer to express myself with pictures rather than words. In addition, I can reach a wider audience with pictures than with words.

    The first book with the half pages was, I think, Adventures of Paddy Pork. *It was such a long time ago that I forget how the device came into being, but I recall that I saw it used in an old Victorian book and therefore it does not belong to me, exclusively. It struck me that it had such universal appeal, including non-English speaking countries, in terms of telling stories, without words, that it was worth developing.*

—John S. Goodall

ABOUT THE AUTHOR

John Strickland Goodall was born on June 7, 1908, in the small English village of Heacham in Norfolk, where his parents had a country house. His family had been in the health professions for seven generations, and his father was the first English physician to specialize in heart diseases.

Goodall was interested in drawing and painting from a young age. After completing his education at the Harrow School, he studied art privately with three well-known instructors before spending four years at the Royal Academy of Art in London. He worked as an illustrator of books, magazines, and advertising before serving in the British Territorial Army. He began painting watercolor landscapes while he was in India and the Far East. Upon military discharge, he continued illustrating books by other authors and painted landscapes. He has had numerous exhibits, and his paintings have won many awards.

John S. Goodall's first book, *The Adventures of Paddy Pork*, which he created for his granddaughter, became the first in a series of successful wordless books. In 1969, this title received the Boston Globe-Horn Book Award for Excellence in Illustration and was an American Library Association Notable Book. Three of his other books were included in the Children's Book Showcase: *Paddy's Evening Out* in 1974, *Creepy Castle* in 1976, and *Paddy Pork's Holiday* in 1977.

Goodall and his wife have one daughter—and a granddaughter named Lavinia. His studio is located in the garden near his cottage in Wiltshire, England.

GOODALL'S BOOKLIST

Selected Books by the Author

Dr. Owl's Party. Blackie & Son, 1954.

Field Mouse House. Blackie & Son, 1954.

Great Days of a Country House. McElderry, 1992.

Selected Books Illustrated by the Author

Alice in Wonderland by Lewis Carroll. Blackie & Son, 1965.

Fairy Tales of England by Barbara Ker Wilson. Dutton, 1960.

Five Children and It by Edith N. Bland. Looking Glass Library, 1959.

Phoenix and the Carpet by Edith N. Bland. Looking Glass Library, 1960.

Story of the Amulet by Edith N. Bland. Looking Glass Library, 1960.

Wordless Books by the Author

Above and Below Stairs. Atheneum, 1983.

The Adventures of Paddy Pork. Harcourt Brace Jovanovich, 1968.

The Ballooning Adventures of Paddy Pork. Harcourt Brace Jovanovich, 1969.

Before the War: 1908-1939: An Autobiography in Pictures. Atheneum, 1981.

Creepy Castle. Atheneum, 1975.

An Edwardian Christmas. Atheneum, 1978.

Edwardian Entertainments. Atheneum, 1982.

An Edwardian Holiday. Atheneum, 1979.

An Edwardian Season. Atheneum, 1980.

An Edwardian Summer. Atheneum, 1976.

Escapade. Publisher unknown. 1980.

Jacko. Harcourt Brace Jovanovich, 1972.

John S. Goodall's Theatre: The Sleeping Beauty. Atheneum, 1979.

Lavinia's Cottage: Imagined by Her Devoted Grandfather. Atheneum, 1982.

Little Red Riding Hood. McElderry, 1988.

The Midnight Adventures of Kelly, Dot, and Esmeralda. Atheneum, 1972.

Naughty Nancy. Atheneum, 1975.

Naughty Nancy Goes to School. McElderry, 1985.

Paddy Finds a Job. Atheneum, 1981.

Paddy Goes Traveling. Atheneum, 1982.

Paddy Pork—Odd Jobs. Atheneum, 1983.

Paddy Pork's Holiday. Atheneum, 1976.

Paddy's Evening Out. Atheneum, 1973.

Paddy's New Hat. Atheneum, 1980.

Paddy to the Rescue. Atheneum, 1985.

Paddy Under Water. Atheneum, 1984.

Puss in Boots. McElderry, 1990.

Shrewbettina Goes to Work. Atheneum, 1981.

Shrewbettina's Birthday. Harcourt Brace Jovanovich, 1970.

The Story of a Castle. McElderry, 1986.

The Story of a Farm. McElderry, 1989.

The Story of a Main Street. McElderry, 1987.

The Story of an English Village. Atheneum, 1978.

The Story of the Seashore. McElderry, 1990.

The Surprise Picnic. Atheneum, 1977.

Victorians Abroad. Atheneum, 1980.

ABOUT GOODALL'S WORDLESS BOOKS

John S. Goodall is a distinguished English artist whose numerous wordless books include historical works as well as adventure and fantasy fiction. His work is marked by the use of a technique in which a half page, cleverly designed to change setting or action when it is turned, is inserted in each full-page illustration. This technique forwards the plot, produces humorous effects in the fiction, and shows activity and various aspects of the historical themes.

Goodall's books of fiction feature animal characters dressing and acting like people. These books have strong plots and contain lots of action, humor, mishaps, and chase scenes. The Paddy Pork books were the first of these works. The first two books in this series about an adventurous young pig are illustrated in black line drawings, and the other eight titles use full-color paintings to tell the comical stories. Other humorous works feature a shrew named Shrewbettina, a young mouse named Nancy, and a mother cat and her kittens who have an unexpected adventure in *The Surprise Picnic*. *Jacko*, the story of a monkey escaping captivity to return to his family in the wild, has more serious overtones. Fantasy elements distinguish *Creepy Castle*, in which two mice explore a castle, and *The Midnight Adventures of Kelly, Dot, and Esmeralda*, in which toys come to life and magically enter a painting. Both of these fantasy adventures are dramatic and contain strong villains.

In two traditional fairy tales as retold by Goodall, to convey the feeling of "once upon a time...," the richly colored paintings are more impressionistic than finely detailed. In *Little Red Riding Hood*, a charming mouse child plays the title role. *Puss in Boots* features a large ginger cat with a sweeping feather in his hat.

Each of the nonfiction works is a historical and cultural look at an aspect of English life. Sumptuous water-colors include exquisite details of custom and costume, architecture and activities, in an artistic account of the past. In the Story of... titles, a single focus—sometimes even a single scene—is used; and as time is shown to have passed, the changes that have occurred are portrayed. For instance, *The Story of a Main Street* begins with a huddle of wattle and daub houses and a market cross in medieval times. The same street is shown in Elizabethan, Restoration, Georgian, Regency, Victorian, Edwardian, and present times. An exterior street view alternates with the interior of one of the shops or houses. The final scene shows the centuries-old market cross still standing on a busy present-day street corner. The way in which the present is built on the past is a recurring theme, as is the concept of time bringing change. Each of the historical works is well researched, and the visual narrative re-creates each time period in a lively and colorful manner. The special fascination the Edwardian period holds for Goodall is seen in the series of books that detail life in that secure and peaceful time. *Above and Below Stairs* gives an unusual look at the class structure in England throughout the ages. In all these books, intriguing details re-create the past, sometimes with nostalgic echoes for a bygone way of life, but always with the artist's eye for the personality of history.

ACTIVITIES

Arts/Crafts

1. The author uses art to record architecture, costumes, and activities of the past. Have students create a school or class social history similar to a title by Goodall. Students can draw the school building or the library building, clothes they are wearing, and typical activities.

2. Goodall's works have been compared to the British landscape painter John Constable, who lived from 1776 to 1837. Show students examples of works by both artists to compare and contrast.

3. *Lavinia's Cottage, Shrewbettina Goes to Work*, and *Paddy Finds a Job* are all movable pop-up books. Share these books and show students how they can make a picture with a movable part.

4. Goodall's books are noted for the half-page inserts he uses to move the action. Share several of these titles and have students make their own full-page picture with a half-page insert.

Bulletin Board/Display

5. Make a display of books illustrated by John S. Goodall. Use a photocopier to enlarge his photograph and use as the center of the display.

6. Drape the bulletin board with red fabric to create the effect of stage curtains. Label the board "Now Appearing—John S. Goodall." Students can make representations of the characters that appear in these books to display on the stage.

7. Create a class mural labeled "The Story of..." (Our School, Our Community, Our City). Each section of the mural can be a different time period in the history of the topic. Students can work in small groups to learn about the various time periods and translate their information into illustrations.

8. Place cards around the board, each bearing the title of a John S. Goodall book. Label the board "Who Is It?" and each day provide hints about a character or one of the books. (Example: Preparations for birthdays can take all day [*Shrewbettina's Birthday*].) One end of a long string can be attached near the label, and students can move the other end to position it near the correct book title.

Geography

9. John S. Goodall was born in Heacham, Norfolk, England, and now lives in Tisbury, Wiltshire, England. Use an atlas to locate these two places in England. Students can use library reference materials to learn about England. Research the country's geographical features and climate. What foods do the English eat? What are some famous English landmarks?

Language Arts

10. Using one of the fiction titles, diagram the story's plot on the chalkboard. When the plot diagram is completed, have students share information on each event: What characters were involved in the event? What was each of the characters feeling? What was the cause and effect of the event?

11. Have students create a newspaper classified ad for one of the characters. Examples: Lady shrew offers reward for missing purse (*Shrewbettina's Birthday*). Experienced scuba diver available for deep sea treasure hunting; contact Paddy Pork (*Paddy Under Water*).

12. Discuss résumés and how they are written and used. As a class, develop a résumé for Paddy Pork based on the jobs he has in his books.

13. Have students, working individually or in pairs, select one of the books about Paddy Pork, Shrewbettina, or Naughty Nancy and write dialogue to go with the story. The dialogue can be used for a play or puppet show.

14. Discuss with the class characterization in fiction using examples from books about Paddy Pork, Naughty Nancy, and Shrewbettina. Select one of the characters and have students describe characteristics of that character based on incidents in the book. List on the chalkboard the characteristics of each character. Students can use these characteristics to develop new characters for stories they will write.

15. Discuss the oral tradition and traditional folktales and fairy tales. Compare various versions of "Puss in Boots" and "Little Red Riding Hood" with the retellings by John S. Goodall. Students can tell or write their own modern version of one of these stories.

16. *An Edwardian Summer* shows many summertime activities enjoyed by the English in Edwardian times. Have students compare and contrast their summer activities with those shown in this book; comparisons can be in verbal or written form.

17. Theater is frequently portrayed in both fiction and nonfiction titles by John S. Goodall. Have students help make a class catalog of theater entertainments found in these books. Discuss the importance of theater and live entertainment. What kinds of theater are available in your community?

Library Research

18. Have students use the author catalog to locate books by John S. Goodall.

19. Have students research the Victorian or Edwardian time periods and discuss how these times are reflected in Goodall's books.

20. Share *The Story of a Farm* before having students research American farms and their history. Have students discuss how American and English farms differ in their history.

21. After carefully studying the Story of... books, use a variety of older city directories at the public library to have students trace the history of a specific house or building in your community.

22. The Story of... books show the changes that have occurred in one location over a period of time. Show students how to use microforms (microfiche or microfilm) to look at old newspapers from your area to read about some of the changes that have taken place in your community over the years.

Math

23. The Story of... books take the reader through several centuries in the history of a location. Use these books to begin a discussion on the concepts of centuries and of 100 years. Count by ones to 100, 1,000, and 2,000.

24. Use the dates in the Story of... books to determine how many years pass from sequence to sequence. Discuss the ways that years are measured (days, weeks, months) and how the calendar was developed. Discuss alternate calendars and how they measure time.

Music

25. The Story of... books all have scenes portraying musical events. Locate the scenes in each book and play music appropriate to that event and that time period. Discuss the importance of music as a form of entertainment, then and now.

26. *Edwardian Entertainments* shows many types of music being played. Discuss the types of instruments shown. Play examples of music that might have been played in Edwardian England.

27. Invite local musicians who play period instruments to discuss their instruments, how they became interested in those instruments, how they acquired them, and how they learned to play them. After they have played for the class, invite the class members to discuss how these instruments sound compared to current musical instruments.

28. Have students work in small groups to research the history of a particular instrument and develop a Story of... book about that instrument. How was the instrument first made? What cultures play the instrument?

Science

29. After sharing *The Ballooning Adventures of Paddy Pork*, study the principles of hot air and how hot air balloons work. Do a simple demonstration in which hot air is used to cause something to rise.

30. Share *Paddy Under Water* and have students point out which things are real and which things are unreal in the book (examples: the scuba equipment is "real"; the mermaids are unreal). View films, videos, or filmstrips that show underwater exploration.

31. Use the Story of... books to introduce a unit of study on the way humans and human activity have affected and changed the environment. As you share each book, have students notice the human activities and how they change from time period to time period. How do those activities affect their environment?

32. Use *The Story of the Seashore* to begin an exploration of coasts and coastal environmental problems. What is the impact of human activity on beaches? Choose a U.S. coastline to study and determine the ways in which the beach environment has changed over the past 100 to 150 years.

33. As a class, develop a scientific timeline entitled "The Story of Science." Make a timeline about 500 years long, divided into 50-year sections, and have students research the scientific events that were occurring at each interval.

Social Studies

34. Locate in the Story of... books universal human activities (eating, entertaining, getting food, and so forth). List these activities on the chalkboard and discuss how they are performed today.

35. Use the nonfiction titles to study costumes from different time periods, including why and how they have changed. What inventions, discoveries, and societal trends have been important in changing what people wear (zippers, buttons, the sewing machine, the availability of different fabrics, inexpensive labor, leisure time, and so forth)?

36. Share *Creepy Castle* and *The Story of a Castle*. Invite student discussion about Goodall's treatment of castles and medieval times in each book.

37. Use the Story of... books to develop a history of transportation modes that have been used in England. On the chalkboard create a timeline based on the time periods found in the books. Under each time period have students list the methods of transportation that were used.

38. Use the Story of... books to make a class list of entertainment and leisure activities portrayed by the author. Compare and contrast this list of activities to those people enjoy today.

39. As you share the Story of... books, discuss the work or jobs that people are involved in. How does human labor change over a lengthy time period? Invite student discussion of how jobs continue to change (example: the use of computers).

40. Use *The Story of a Castle* to discuss how the use of buildings can change from one time period to the next. As you share the book, have students discuss the ways the castle was used from time period to time period and why it was used in those ways. Discuss buildings in your community that have had several uses (example: a large single-family home that was divided into apartments after World War II and is now used as an office building).

41. Use the nonfiction titles to see how the author has portrayed the British class system. How did the class structure limit people's lives? How were people's lives enhanced? Is there a class system in the United States?

42. Introduce the concept of servants by sharing the book *Above and Below Stairs*. Have students look through other nonfiction books by John S. Goodall to find examples of servants. Discuss servants in current times.

43. It has been suggested that John S. Goodall portrays the good that happens during each time period. Challenge students to discover what negative events might have been left out of each time period. Discuss what historians include and what they leave out of their accounts of history.

44. Goodall's illustrations are similar to colored photographs because they are historically accurate and contain many details. Discuss the way that old photographs can be used to tell about a time period. Bring in old photographs for student observation.

Group Activities

45. In many of Goodall's books, children and adults are shown playing games. Make a list of games shown and learn how to play them. Have a special day during which students and teachers play games from the past.

46. Have students research a time period depicted by John S. Goodall. Culminate the research with a pageant. Each student can design a period costume after tracing his or her outline on a large piece of paper. These "paper doll" costumes can be pinned to the front of students for the pageant, while the students present some of their research findings to the rest of the class.

47. The author creates a visual time capsule in the Edwardian books. Have students create their own class time capsule. What things would be included?

Other

48. Develop a health unit that focuses on disease and disease control through the ages. As you share these nonfiction books, discuss diseases of the times, disease control or the lack of, and medical treatments for disease.

49. Paddy Pork has many adventures. Have students work in small groups to develop board games based on Paddy Pork's adventures. Then the groups can share and compare their games. Students can play the games, or another class can be invited to play them to learn about Paddy Pork.

50. John S. Goodall's books are rich in detail. Have students work in pairs to observe and note the details they find on a two-page spread, including the half page.

51. Students can work individually or in pairs to make a diorama of one of their favorite scenes from any of John S. Goodall's books.

Ways to Use Activities

For an author study. *See* 2, 5, 6, 9, 18

For *Above and Below Stairs*. *See* 19, 24, 35, 41, 42, 43

For *The Adventures of Paddy Pork*. *See* 13, 14, 49

For *The Ballooning Adventures of Paddy Pork*. *See* 13, 14, 29, 49

For *Before the War*. *See* 35, 44

For *Creepy Castle*. *See* 36

For *An Edwardian Christmas*. *See* 19, 35, 41, 48

For *Edwardian Entertainments*. *See* 19, 26, 35, 41, 47

For *An Edwardian Holiday*. *See* 19, 35, 41, 47

For *An Edwardian Season*. *See* 19, 35, 41, 47

For *An Edwardian Summer*. *See* 16, 19, 35, 41, 47

For *John S. Goodall's Theatre: The Sleeping Beauty*. *See* 15, 17

For *Lavinia's Cottage*. *See* 3

For *Little Red Riding Hood*. *See* 15

For *Naughty Nancy*. *See* 13, 14

For *Naughty Nancy Goes to School*. *See* 13, 14

For *Paddy Finds a Job*. *See* 3, 12, 13, 14, 49

For *Paddy Goes Traveling*. *See* 13, 14, 49

For *Paddy Pork—Odd Jobs*. *See* 12, 13, 14, 49

For *Paddy Pork's Holiday*. *See* 13, 14, 49

For *Paddy's Evening Out*. *See* 13, 14, 49

For *Paddy's New Hat*. *See* 12, 13, 14, 49

For *Paddy to the Rescue*. *See* 13, 14, 49

For *Paddy Under Water*. *See* 13, 14, 30, 49

For *Puss in Boots*. *See* 15

For *Shrewbettina Goes to Work*. *See* 3, 13, 14

For *Shrewbettina's Birthday*. *See* 13, 14

For *The Story of a Castle*. *See* 7, 21, 22, 23, 24, 25, 28, 31, 34, 35, 36, 37, 38, 39, 40, 41

For *The Story of a Farm*. *See* 7, 20, 21, 22, 23, 24, 25, 28, 31, 34, 35, 37, 38, 39, 41

For *The Story of a Main Street*. *See* 7, 21, 22, 23, 24, 25, 28, 31, 34, 35, 37, 38, 39, 41

For *The Story of an English Village*. *See* 7, 21, 22, 23, 24, 25, 28, 31, 34, 35, 37, 38, 39, 41

For *The Story of the Seashore*. *See* 7, 21, 22, 23, 24, 25, 28, 31, 32, 34, 35, 37, 38, 39, 41

For *Victorians Abroad*. *See* 19, 35, 37, 41

For all titles by Goodall. *See* 1, 4, 8, 10, 11, 17, 27, 33, 41, 42, 43, 44, 45, 46, 48, 50, 51

Tana Hoban

I do wordless books because I am attempting to activate minds. I don't want my books to be passive experiences. I want to make the wheels turn in readers' heads, so I try to make my photographs stimulate imagination and possibly creativity. Sometimes, if the word is there, it blocks or might arrest the flow of thought since it makes the perception of the photograph a "fait accompli."

My books are about awareness. We are constantly exposed to things that desensitize us. I would like to think my books will help young people to observe and discover things that we take for granted in our daily lives ... and might easily overlook. By sharing what I see with my readers, I hope to sharpen their powers of observation and perception.

— Tana Hoban

ABOUT THE AUTHOR

Tana Hoban was born to Russian immigrant parents in Philadelphia, Pennsylvania. She was raised and educated in Lansdale, a suburb of Philadelphia. Her father influenced her to have a career so that she would not ever have to be dependent on anyone. He enrolled Tana in art classes when she was a young girl, and she sketched all the way through school. She attended Moore College of Art on a scholarship, and after graduation she received a fellowship to paint in Europe.

Tana Hoban began her career working as a freelance artist, doing advertising and magazine illustration. When she took up photography, her painting and sketching background influenced her work. She worked successfully in advertising for many years, and one year her photographs appeared on the covers of 16 magazines. She won numerous awards as a filmmaker, photographer, and commercial consultant before she began working on books for children. Her interest in child development led her to design and write books for young people. *Shapes and Things* and *Look Again!* were published in 1971, and she has been writing and photographing her own books ever since.

Considered a gifted photographer, Tana Hoban has won numerous awards for her books, most recently the 1983 Drexel University Citation for a body of creative work; the 1985 Boston Globe-Horn Book Award for *1,2,3*; the 1988 *New York Times* best illustrated book award for *Look! Look! Look!* and the Parents' Reading Magic Award for *All About Where*. In 1990, *Shadows and Reflections* received the Boston Globe-Horn Book Award and the Parents' Choice Foundation Award and was included on the American Library Association Notable List. Her works have been included in a number of exhibits, most recently in New York, Philadelphia, and Arles, France, and are part of the Kerland Collection at the University of Minnesota and other collections in the United States and France.

Tana Hoban currently lives in Paris. She has a grown daughter.

HOBAN'S BOOKLIST

Selected Books by the Author

Black on White. Greenwillow, 1993.

A Children's Zoo. Greenwillow, 1985.

Count and See. Macmillan, 1972.

I Walk and Read. Greenwillow, 1984.

More Than One. Greenwillow, 1981.

One Little Kitten. Greenwillow, 1979.

1,2,3. Greenwillow, 1985.

Over, Under and Through! And Other Spacial Concepts. Macmillan, 1973.

Panda, Panda. Greenwillow, 1986.

Push-Pull, Empty-Full. Macmillan, 1972.

Red, Blue, Yellow Shoe. Greenwillow, 1986.

Where Is It? Macmillan, 1974.

White on Black. Greenwillow, 1993.

Selected Books Illustrated by the Author

The Moon Was the Best by Charlotte Zolotow. Greenwillow, 1993.

The Wonder of Hands by Edith Baer. Rev. ed. Macmillan, 1992.

Wordless Books by the Author

A, B, See! Greenwillow, 1982.

All About Where. Greenwillow, 1991.

Big Ones, Little Ones. Greenwillow, 1976.

Circles, Triangles, and Squares. Macmillan, 1974.

Dig, Drill, Dump, Fill. Greenwillow, 1975.

Dots, Spots, Speckles, and Stripes. Greenwillow, 1987.

Exactly the Opposite. Greenwillow, 1990.

I Read Signs. Greenwillow, 1983.

I Read Symbols. Greenwillow, 1983.

Is It Larger? Is It Smaller? Greenwillow, 1985.

Is It Red? Is It Yellow? Is It Blue? An Adventure in Color. Greenwillow, 1978.

Is It Rough? Is It Smooth? Is It Shiny? Greenwillow, 1984.

Look Again! Macmillan, 1971.

Look! Look! Look! Greenwillow, 1988.

Look Up, Look Down. Greenwillow, 1992.

Of Colors and Things. Greenwillow, 1989.

Round and Round and Round. Greenwillow, 1983.

Shadows and Reflections. Greenwillow, 1990.

Shapes and Things. Macmillan, 1970.

Shapes, Shapes, Shapes. Greenwillow, 1986.

Spirals, Curves, Fanshapes and Lines. Greenwillow, 1992.

Take Another Look. Greenwillow, 1981.

26 Letters and 99 Cents. Greenwillow, 1987.

What Is It? Greenwillow, 1985.

Media from Books by the Author

"Catsup" in *Dogs, Cats and Rabbits*. 16mm film/video. Texture Films, 1983. Distributed by Films Inc. Video.

One Little Kitten. Live action. 16mm film. Texture Films, 1980.

Where Is It? Live action. 16mm film. Texture Films, 1980.

ABOUT HOBAN'S BOOKS

Two themes prevail in the works of this incredibly intelligent and gifted photographic artist. One is a fascination with the attributes that define matter: form, size, texture, number, pattern, and color. A second unifying theme is the transformation of ordinary images into something extraordinary through the artist's perception. Tana Hoban's photographic works have a fresh feeling of discovery and educate the eye of the reader to observe in a similar manner.

Tana Hoban uses in her works color photographs and sometimes black-and-white photographs; she did two books completely with photograms, which are described later in this discussion. The simplest of pictures contains complexities waiting to be discovered, and the arrangement of pictures within each book provides further resonance to the individual work. These are photographs to be examined carefully and to be reflected upon, since they challenge readers to see more deeply each time they read them. The images are predominantly urban. The photographer takes ordinary objects—cranes, high-tension wires, bicycles, fire trucks, children at play—and makes each one an eye-opening experience.

Three of the books use a window device to turn visual discrimination into a game. *Look Again!*, *Take Another Look*, and *Look! Look! Look!* mask all but a significant portion of a photograph by means of a hole cut into the page. As the page is turned, a larger picture is revealed, and a third page shows the object or animal pictured in context.

Color photographs organized around a concept are found in several titles: *Round and Round and Round*; *Shapes, Shapes, Shapes*; *Is It Larger? Is It Smaller?*; *Is It Red? Is It Yellow? Is It Blue?*; *Is It Rough? Is It Smooth? Is It Shiny?*; *Dots, Spots, Speckles, and Stripes*; and *Exactly the Opposite*. Each contains a direct concept for the simplest use, and each is arranged for comparison and contrast within the scope of the concept as well as for the additional exploration of textures, patterns, and other attributes. *Shadows and Reflections* is one of the most sophisticated of these books, raising questions about the nature of reality and inviting older readers to consider appearances and illusions. The self-portrait at the end of this book is a spectacular photograph.

The black-and-white images found in *Big Ones, Little Ones*; *Circles, Triangles, and Squares*; and *Dig, Drill, Dump, Fill* are no less sophisticated than the color photographs. For example, in the first picture in *Circles, Triangles, and Squares*, a child blows round bubbles underneath a round brass door knob. The bubbles, blower, and door knob all reflect a certain roundness, but the contrast in weight, texture, and transparency is obvious. A closer look shows that one of the bubbles is not round but curling, and the child's hair curls and one of her fingers are curling. The half-moon shape of the child's mouth is like the shape of the keyhole. All of these rounded shapes complement the concept of circle.

Of Colors and Things and *26 Letters and 99 Cents* use isolated photographs of individual objects set against a neutral background. Both have brilliant color and are arranged to enhance early learning.

Photograms are three-dimensional objects recorded on light-sensitive paper without the use of a camera. This technique is used in *A, B, See!* and *Shapes and Things*, as white on black silhouetted images are presented in visual games.

I Read Symbols is an unusual collection of the common symbols of city streets—from the crossing sign of a man walking, to the red upraised hand that indicates Do Not Walk. Companion books, *I Walk and Read* and *I Read Signs*, show the words on signs throughout the city.

Many of Tana Hoban's other books are not quite wordless, but contain labels. *Count and See*; *Over, Under and Through!*; and *Push-Pull, Empty-Full* can be enjoyed without interpreting the limited text.

ACTIVITIES

Arts/Crafts

1. Share the books *Look Again!*, *Look! Look! Look!*, and *Take Another Look*. Give students cardboard or heavy paper squares that have a square or hole cut out and invite them to look at the environment, using the cutout to isolate a portion of what they view, similar to the pictures in the three books they have seen. Then have students make their own window pictures using magazine photographs. The magazine pictures can be glued on paper. A round or square window can be cut out from the overlay page to show a portion of the picture underneath.

2. Share the book *Of Colors and Things* and have students notice how the objects shown on each page match the color highlighted for that page. Each student then selects a favorite color and divides a large sheet of paper into four sections using paint or thick-line markers. Students can locate objects in their chosen colors in magazine pictures, cut them out, and glue them in the squares; or they can draw and paint their own objects.

3. Study photography as an art form with students. Discuss composition, the use of light, and other esthetic elements in photography, using examples from Tana Hoban's books. Have students discuss the work of this photographer by carefully examining both her color and black-and-white photographs.

4. Have students create photograms using light-sensitive paper and objects commonly found in the classroom or around the school.

5. Students can use crayons or paints to make original designs of things that have dots, spots, speckles, and stripes.

Bulletin Board/Display

6. Make a display of books written and/or illustrated by Tana Hoban. Use a photocopier to enlarge her photograph for the center of the display.

7. Have students create pictures to illustrate one of Tana Hoban's concept books, and develop a bulletin board display. For example, for *Round and Round and Round*, students can draw pictures on paper cut in circles to illustrate round objects; pictures can be displayed in a circle with the title of the book in the center.

8. Make labels of titles of Tana Hoban's books and hang them around the room, leaving plenty of room by each label so that students can bring in images based on the books to put by each label. For example, for *Is It Rough? Is It Smooth? Is It Shiny?* students can bring in examples of different textures to put near the title.

9. Make a display shelf or display box with four sections and a white background, similar to the format in *Of Colors and Things*. Each day select a different color and place three-dimensional objects in that color in the appropriate section.

Geography

10. Tana Hoban was born in Philadelphia, Pennsylvania. She currently lives in Paris, France. Divide the class into two groups so that one can study Philadelphia and one can study Paris. Have students use library resources to learn as much as they can about each city: its geography, climate, landmarks, history, foods, customs, and so forth. Have students learn why both cities are historically important in their countries. Each group can develop an informational book about its city that can be shared with the other group.

Language Arts

11. Share the book *26 Letters and 99 Cents* and have students draw or bring in objects that begin with each letter. Or, create a large-size class book titled *26 Letters* and have each student add one object to each page.

12. Have students select a photograph from one of Tana Hoban's books and carefully examine it, paying particular attention to the details. The details can be used to write a story to go with the photograph.

13. Use *I Read Symbols* to begin a discussion on how symbols convey meaning and how they can be read. Brainstorm a class list of additional symbols and what they mean.

14. Use *I Read Signs* to begin a discussion on the information that common signs convey in a brief format. Have students discuss signs they see frequently around the school or neighborhood. Students can design their own sign and write about how it would be used.

15. Use the word lists in *All About Where* as an example of how vocabulary can be developed by looking at photographs. Select another book by Tana Hoban and have students develop a class or group word list of descriptive words.

16. The natural images in the photographs of Tana Hoban capture a moment's insight in the same way that haiku poetry often does. After introducing the haiku form (three lines of five, seven, and five syllables), and sharing examples of this type of poetry, children can select a photograph from one of the books and write haiku based on the images in the photograph.

17. As a group, select a favorite photograph from one of Tana Hoban's books. Decide on a central theme or image from the photograph. Have each student write or dictate a sentence about the central theme or image, and organize these sentences or phrases into a class poem.

18. Have students write individual descriptions while looking at a selected photograph in one of Tana Hoban's books. Each writer creates lists of words in specified categories. Parts of speech might be one category, under which would be listed all the nouns, adjectives, or verbs that could be used to describe the photograph. Categories of descriptive words might relate to the senses, such as words used to describe textures, colors, shapes, and sounds. Positional or relative categories could be used. Introduce the use of a thesaurus, and try to expand each list by using the thesaurus to discover new words. After the word lists are produced, the writer can use these lists to write a creative description of the photograph and his or her response to it.

Library Research

19. Have students use the author catalog to locate other books by Tana Hoban. Develop a set of books by this author for use in the library or classroom.

20. Print the title of each of Tana Hoban's books on 3-by-5-inch cards. Have students practice their alphabetizing skills by putting these cards in alphabetical order.

21. As students look through books by Tana Hoban, have them locate a photograph of something they would like to know more about and use library resources to gather information. For examples, *Dig, Drill, Dump, Fill* has photographs of different types of machinery a student may want to learn about; *Big Ones, Little Ones* has a variety of animals that would be interesting to research.

22. Have students use the subject catalog and subject booklists to develop sets of alphabet books, or books about a specific concept such as size, shape, or color.

Math

23. *26 Letters and 99 Cents* can be used to begin a discussion of coins and how they can be added and subtracted. Use coins or paper coin cutouts in different denominations for students to manipulate. Students can decide how many pennies make a nickel, how many nickels make a dime, and so forth.

24. Share the book *Shapes, Shapes, Shapes* and have students locate and name the different geometric shapes in the book. Make a stack of 3-by-5-inch cards with the different shapes, one per card, for a classroom shape hunt. Each student can select one card to locate things in the classroom that match the shape on his or her card. Students can make a list of their findings to share with the class.

25. While sharing the book *Circles, Triangles, and Squares*, have students draw simple sets of the circles and other shapes they see. Students can cut out the shapes and use them to practice addition and subtraction.

Music

26. Most of Tana Hoban's photographs depict an urban setting. Listen to a recording of urban sound effects and find a picture that might have those sounds.

27. The books *Look! Look! Look!*; *Look Again!*; and *Take Another Look* all lead the reader from a part of a picture to a whole. Use these books to introduce the idea of listening to a part of a piece of music and then identifying the whole. Play a preselected piece of familiar music briefly and invite students to identify the music. Continue with several examples of familiar songs or other music.

Science

28. Use these books to begin a discussion on how eyes are like cameras and how the lenses in eyes and cameras work.

29. Have students close their eyes and listen to the sounds around them. What sounds can they identify? Take a listening walk around the school or the neighborhood and invite students to become aware of the sounds they hear. Look at several of Tana Hoban's books and have students suggest the types of sounds the author might have heard while she was taking particular photographs.

30. After sharing the book *Shadows and Reflections*, have the class divide into two groups—one to explore shadows, the other reflections.

31. Scientists and photographers are both careful observers of their environments. Have students carefully observe their environment either in the classroom or around the school. What is present? What is absent? What objects are natural? What are made by humans? What might a scientist find interesting? What might a photographer find interesting?

32. Scientists use categorization as one of their research tools. Select a category such as a specific color, texture, or shape, and have students go through several of Tana Hoban's books locating items that would fit in the selected category.

33. Share the book *Is It Rough? Is It Smooth? Is It Shiny?* and then have students explore texture. Before class, place textured objects or pieces of fabric in empty margarine or other plastic tubs, and put the tubs in the bottom of a long tube sock. Because students cannot see what is at the bottom of the sock as they put their arms in, they can discover textures by touch.

Social Studies

34. As you share an individual photograph from one of these books, invite students to look at the artifacts in the picture to determine what they tell about the culture in which the photograph was taken. What objects are culture specific? What objects might be used in many societies?

35. As you share one of Tana Hoban's books, have students decide which photographs might have been taken in their neighborhood or city and which ones were obviously not taken in their area. Invite student discussion about how the photographs are like or unlike their area and why.

36. Take a classroom photo walk. Take cameras and have students take pictures to make a class book or display of photographs that depict their neighborhood.

Group Activities

37. Use the books *Is It Larger? Is It Smaller?* and *Is It Rough? Is It Smooth? Is It Shiny?* to introduce a classroom game similar to Twenty Questions. A student can silently select something in the classroom, and other students can use descriptive phrases to try to determine what it is. Examples: Is it larger than a pencil? Is it smaller than a desk? Is it as smooth as the chalkboard?

38. Have a classroom concept scavenger hunt after sharing a variety of Tana Hoban's books. Develop a class list of concepts and have students work individually or in pairs or small groups to locate other things that might be used to picture that concept.

Other

39. As a class, visit a photography lab and discover how film is developed, how photographs are enlarged, and so forth.

40. Invite a newspaper photographer or other professional photographer to visit the classroom to discuss photography as a career. What do photographers have to know? Where do they learn about photography? What different career opportunities are available for photographers?

Ways to Use Activities

For an author study. *See* 6, 10, 19

For *A, B, See!* *See* 4

For *All About Where.* *See* 15

For *Big Ones, Little Ones.* *See* 7, 21

For *Circles, Triangles, and Squares.* *See* 7, 25

For *Dig, Drill, Dump, Fill.* *See* 21

For *Dots, Spots, Speckles, and Stripes.* *See* 5

For *Exactly the Opposite.* *See* 7

For *I Read Signs.* *See* 14

For *I Read Symbols.* *See* 13

For *Is It Larger? Is It Smaller?* *See* 7, 37

For *Is It Rough? Is It Smooth? Is It Shiny?* *See* 8, 33, 37

For *Look Again!* *See* 1, 27

For *Look! Look! Look!* *See* 1, 27

For *Look Up, Look Down.* *See* 7

For *Of Colors and Things.* *See* 2, 19

For *Shadows and Reflections.* *See* 7, 30

For *Shapes and Things.* *See* 4, 7

For *Shapes, Shapes, Shapes.* *See* 7, 24

For *Spirals, Curves, Fanshapes and Lines.* *See* 7

For *Take Another Look.* *See* 1, 27

For *26 Letters and 99 Cents.* *See* 11, 23

For all titles by Hoban. *See* 3, 4, 7, 8, 12, 16, 17, 18, 20, 21, 22, 26, 28, 29, 31, 32, 34, 35, 36, 38, 39, 40

Mario Mariotti

My work is dedicated to many, almost too many, who do not want to know art or have anything to do with it... But to those who will be happy, even if with an instinctive mistrust, just to appreciate something extraordinary.

—Mario Mariotti
(translated by Jo Ann Thweatt)

ABOUT THE AUTHOR

Mario Mariotti was born in Italy in 1936. He studied art at the Accademia di Belle Arti in Florence. He works primarily as a fine artist using a variety of media, including paint, sculpture, photography, and found objects. He has a "glorious studio" in Florence and also shows his art in Europe and at a gallery in Soho, New York City.

Mario Mariotti is best known in the United States for his wordless "hand books," which were first published in Italy.

MARIOTTI'S BOOKLIST

Wordless Books by the Author

Hand Games. Kane/Miller, 1992.

Hands Off! Kane/Miller, 1990.

Hanimals. Green Tiger, 1980.

Hanimations. Kane/Miller, 1989.

Humages. Green Tiger, 1984.

Humands. Green Tiger, 1983.

ABOUT MARIOTTI'S WORDLESS BOOKS

In these works, the eye of the artist finds an array of images hidden in the human hand. The first book, *Hanimals*, introduces the unusual technique that is also used in each succeeding book. The artist has painted and arranged his hands to resemble various animals. Close-up color photographs give life to the imaginative creations. The work of the artist and of the photographer, Roberto Marchiori, combine smoothly.

In *Humands*, the hands are painted and posed to represent people, more animals, and objects. Here the full orchestra appears, complete with soloists, singers, and conductor. A departure is made in *Humages*, in which the face and feet are also used in producing the sometimes unsettling images. The artist uses both his own hands and the hands of his daughter, Francesca, in *Hanimations*. Returning to the zoological realm, the artist and his daughter increase both the number and complexity of the "hanimals."

Sports fans will enjoy Mariotti's two newest books. In *Hands Off!* hands become the best of the world's soccer teams, fans, and officials, in honor of Italy hosting the World Soccer Cup. *Hand Games* celebrates the athletes and events of the summer Olympics.

Many of the images from these books have been exhibited as individual works of art. Each separate illustration or short sequence represents a distinct artistic creation and can be viewed or shared independently.

ACTIVITIES

Arts/Crafts

1. After sharing these books, have students paint their own hands to resemble animals or people.

2. Have students trace one of their hands onto a piece of construction paper and then decorate the tracing to represent some form of person or creature.

3. Have students make handprint pictures by inking their hands and pressing down on a blank sheet of paper.

4. Make reverse handprint pictures by placing the hand on a blank sheet of paper and splatter painting over the hand, creating on the paper a silhouette of the hand surrounded by paint.

5. Make thumbprint pictures using an ink pad. Students can add features to create animals or scenes.

6. Mario Mariotti uses paint on his hands to create. Students can use their hands to paint with finger paint and make handprints.

Bulletin Board/Display

7. Have students create a classroom mural with their handprints. Cover the board with colored paper and have students individually ink or paint their hands and place them on the mural. Students can write their names by their handprints.

8. Make a display of books by Mario Mariotti. Use a photocopier to enlarge his photograph and use it as the center of the display.

Geography

9. The artist was born in Italy and now lives in Florence, Italy. Use a world atlas to locate Florence. Have students use library resources to learn about that city—its geography, climate, famous landmarks, art, and foods.

Language Arts

10. Have each student select a page from one of Mariotti's books to copy and use to create a story or to illustrate a scene based on the image on that page.

11. Invite students to draw a face on the tip of their pointer finger or thumb and allow the "character" to tell about its life.

12. As you share the books *Hanimals* and *Hanimations*, have students determine whether each page represents a real or an imaginary animal. Compare the ones that represent real animals with photographs of those animals.

13. Develop a class list of vocabulary words or phrases related to hands, such as *hands up, hands-on experience, hands off, handy, handicrafts, handcuffs*.

Library Research

14. Have students use reference materials and nonfiction sources to learn about hands.

15. After sharing *Hands Off!* have students use library resources to learn about soccer. What is its history? How is the game played? What are the rules of the game? Who are famous soccer players? What is the World Cup?

16. After sharing *Hand Games*, have students use library resources to learn about the summer Olympics. What events are played? How do they differ from the winter Olympics? How often are they held? Where are they held? Which countries participate? Where can you find the names and sponsoring countries of the winners of each event?

Math

17. Discuss how counting was originally organized, using the 10 fingers, and how units of 10 are used in a counting system.

18. Discuss the use of hands as calculators and teach students the basics of the Chisenbop method using their 10 fingers.

19. Have students discuss how the score is kept in a soccer game.

20. Have students discuss how sports records are kept and what math is required for sports statistics. The class can be divided into small groups, and each group can learn about scoring for a particular sport played during the summer Olympics.

Music

21. After sharing the music section in *Humands*, discuss the instruments of the orchestra portrayed and play recordings so that students can hear the sounds they make. Portrayed in the book are the soloist, the chorus, and the conductor; discuss the role of each.

22. *Humands* portrays choir members singing. Discuss the way the different voices blend in a choir. Divide the class into parts—soprano, alto, and tenor—and teach them a simple song.

Science

23. Share the x-ray picture of hands from *Hanimations* and discuss the bones and joints in our hands and how hands are constructed. Discuss why fingers are able to bend, and why hands can bend at the wrists. Discuss x-rays and how they work to show the bones in our bodies.

24. Make a class list of animals that have handlike appendages (people, apes, raccoons, squirrels, and so forth). Discuss the importance of those "hands" and how they can be used. What can each animal do with its "hands"? What is it unable to do?

25. How many students use their right hand? How many use their left hand? Discuss the reasons for these differences.

Social Studies

26. Examine *Humands* and determine the societal role that each hand character is portraying. Discuss the importance of each of these roles.

27. Study the way that hand decorations vary in different cultures (rings, gloves, tattoos, and so forth).

Group Activities

28. As a class, learn to play soccer.

29. Plan a Mario Mariotti Day and invite another class to attend. Share Mariotti's books and art projects the class has made.

30. Have students carefully plan and present a puppet play, painting their hands to represent the characters.

31. Show students how to cast hand shadows behind a sheet. Invite students to make their own hand shadows and have other students determine what they are showing.

Other

32. Hands are often used in different forms of communication. Discuss uses of hands in classroom communication. Discuss sign language and invite an interpreter to show students a conversation in sign and to teach them a few words.

33. Have students look at one of the photographs in a book by Mariotti and hold their hand in the same position as the hand in the photo. Challenge students to use their imaginations to see what the artist saw in his hands before he added the paint. What other images are they able to see as they change the position of their hands?

Ways to Use Activities

For an author study. *See* 8, 9, 29

For *Hand Games*. *See* 16, 20

For *Hands Off!* *See* 15, 19, 20, 28

For *Hanimals*. *See* 12

For *Hanimations*. *See* 12, 23

For *Humands*. *See* 21, 22, 26

For all titles by Mariotti. *See* 1, 2, 3, 4, 5, 6, 7, 10, 11, 13, 14, 17 18, 24, 25, 27, 30, 31, 32, 33

Mercer Mayer

I find it quite odd to be included among authors. For it is hard to conceive of myself as one. I tell stories with pictures, and quite often I even add words. I am and always have been mostly visual. My verbal skills are almost nil.

—Mercer Mayer

ABOUT THE AUTHOR

Mercer Mayer was born on December 30, 1943, in Little Rock, Arkansas. As a boy he caught frogs in the swamps and forests near his home. From the time he was very small he enjoyed illustrated picture books, particularly those of Arthur Rackham, and the worlds they showed. He decided at a young age that he wanted to be an illustrator of children's books.

Mercer Mayer's father was in the navy, so the family moved around the United States as he was growing up. They moved to Hawaii when Mercer was a teenager, and he graduated from high school there. He attended the Honolulu Academy of Arts for one year, where he was told that he would be a very good book illustrator but that there was little need for illustrators.

He moved to New York but couldn't afford to take art classes, so he assisted the teacher at the Art Students' League for six months. During his early years in New York, Mercer Mayer sold fire alarms, designed tags for a textile firm, and worked for an advertising agency. During his spare time he made sketches of odd creatures and scenes from his childhood. He used these sketches to interest children's book publishers in his work.

A Boy, a Dog, and a Frog was Mercer Mayer's first book. Because of this book, many people have considered Mayer to be one of the first creators of wordless picture books for children. His first book with words was *There's a Nightmare in My Closet*. He has worked on more than 60 books of various types, including nonsense, fantasy, folktales, and realistic stories, using different artistic styles for his illustrations. The author is best known for his Little Critter books and his wordless adventures about a boy, a dog, and a frog.

Mercer Mayer has received a number of awards for his illustrations. *A Boy, a Dog, and a Frog* received the 1970 Society of Illustrators Annual National Exhibit Citation and the 1974 International Books for Children Award from the Association for Childhood Education. In 1974, *Frog Goes to Dinner* was considered one of the Ten Notable Children's Books by the *New York Times*. *Everyone Knows What a Dragon Looks Like* won the 1978 *New York Times* award for best illustrated book.

Mercer Mayer is married and has three children. The family lives in Bridgeport, Connecticut.

MAYER'S BOOKLIST

Selected Books by the Author

Astronaut Critter. Simon & Schuster, 1986.

Baby Sister Says No. Western, 1987.

East of the Sun and West of the Moon. Four Winds, 1984.

I Just Forgot. Western, 1988.

Liverwurst Is Missing. Illustrated by Steven Kellogg. Morrow, 1990.

Liza Lou and the Yeller Belly Swamp. Four Winds, 1984.

The Pied Piper of Hamlin. Macmillan, 1987.

The Sleeping Beauty. Macmillan, 1984.

Terrible Troll. Dial, 1968; 1981.

There's an Alligator Under My Bed. Dial, 1987.

There's a Nightmare in My Closet. Dial, 1990.

What Do You Do with a Kangaroo? Scholastic, 1987.

Whinnie the Lovesick Dragon. Illustrated by Diane Hearn. Macmillan, 1986.

Selected Media from Books by the Author

There's a Nightmare in My Closet. Live action. 16mm film/video. Phoenix/BFA Films and Video, 1987.

Selected Books Illustrated by the Author

Everyone Knows What a Dragon Looks Like by Jay Williams. Four Winds, 1984.

The Figure in the Shadows by John Bellairs. Dial, 1975.

The Gillygoofang by George Mendoza. Dial, 1982.

The Great Brain by John Fitzgerald. Dial, 1985.

Me and My Little Brain by John Fitzgerald. Dial, 1985.

Wordless Books by the Author

A Boy, a Dog, a Frog, and a Friend. With Marianna Mayer. Dial, 1971.

A Boy, a Dog, and a Frog. Dial, 1967.

AH-CHOO. Dial, 1976.

Bubble, Bubble. Four Winds, 1973.

Frog Goes to Dinner. Dial, 1974.

Frog on His Own. Dial, 1973.

Frog, Where Are You? Dial, 1969.

The Great Cat Chase. Four Winds, 1974.

Hiccup. Dial, 1976.

One Frog Too Many. With Marianna Mayer. Dial, 1975.

OOPS. Dial, 1977.

Two Moral Tales. Four Winds, 1974.

Two More Tales. Four Winds, 1974.

Media from Books by the Author

A Boy, a Dog, and a Frog. Live action. 16mm film. Phoenix Films, 1981.

A Boy, a Dog, and a Frog. Sound filmstrip. SVE.

Frog Goes to Dinner. Live action. 16mm film/video. Phoenix/BFA Films and Video, 1985.

Frog on His Own. Sound filmstrip. SVE.

Frog, Where Are You? Sound filmstrip. SVE.

ABOUT MAYER'S WORDLESS BOOKS

The strength of Mercer Mayer's humorous wordless books can be found in the expressive drawing of facial expressions and body language. Elements of slapstick humor, such as exaggeration and anticipation of a coming mishap, enliven the funny plots. Brown or black line drawing in a vigorous, lively style conveys the emotions and reactions of characters. Color rarely appears and is secondary to the drawing when it is used.

A trio of "disaster" books feature a winsome lady hippo. She sets off on a picnic with a gentleman hippo in *Hiccup*. His attempts to cure her hiccups make for a wild boating expedition. In *OOPS*, she is unperturbed as she moves from disaster to disaster, upsetting a fruit stand, shattering china in a shop, and causing a train wreck. She finally meets her equal in *AH-CHOO*, when an elephant with a giant allergy sneezes down houses, courtrooms, and a jail before finally finding his match when the lady hippo comes along.

The best known of Mercer Mayer's wordless book series features a boy, a dog, and various frogs. When a boy and his dog go to the pond to catch a frog, they end up wet and disgusted after various failed attempts. The frog, while not caught, nonetheless becomes a friend. In the first sequel, the frog leaves while the boy and his dog are sleeping. Their search leads to the discovery of the frog at home with his family. Although the first frog prefers to stay in the pond, a young and compatible frog goes off with the boy and dog. A turtle joins the group in *A Boy, a Dog, a Frog, and a Friend*. In *Frog on His Own*, Frog has adventures in a city park. In *Frog Goes to Dinner*, Frog sneaks into the boy's pocket to be taken to a fancy restaurant, where he enjoys the chaos he creates. Frog is not at all pleased, however, when a surprise package arrives that contains a new, smaller frog in *One Frog Too Many*.

In the moral tales series, two little stories are bound back-to-back, so that the reader can begin at either end. In fable fashion, animals act out the brief and humorous sequences. A bear finds old items of clothing and fancies himself well dressed until a goat laughs at him; a top hat that appears funny on a furry bird becomes the nest for another bird until it is reclaimed; two young pigs dress for a romantic evening and end up in a mud puddle; and a fox tricks elegant ladies into purchasing discounted furs and hats, which are actually live animals that return to him.

Two of Mayer's books are not in a series: *Bubble, Bubble*, recently rereleased with text, and *The Great Cat Chase*. Both of these titles deal with imagination. *Bubble, Bubble* concerns a boy who buys a magical bubble mixture from which he blows increasingly amazing and threatening creatures. *The Great Cat Chase* shows children engaged in pretend play as they pursue a cat who does not want to participate in their play activities.

ACTIVITIES

Arts/Crafts

1. As you share the books *OOPS* and *Hiccup*, have students notice the hats the lady hippo wears. Have students cut out a lady hippo and glue her to a large sheet of construction paper. Then have each student design a new hat for the hippo.

2. Teach students to fold newspaper hats such as the one the boy wears in *One Frog Too Many*.

3. Share the book *Bubble, Bubble*. Mix a little powdered tempera paint into a bubble solution. As bubbles are blown, students can catch them on sheets of construction paper. As the bubbles pop, they leave the outline of a shape on the paper, creating a design. These shapes can be displayed as they are, or students can add features to make creatures similar to the ones in the book.

4. The use of line is often taken for granted since it is such an inherent part of every illustration. Discuss line as an element of design and how horizontal, vertical, and diagonal lines can be used to convey meaning. Use an opaque projector to enlarge one of Mayer's wordless books so that the whole class can view it and discuss the way Mayer uses line.

5. Divide the class into small groups and give each group one of Mayer's wordless titles. Have students look carefully at the way the artist conveys facial expressions and feelings using only black line drawings. Students can take turns expressing an emotion while the others in their group use them as models to practice drawing facial expressions.

6. Frog is very energetic and is always popping out of unusual places. Show students how to make folded paper pop-up pictures, and invite them to create a new situation for Frog where he can pop up.

Bulletin Board/Display

7. Make a display of books illustrated and/or written by Mercer Mayer. Use a photocopier to enlarge his photograph and use as the center of the display.

8. Enlarge and laminate pictures of the boy, the frog, and the dog and use them as part of a display of student work about this series of books.

9. Create a pond scene on the bulletin board, with the forest in the background. As students read Mercer Mayer's books, have them put the title of a book and their name on a construction paper frog or turtle and place it in or around the pond.

Geography

10. Mercer Mayer was born in Little Rock, Arkansas. He has also lived in Honolulu, Hawaii, and New York City. He currently lives in Bridgeport, Connecticut. Locate these four locations on a map of the United States. Divide the class into four groups and have each group use library resources to learn about one of these cities. You may want to have each group write a letter to the chamber of commerce to request additional information. Place the map in the middle of a bulletin board, marking each of the cities with a colored pin and attaching them with yarn to the side where group reports are shown.

Language Arts

11. *AH-CHOO, OOPS,* and *Hiccup* all portray humorous catastrophes. After sharing these books, have students write their own stories about catastrophes, using one-word titles.

12. After sharing *Frog Goes to Dinner*, make a menu for the restaurant. Use sample menus from local restaurants to discuss format. Decide on the type of restaurant, the foods it would serve, and the cost of each item. Give the restaurant a name and a location.

13. Have students make individual books with further adventures about the boy, the dog, and the frog. Books can be shared with classmates.

14. Frog gets himself into a lot of unintentional trouble. Many pets create troublesome situations. Have students write and/or illustrate their own stories about a real or imaginary pet that gets into trouble or causes trouble for others.

15. On the first page of *One Frog Too Many*, the boy receives a large package with air holes. Enlarge this page so that the class can view it, and have students write about what they think might be inside the box. Students can share what they wrote with the class before the rest of the book is shared.

16. As you share the series of books about the boy, the dog, and the frog, make a class list of the emotions that are conveyed (hope, frustration, anticipation, and so forth). Have each student select one of the characters and use first-person narrative to tell about that character's feelings as he or she goes through the book.

17. Discuss the conflict or problem presented in each of several titles. After identifying the conflict, discuss how it was resolved. Is the resolution satisfactory? What other ways might the conflict have been resolved?

18. Discuss news stories and their attention-grabbing captions. Each student can select one of Mayer's wordless books and write a humorous or sensationalistic news story with a caption (examples: "Frog Destroys Picnic in Park"; "Boy Receives Unusual Gift"). When completed, the stories can be compiled into a class newspaper or placed on a news board display.

19. Begin a discussion of moral tales with the titles by Mayer. Share other moral tales with the class and then have students write their own moral tales based on current classroom or societal concerns.

Library Research

20. Have students use the author catalog to locate other books by Mercer Mayer. After students have gathered together a variety of books, have them discuss the different types of characters, stories, and artistic styles.

21. Have students use the subject catalog or booklists to develop a collection of fiction and picture books that have hippos as main characters. Each student or small group of students can read one of these books and compare it with the hippo in *Hiccup* and *OOPS*.

22. Have students use the subject catalog or booklists to develop a collection of fiction and picture books that have frogs as characters. Students can compare the frogs in these books with the frog in Mayer's series.

23. Have students use the subject catalog and reference sources to locate nonfiction information about frogs and turtles.

24. There are six books in the series about the boy, the dog, and the frog. Introduce the idea of book sequels and books in series using these books as an example. Have students locate other books that have sequels or are part of a series.

Math

25. Begin a discussion on exponential growth with the question, how many frogs is one too many? Use this concept to explain how animal populations can grow too large for the resources in their environment.

26. Frog jumps all over the place in these books. There are frog-jumping contests around the country that are famous. Use frog jumping as a way to discuss measurement. Have students pretend they are frogs and see who can jump the farthest. Mark a starting line and mark where each student lands. Have students use a measuring tape to determine how far they jump and record the results.

27. Have students create formulas to describe a character in a book and then have others in the class see if they can tell who has been described. Example: 2 eyes + 2 ears + 1 mouth + 4 legs + 1 tail = dog.

Music

28. In *Frog Goes to Dinner*, there is a group of musicians playing dinner music. Look at the instruments and listen to the type of dinner music they might play.

29. Collect frog songs to sing as a group. Examples: "Froggy Went a' Courtin'," "Little White Duck," "Glump, Glump Went the Little Green Frog," "I'm in Love with a Big Blue Frog."

Science

30. After sharing *Bubble, Bubble*, make a bubble mixture and have students blow bubbles, noting the colors and the variety of sizes and shapes.

31. Study the ecosystem of a pond and the role frogs play in it. If possible, take a field trip to a pond and observe the different animal and plant life.

32. Use the series of books about the boy, dog, and frog to introduce auditory perception and sounds. Listen to recordings of pond life and frogs croaking; listen to the barking of dogs. How do animals make their different sounds? What do the sounds mean? Make a class list of the different sounds the boy might hear when he is at the pond, at the restaurant, and at home.

Social Science

33. These books by Mercer Mayer portray a variety of friendships. Discuss friendship and its importance in our lives. Do friends have to be human? The same age? Invite students to tell what they think is the most important part of being a friend.

34. In *Hiccup*, the hippos become involved in a conflict that turns into one-upmanship. Discuss retribution and one-upmanship and whether these are effective ways to resolve conflicts. What other interactions might have been helpful to these characters?

35. In *The Great Cat Chase*, children dress up in adult clothes and pretend that they are a policeman, a nurse, a cowboy, and a mother. Discuss occupational clothing and how we can often tell what a person does by the clothes they are wearing.

Group Activities

36. Have students work in small groups to develop dialogue for a play, using one of Mayer's books. Students can determine how many characters are in the story and make simple masks of construction paper glued to a stick that can be held in front of the face. After rehearsing the script several times, the group can present the play in front of the class.

37. The boy goes to the pond to fish. Have children use their imaginations and draw something he might catch in the pond. Cut the objects out and put a paper clip on them before putting them in a small "pond." Students can take turns "fishing" with a small pole and string that has a magnet at the end.

38. Celebrate Mercer Mayer and his books by having a Mercer Mayer Day. Read aloud selected books and show videos and filmstrips of other works. There are rubber stamps of characters from Mayer's books that can be ordered from the Kidstamps catalog. Students can use the rubber stamps and ink pads to make bookmarks.

Other

39. Use the books about the boy, dog, and frog and the books about the hippos to discuss water safety at a pond, at a lake, and at home. As you share the books, have students notice which things would not be safe (swimming in a pond alone without another person around, pushing someone off a boat into the lake, and so forth).

40. The lady hippo hiccups, which causes her many problems. What are some home remedies for hiccups? Discuss home remedies that are used by students' families for other simple ailments such as sneezing, bee stings, stomachaches, and headaches.

Ways to Use Activities

For an author study. *See* 7, 10, 20, 38

For *A Boy, a Dog, a Frog, and a Friend. See* 6, 8, 9, 13, 16, 22, 23, 24, 26, 29, 31, 32, 37

For *A Boy, a Dog, and a Frog. See* 6, 8, 9, 13, 16, 22, 23, 24, 26, 29, 31, 32, 37

For *AH-CHOO. See* 11

For *Bubble, Bubble. See* 3, 30

For *Frog Goes to Dinner. See* 6, 8, 9, 12, 13, 16, 22, 23, 24, 26, 28, 29, 32

For *Frog on His Own. See* 6, 8, 9, 13, 16, 22, 23, 24, 26, 29, 31, 32

For *Frog, Where Are You? See* 6, 8, 9, 13, 16, 22, 23, 24, 26, 29, 31, 32

For *The Great Cat Chase. See* 35

For *Hiccup. See* 1, 11, 21, 34, 39, 40

For *One Frog Too Many. See* 2, 6, 8, 9, 13, 15, 16, 22, 23, 24, 25, 26, 29, 31, 32

For *OOPS. See* 1, 11, 21

For *Two Moral Tales. See* 19

For *Two More Tales. See* 19

For all titles by Mayer. *See* 4, 5, 9, 14, 17, 18, 27, 33, 36, 39

Emily Arnold McCully

Picnic *was a major breakthrough for me. I had illustrated for years and written adult fiction and a children's text seemed to fall somewhere between. I wasn't able to interest any editors in the stories I showed them. Finally, I began fooling with a dummy before writing a text.* Picnic *was the result and at that time, I felt that I should apologize for not having provided words, since it seemed to be shortchanging the children. However, as soon as I witnessed a "reading" of the book by a five year old and heard more of the experiences of parents, children and teachers, with the series, I was thrilled by the tremendous potential for invention and interpretation. As for language, how much* more *emerged than would have been contained in a conventional book.*

—Emily Arnold McCully

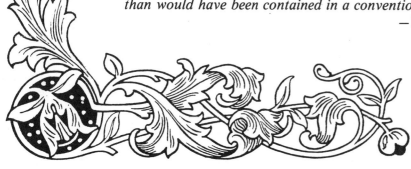

ABOUT THE AUTHOR

Emily Arnold McCully was born July 1, 1939, in Galesburg, Illinois. Her mother was a teacher and her father was a writer. When Emily was four years old, her family moved to New York, where her father wrote and produced radio shows. Although she grew up living on Long Island and lived in the Midwest for only a few years, she considers herself to be a midwesterner, since she visited there often as she was growing up. As a child she made her own books—writing, illustrating, and binding them. Her stories were usually about boy heroes, and today she is very conscious of sex stereotyping in children's books.

Emily Arnold McCully graduated from Brown University, and she attended graduate school in art history at Columbia. Prior to illustrating children's books, she worked at several jobs, including mat cutting for a large advertising agency and freelance magazine illustration and book jacket design. She was invited to illustrate a children's book in 1966 after an editor from Harper & Row saw a subway poster she had designed. Since that time, she has illustrated and written more than 70 books.

Awards and honors include a gold medal from the Philadelphia Art Director's Club in 1968. *A Journey from Peppermint Street*, which she illustrated, won the 1969 National Book Award, and *Hurray for Captain Jane!* was a Children's Book Showcase title in 1972. *MA nDA LA* was included in the 1975 Brooklyn Art Books for Children. *Mirette on the High Wire* won the 1993 Randolph Caldecott Medal.

According to McCully, the high point of her school appearance experience came when she visited the Parkway School District outside of St. Louis. She was greeted by class after class in which each child owned one of her wordless books and had written versions of the stories, often with new illustrations.

Emily Arnold McCully has two sons, Nathaniel and Thaddeus. She is no longer married. Her hobbies include restoration of old houses and organic gardening. She lives in Brooklyn, New York.

MCCULLY'S BOOKLIST

Selected Books by the Author

The Evil Spell. HarperCollins, 1990.

The Grandma Mix-Up. HarperCollins, 1988.

Grandma's at Bat. HarperCollins, 1993.

Grandma's at the Lake. HarperCollins, 1990.

Help! from Camp Whatsis. Western, 1983.

Mirette on the High Wire. Putnam, 1992.

Speak Up Blanche! HarperCollins, 1991.

Zaza's Big Break. HarperCollins, 1989.

Selected Books Illustrated by the Author

Alice and the Boa Constrictor by Laurie Adams and Allison Coudert. Houghton Mifflin, 1983.

The Bed Book by Sylvia Plath. HarperCollins, 1976.

Best Friend Insurance by Beatrice Gormley. Dutton, 1983.

Black and Brown Is Tan by Arnold Adoff. HarperCollins, 1973.

The Boston Coffee Party by Doreen Rappaport. HarperCollins, 1988.

The Butterfly Birthday by Ann Herold. Macmillan, 1991.

The Explorers of Barkham Street by Mary Stolz. HarperCollins, 1985.

Fifth Grade Magic by Beatrice Gormley. Dutton, 1982.

Friday Night Is Papa Night by Ruth Sonneborn. Puffin, 1987.

Gertrude's Pocket by Miska Miles. Peter Smith, 1984.

Go and Hush the Baby by Betsy Byars. Viking, 1971.

How to Eat Fried Worms by Thomas Rockwell. Watts, 1973.

Hurray for Captain Jane! By Sam Raevin. Parents Magazine Press, 1971.

A Journey from Peppermint Street by Meindert De Jong. Harper & Row, 1968.

MA nDA LA by Arnold Adoff. Harper, 1971.

Maxie by Mildred Kantrowitz. Macmillan, 1970; 1984.

Molly at the Library by Ruth Radlauer. Simon & Schuster, 1988.

Wordless Books by the Author

The Christmas Gift. Harper & Row, 1988.

First Snow. Harper & Row, 1985.

New Baby. Harper & Row, 1988.

Picnic. Harper & Row, 1984.

School. Harper & Row, 1987.

Media from Books by the Author

Picnic. Video. Weston Woods.

ABOUT MCCULLY'S WORDLESS BOOKS

Emily Arnold McCully's five wordless picture books are about a large family of mice and focus on the youngest of the nine siblings. This little mouse is distinguished in some way from the others in each book—by a pink hat and scarf, by the toy she carries, or by the watch she wears. In *Picnic*, the littlest mouse is lost as the family travels to a favorite picnic spot; in *First Snow*, she is frightened by the high sledding hill; in *School*, she follows her older siblings on the first day of school. When the new baby arrives in the fourth book, the little mouse must deal with the emotions of no longer being the baby of the family. The final book shows the family celebrating Christmas. The little mouse breaks her wonderful new present and receives a replacement gift from her grandparents' attic.

The active mouse family is shown enjoying one another and interacting in many ways. The siblings, the parents, and the grandparents are all involved and caring. The clear, easy-to-follow plots revolve around an incident for the central character, but additional stories are going on with other family members as the bustling activity of a large household fills each page.

Taken together, the first four books cover the seasons of the year. McCully says, "*Picnic* was inspired by an actual truck parked in the New York State Berkshire-Taconic hills. It prompted a winter story in the same setting and then 2 more, with the seasons as characters." The dominant colors in each book portray the season: *Picnic* is summery green, while the reds and oranges of autumn predominate in *School*. In *First Snow*, cool blues and grays highlight the white snow, and *New Baby* is full of the pastels of a floral spring. The theme, activities, and mood of each book match typical ones for each season. The illustration technique combines a delicate pen-and-ink line with bold watercolors.

One of the most obvious aspects of each book is the importance of emotions and feelings. Corresponding to the concerns and interests of early childhood, these emotions are readily interpreted by children from kindergarten to third grade. The rural environment with its outdoor activities enhances the innocence of pleasures and tragedies in each plot. A warm and affectionate family is shown with gentle humor, and each simple story provides a sense of security and satisfaction in its resolution. Although the concerns are universal—the fear of being abandoned; the desire to grow up and do what older kids do; the fear of a new experience; loneliness; jealousy; and disappointment—they are shown in a nonthreatening way through the warmth of the illustration. The small female main character shows resourcefulness and initiative as she overcomes fears and bad feelings and becomes successful in her interactions with others.

ACTIVITIES

Arts/Crafts

1. Students can make a stick puppet of their favorite mouse. The puppet can be used to tell one of the stories from that character's point of view.

2. Students can model a mouse figure from a modeling compound.

3. Have students look at the dominant color in each book and discuss how it gives the feeling of the season in which the story is set. Invite students to create original drawings, selecting a season and a color for that season. What happens when inappropriate colors are used for a drawing of a season?

4. Have students observe the decorative art used for the title of each book. Invite students to use decorative art to make a drawing of their own first name.

Bulletin Board/Display

5. Using the five books about the mice family, have students create a map mural. Where is their house? Where is the grandparents' house? Where is the school? Where did they picnic (include a pond, etc.)? Where are the hills where they go to play in the snow? Other buildings can be added, such as a grocery store or gas station.

6. Use the overhead projector to make large pictures of each of the characters in the books. Color or paint each character and include a label for the name of each mouse. Invite class members to name the young mice. Laminate the characters and display them with multiple copies of the books.

Geography

7. The author was born in Galesburg, Illinois, grew up on Long Island, New York, and currently lives in Brooklyn, New York. Pinpoint these three locations on a map of the United States. Use library resources to study the two states and to determine differences McCully might have found between living in Illinois and living in the New York City area.

Language Arts

8. As you share the books with a group, have participants determine how they can tell which mouse is the smallest (by her special toy, her watch, and so forth). Have each student tell something that is special about the child sitting next to him or her.

9. As you read each book, identify and discuss the feelings the little mouse shows in each story. Develop a class list of vocabulary words for feelings—lonely, jealous, disappointed, proud, happy, afraid, and so forth.

10. Use the vocabulary words for feelings and the feelings expressed in one of the books, and invite students to write or tell about a time when they had similar feelings, such as being lost or left out.

11. Use one of the books as a discussion starter to have class members tell about favorite recollections from life in their own families.

12. The smallest mouse is the focal character in all five of these books. Write or tell one of the stories from another character's point of view.

Library Research

13. Have students use the subject catalog or booklists to develop a collection of fiction or picture books that have mice as main characters. Each student can read one of these books and tell how the characters are the same or different from the mice in Emily Arnold McCully's books.

14. Have students use the author catalog to locate books illustrated by Emily Arnold McCully. In class, have students look at her illustrations in a variety of titles to compare them and to determine how they add to the story being told.

Math

15. Make simple mice cutouts from construction paper and use them for simple addition and subtraction problems. For example: Three mice plus four mice equal how many mice?

16. As students look at one of the books, have them create sets of mice for each page according to what the mice are doing, whether they are adults or children, and so forth. Example: How many mice are sitting on the page? How many mice children are on the page? How many adult mice are missing from the page?

Music

17. What songs could the mice sing while they are traveling to and from their picnic? Learn songs to sing in the car or on the school bus.

18. What Christmas carols could the mice sing while they are by the Christmas tree? Learn, or adapt, Christmas songs.

19. What lullabies could be sung to the new baby mouse? Listen to lullabies and/or sing lullabies.

20. What school songs can you sing? Learn to sing "School Days, School Days."

21. Grandpa Mouse plays a banjo. Discuss banjos and bring a banjo, or show a picture of one. Play a record or tape of banjo music for students to listen to.

Science

22. Relate these books to each season of the year. Discuss the seasons and how they differ in your area. What causes the seasons? What effect does each season have on the people in your area (clothes, activities, and so forth)?

Social Studies

23. Use these books to begin a discussion on family structures. Who are the family members in these books? What are siblings? What is the sibling order of the mice children? What are extended families? How is this family structure like or different from family structures of class members?

24. Make a class list of the leisure-time activities found in these books. Discuss leisure time and the importance of play. Invite students to discuss how their families spend their leisure time and what they enjoy.

Group Activities

25. Plan and go on a picnic—either outdoors or in the classroom.

26. Make mouse ears and have students wear them for the day as they enjoy these books.

27. At recess, play mouse baseball with all students wearing their ears.

Ways to Use Activities

For an author study. *See* 7, 14

For *The Christmas Gift*. *See* 18

For *First Snow*. *See* 17

For *New Baby*. *See* 19

For *Picnic*. *See* 17, 21, 25

For *School*. *See* 17, 20

For all titles by McCully. *See* 1, 2, 3, 4, 5, 6, 8, 9, 10, 11, 12, 13, 15, 16, 22, 23, 24, 26, 27

Peter Spier

The question about why I have done some wordless picture books is an easy one to answer: because they did not need words. In the case of Noah's Ark *the sequencing of the story is so well known, and in the others I felt that words would have been superfluous. Yet the curious thing is that in, for example, Sweden and Italy, wordless books are not acceptable, and when I sell a publisher there one of these books ... they add a silly text.*

I feel in any case that writing and drawing are so closely related that both forms of expression are identical in many ways. And then there are, of course, books that cannot be done without words. I have sometimes thought that the perfectly written book does not require any pictures, and the perfect picture book no words. But I suppose one could argue that!

—Peter Spier

ABOUT THE AUTHOR

Peter Spier was born in Amsterdam, the Netherlands, on June 6, 1927. He grew up in the small romantic village of Broek in Waterland and traveled by train to school in Amsterdam. His father was a famous journalist and illustrator who worked at home, so young Peter grew up surrounded by books, art, and illustration. When he was 18, he decided to make this his career and attended the Rijksacademie voor Belldende Kunsten in Amsterdam. Upon completion of school he was drafted into the Royal Netherlands Navy, where he was an officer. He then went to work for *Elsevier's Weekly*, the largest Dutch newspaper.

Peter Spier came to the United States in 1952 to work for Elsevier Publishers in Houston, Texas. He then moved to the New York City area, where he began illustrating magazines and children's books and later wrote and illustrated his own books. Peter Spier is a naturalized U.S. citizen and lives in Shoreham, New York. He is married and has two grown children.

Peter Spier's illustrations are known for their historical accuracy and myriad of meticulous details. Most of his picture books have a historical or local setting. He learns as much as possible about a subject or a region through extensive research and by traveling there to make sketches and take notes of colors. His books often include historical notes or other scholarly information.

Peter Spier illustrated over 100 books by other authors before writing and illustrating his first book, *The Fox Went Out on a Chilly Night*, which won the 1962 Caldecott Honor Book Award. He received almost 30 major awards and honors for his works between 1957 and 1987. *Noah's Ark* received the 1978 Randolph Caldecott Medal, the Lewis Carroll Shelf Award, the Christopher Award, the 1977 *New York Times* Choice of Best Illustrated Children's Books of the Year Award, the International Board on Books for Young People (IBBY) Honor List Award in 1980, and the American Book Award in 1982. *London Bridge Is Falling Down* received the 1967 Boston Globe-Horn Book Award, and *The Erie Canal* received the 1970 Christopher Award.

SPIER'S BOOKLIST

Selected Books by the Author

The Book of Jonah. Doubleday, 1985.

Bored—Nothing to Do! Doubleday, 1978.

Crash! Bang! Boom! Doubleday, 1972.

The Erie Canal. Doubleday, 1970.

Fast-Slow High-Low. Doubleday, 1972.

The Fox Went Out on a Chilly Night. Doubleday, 1961.

Gobble, Growl, Grunt. Doubleday, 1971.

London Bridge Is Falling Down. Doubleday, 1972.

Oh, Were They Ever Happy. Doubleday, 1978.

People. Doubleday, 1980.

The Star-Spangled Banner. Doubleday, 1973.

Tin Lizzie. Doubleday, 1975.

To Market! To Market! Doubleday, 1967.

We the People: The Constitution of the United States. Doubleday, 1987.

Selected Media from Books by the Author

Bored: Nothing to Do! Video. Great Plains National Instructional Television Library. (Reading Rainbow Series #64)

The Erie Canal. 16mm film/video. Weston Woods.

The Fox Went Out on a Chilly Night. 16mm film/video. Weston Woods.

The Star-Spangled Banner. 16mm film/video. Weston Woods.

Selected Books Illustrated by the Author

The Cow Who Fell in the Canal by Phyllis Krasilovsky. Doubleday, 1957.

Last Hurdle by F. K. Brown. Shoe String, 1953; 1988.

The Little Riders by Margaretha Shemin. Putnam, 1988.

100 More Story Poems. Compiled by Elinor Parker. Crowell, 1960.

Wordless Books by the Author

Dreams. Doubleday, 1986.

Noah's Ark. Doubleday, 1977.

Peter Spier's Christmas. Doubleday, 1983.

Peter Spier's Rain. Doubleday, 1982.

Media from Wordless Books by the Author

Award Puzzles: Noah's Ark. JTG of Nashville, 1990.

Noah's Ark. Video. Hi-Tops Video, 1989. (Stories to Remember Series)

Peter Spier's Christmas. Sound filmstrip. Spoken Arts/SVE.

Peter Spier's Rain. Sound filmstrip. Spoken Arts/SVE.

ABOUT SPIER'S WORDLESS BOOKS

Three of Peter Spier's wordless books depict ordinary people in everyday situations, which through observation and imagination are made worthy of careful examination. In the fourth book, *Noah's Ark*, Spier takes an extraordinary life and illuminates the daily, ordinary parts of it that are not normally part of the account. In every book, abundant detail reflects the artist's close attention and delight in recording the minutia of his observations. The clean line of his ink drawing and the clear colors of the watercolor washes he uses are characteristically humorous and full of vitality.

Dreams, Rain, and *Christmas* all show siblings enjoying their interactions with each other and with a warm traditional family. A boy and girl wander out to a grassy meadow to watch clouds in *Dreams*. The warmth of a sunny summer day surrounds them as they lie back to daydream about the cloud forms. Vague cloud masses on one page become elaborate pictures on the next as the children transform the sky with their imaginations. In the air, birds, insects, aircraft, and hot air balloons join the clouds in creating each picture.

As spring storm clouds gather in *Rain*, a brother and sister play outside. They don boots and rain gear to explore their world in the downpour, enjoying the many aspects of rain and wetness. The artist invites the reader to join them in the wonder of seeing the world in a fresh and curious way. Wet weather activities outside are followed by a warm bath and cozy indoor activities until bedtime. The passage of the storm during the night is especially effective.

An affectionate look at Christmas traditions rounds out this group of books. A family of five makes elaborate preparations for the celebration, beginning with the withdrawal of Christmas Club savings. Holiday activity throughout their community and neighborhood supports the family's special traditions. Occasional quiet and contemplative scenes contrast with the ongoing hectic activity of the season. Shopping, decorating, singing, and cooking lead to the day itself, and the aftermath of dirty dishes and stacks of trash. The season's activities are completed with exchanging presents, taking down decorations, and opening a new savings account.

Noah's Ark takes the well-known story of the Great Flood and illuminates it with everyday detail. Bustling activity and the problems, chores, and hard work involved in taking care of so many animals are shown with realism and humor. The poignant sequence of the animals left out of the ark is balanced by the abundant life aboard as baby animals of all kinds are born during the voyage. A translation of the Dutch poem "The Flood" by Jacobus Revius appears as an introduction to the wordless story.

ACTIVITIES
Arts/Crafts

1. Show students how to fold and cut paper for paper angel or doll chains similar to the ones on the tree in *Christmas*. Students can make their own chains.

2. Use pieces of sponge and white tempera paints to make sponge cloud paintings on blue paper. Do the clouds form pictures like the ones in *Dreams*?

3. Have students make paper blot art by folding a piece of construction paper in half, then placing a blob of paint inside and folding it so that the paint forms a blot. What does the blot look like?

4. Locate pictures of rainy, cloudy days that other famous artists have painted (for example, Monet, Turner) and invite students to compare and contrast them with the illustrations by Spier.

5. Have students make rainy day pictures using blue or gray crayons to draw their pictures and a watery blue paint wash to paint over them.

6. Talk about the color spectrum and have students make a rainbow by putting colors in the same order as the spectrum. How does their rainbow compare to the rainbow at the end of *Noah's Ark*?

7. Have students, using colored chalks, completely cover a large piece of cardboard or construction paper. Place the paper outside as light rain falls. The raindrops will create a pattern on the paper. On a sunny day, light spray from a hose can be used to create the effect of raindrops.

Bulletin Board/Display

8. Make a display of books written and/or illustrated by Peter Spier. Use a photocopier to enlarge his photograph and place it in the center of the display.

9. Make a large ark out of brown construction paper. Each student can select an animal and make a pair to place in or around the ark. The ark can be set on a green construction paper ground or on a light blue tissue paper sea of water.

10. Cover the bulletin board with a light blue construction paper sky and invite each student to cut out a white construction paper cloud to place in the sky.

11. Make an umbrella mobile by hanging an opened umbrella from the ceiling. Students can cut out and hang "raindrops" with thread. They can write their name on one side of the drop and the title of their favorite book by Peter Spier on the other side.

12. Peter Spier frequently uses small, detailed pictures to highlight different observations from a single situation or circumstance. Have students observe a situation (the classroom, the playground, the neighborhood). Draw a large picture of the situation in the center of a bulletin board or wall mural and invite students to each draw a small picture to highlight details of the situation.

Geography

13. The author was born in Amsterdam, the Netherlands, and grew up in the village of Broek in Waterland. When he came to the United States he first lived in Houston, Texas, and now lives in Shoreham, New York. Locate these four places on a map. Use library resources to discover how Spier's life might have been different in the Netherlands, in Texas, and in New York. Discuss the geography and climate of each and differences in housing, transportation, foods, and clothes.

Language Arts

14. Make a class list of favorite rainy day activities.

15. Read poetry describing rain and have students write their own rain poems.

16. Have students make individual or class books about a particular type of weather day (rain/snow/sunshine/wind).

17. Use *Dreams* to invite children to predict outcomes. What do they really see on a page? Have them predict what the cloud will become before the page is turned.

18. In *Dreams* the two young children appear to be telling stories about the clouds they are looking at. Students can each select a cloud picture that they would like to write an imaginative story about. After writing their story and having another student proof it, they can cut out white paper in the shape of their cloud and carefully copy their story on the cloud for a bulletin board display.

19. In *Christmas* the family prepares for their holiday meal by shopping, baking, and cooking. Discuss the amount of preparation that goes into special holiday meals. Have students write a menu for their favorite holiday meal. Menus can be shared orally, and students can compare foods and how they reflect family preferences.

20. As a class, discuss family holiday traditions and why holidays are important to people. Have students select a holiday of importance to their family and write about what the holiday means to them. Have them include activities traditional in their family and what they do before, during, and after the holiday.

21. Noah took two animals of each type aboard his ark to save them from the ark. Have students think about which 10 animals they would save in case of a disaster. Students can then make a book telling about the type of disaster. They should devote one page to each animal, illustrate the pages, and say why they would save those particular animals.

Library Research

22. Have students use the author index to locate other books written and/or illustrated by Peter Spier. Each student can read one book to share with the rest of the class.

23. Have students use the subject catalog and booklists to locate books on clouds and rain in order to develop a text set that can be used in the library or the classroom. Nonprint materials (filmstrips, videos, study prints) can also be included.

24. Have students select animals from *Noah's Ark* that they would like to learn more about. They can use library resources to learn about those animals.

25. Many cultures include stories about a great flood in their folklore. Use booklists and the subject catalog to locate such stories, and put together a text set of flood stories to compare and contrast as a class.

26. Use materials on holidays and countries to study Christmas customs in the Netherlands and in the United States.

Math

27. The animals went into the ark in pairs. Introduce counting by two's and have students count to 100. Paper cutouts of animals in pairs can be used to help students visualize the concept of 100.

28. Multiply by two. Two animals times two animals equals four animals, and so forth.

29. At the beginning of *Christmas* the children are at the bank, where there is a sign about the Christmas Club. Talk about Christmas Club savings accounts and other ways to save money for holiday purchases. Have students think about how much money they would need for holiday gifts and ways they could earn and save the money. Use the Christmas Club idea to have students calculate the amount they would have if they saved a certain amount each week. Using percentages based on local savings interest rates, have students calculate the amount of interest their money would earn in a year.

30. Using mail order catalogs, have students select one gift for each member of their family. Have them figure out how much it would cost for these gifts, including postage and taxes.

31. Have the class plan a holiday dinner. Decide upon the holiday and then plan a menu. For each item on the menu, list all ingredients and the amounts needed. Remember, some recipes will have to be doubled or tripled to provide a serving for each class member. Make a list of groceries needed. Divide the list so that each student can price several ingredients at the grocery store. Remind students to get both the price per item and the number of servings the item will provide, since it may take several of the item to prepare enough servings for all the students. As a class, figure out what it would cost to prepare the holiday meal. When you have the total cost, divide it by the number of people eating to determine how much it would cost per person.

Music

32. Use percussion instruments to make the sounds of a thunderstorm and rain. Or, locate music with the sounds of rain and storms to play for the group.

33. Improvise the song "It Rained a Mist" to include objects that are rained on in the book *Rain*, or that might be rained on in your neighborhood.

34. Locate and sing folk songs about the story of Noah, such as "Who Build the Ark?" and "One Wide River."

35. Select favorite holiday songs to sing as a group. Since students may celebrate different holidays, they might be able to teach the class new songs.

Science

36. Weather conditions play a role in all four of these wordless books. Have students view the books to determine which types of weather are portrayed. Develop a set of print and nonprint nonfiction resources about weather that students can use to study weather. Discuss types of shelter different animals use to protect themselves from weather conditions in these books and in nature.

37. Study clouds and cloud types. How are clouds formed? What are the names and shapes of different types of clouds?

38. Study the water cycle and clouds. Look for simple experiments that help explain aspects of the water cycle, such as condensation and evaporation.

39. Discuss floods and their causes.

40. Use *Rain* and *Noah's Ark* to locate things that float and those that don't. Discuss why some things float and others don't. Perform simple water experiments with objects that do and do not float.

41. Use these four books to have students identify wet and dry. Which things are wet? Which are dry?

Social Studies

42. Use these books to begin a discussion on family life. Two siblings enjoy a rainy day together. Noah took only his nuclear family on the ark. An extended family enjoys a holiday together. The children in *Dreams* could be siblings or they could be friends.

43. Have students determine the environment in which each of these books takes place. What indications are given as to the culture of each?

44. Use *Christmas* to begin a discussion on the impact of holidays on the economy and the environment. Have students select a holiday and discuss how the economy is affected by that holiday (gift giving, cards purchased, extra groceries, travel, and so forth). What effect does the holiday have on the environment (Fourth of July litter; Christmas tree cutting; number of people using highways, beaches, and parks; and so forth)? Which resources used for holidays are renewable? Which ones are not?

Group Activities

45. On a cloudy day, take a class walk and observe cloud formations and shapes. What do students imagine different cloud shapes to be?

46. Make holiday cutout cookies and invite parents or another class to the room for a holiday celebration.

47. Play a round-robin accumulation game based on the animals going to the ark two by two. The first student names an animal and each child adds an animal after repeating all the prior animals.

48. Celebrate Peter Spier and his books by having a Peter Spier Day. Read aloud selected books, and show videos and filmstrips of other works.

Other

49. Use *Dreams, Rain*, and *Christmas* to discuss appropriate clothing for different seasons and different types of weather. How does our choice of clothing help keep us healthy?

50. Use these books to discuss health and safety during different types of weather. You can make charts for each season or each type of weather and discuss how to stay safe and healthy during each. Sample questions: How do you protect yourself from getting a sunburn on a sunny day? While looking at the clouds, should you look directly at the sun? How might that harm your eyes? Walking in the rain is fun but can be dangerous if there is lightning—what should you do to protect yourself? What would you do to protect yourself if there was a sudden flood in your area? Snow play is fun but can be dangerous. How do you play safely with snowballs and sleds? How do you keep from slipping and falling on ice? Why is it important not to get winter clothes wet and become too cold? What would you do in a blizzard?

51. Peter Spier is known for the numerous details in his books. These details provide a way to explore and improve student visual perception. Divide the class into four groups and have each group work with one of Spier's wordless books to observe the many details on each page. Students, taking turns showing a page, can make a cumulative list of the details they see. Afterward, take a class walk around the school or play-ground and invite students to share details they observe. If you have taken the same walk prior to working with the books, see how students' observation has improved after this activity.

Ways to Use Activities

For an author study. *See* 8, 13, 22, 48

For *Dreams*. *See* 2, 3, 4, 10, 17, 18, 23, 37, 45, 49

For *Noah's Ark*. *See* 4, 6, 9, 21, 24, 25, 27, 28, 32, 34, 39, 40, 47

For *Peter Spier's Christmas*. *See* 1, 19, 20, 26, 29, 30, 31, 35, 44, 46, 49

For *Peter Spier's Rain*. *See* 4, 5, 7, 11, 14, 15, 23, 32, 33, 38, 40, 49

For all titles by Spier. *See* 12, 16, 36, 38, 41, 42, 43, 50, 51

David Wiesner

A wordless book offers a different kind of an experience than one with text, for both the author and the reader. There is no author's voice telling the story. Each viewer reads the book in his or her own way. The reader is an integral part of the storytelling process. As a result, there are as many versions of what happened that Tuesday night as there are readers. For some, the dog in the story is rightfully defending his territory against amphibian invaders, and their sympathy lies with the dog when the frogs get the best of him. For others, the dog is a humorless bully who gets his comeuppance. As the author of a wordless book, I don't have to concern myself about whether the reader's interpretation of each and every detail is the same as mine. My own view has no more (and no less) validity than that of any other viewer. Since my intent was for the book as a whole to make people laugh, all that matters is that the pictures are funny.

A series of individually funny pictures, however, does not necessarily add up to a successful story. The book was very carefully plotted, and details were developed in ways that move the story forward as logically as possible, from the full moon that rises slowly in the sky that first Tuesday night to the gibbous moon that appears a week later at the end. By placing my characters in the context of a familiar reality, I hoped to entice readers to take that great leap of faith and believe that frogs, and perhaps pigs too, could fly—if the conditions were just right!

—David Wiesner

ABOUT THE AUTHOR

David Wiesner was born on February 5, 1956, in Bridgewater, New Jersey. His neighborhood was surrounded by woods, and he and his friends created fantasy worlds as they played in the brooks and streams. Many of his current story ideas come from memories of things he and his friends imagined as children.

David Wiesner has always enjoyed drawing and can still remember how frustrated he felt in kindergarten when a picture he was drawing didn't look like he wanted it to. After high school, he attended the Rhode Island School of Design (RISD), where he majored in illustration. He became interested in the idea of wordless story books during his freshman year, and for his senior project he created a wordless picture book.

The famous children's book illustrator Trina Schart Hyman saw David Wiesner's work when he was a senior at RISD, and he was asked to design a cover for *Cricket* magazine. Since then, he has illustrated children's books and textbooks. He also created E.T. posters for McDonald's when the film was released. *The Ugly Princess* was the first picture book David Wiesner designed and illustrated from cover to cover, and he was invited to exhibit work from the book at the Metropolitan Museum of Art along with well-known children's book illustrators.

David Wiesner has received a number of awards since that time. He and his wife, who is a surgeon, coauthored *The Loathsome Dragon*, which received the 1987 Redbook Children's Picturebook Award. In 1988, *Free Fall* became a Caldecott Honor Book. *Tuesday* received the 1992 Randolph Caldecott Award; it has also been chosen as an American Library Association Notable Book, a Publishers Weekly Best Book of 1991, one of Parenting Magazine's Ten Best Books of 1991, and a Sesame Street Parent's Guide Reviewers' Choice.

Wiesner and his wife, Kim Kahng, have a son, who was born in the spring of 1992. The family lives in Brooklyn, New York.

WIESNER'S BOOKLIST

Selected Books by the Author

Hurricane. Clarion, 1990.

June 29, 1999. Clarion, 1992.

The Loathsome Dragon. With Kim Kahng. Putnam, 1987.

Selected Books Illustrated by the Author

The Boy Who Spoke Chimp by Jane Yolen. Knopf, 1981.

The Dark Green Tunnel by Alan Eckert. Little, Brown, 1984.

Dinosaur Tales by Ray Bradbury. Bantam, 1983.

E.T.: The Storybook of the Green Planet by William Kotzwinkle. Putnam, 1985.

Firebrat by Nancy Willard. Knopf, 1988.

Honest Andrew by Gloria Skurzynski. Harcourt Brace Jovanovich, 1980.

Kite Flyer by Dennis Haseley. Four Winds, 1986.

Man from the Sky by Avi. Knopf, 1980.

Neptune Rising: Songs and Tales of the Undersea Folk by Jane Yolen. Philomel, 1982.

Owly by Mike Thaler. HarperCollins, 1982.

The Rainbow People by Laurence Yep. Harper-Collins, 1989.

The Sorcerer's Apprentice by Marianna Mayer. Bantam, 1989.

Tongues of Jade by Laurence Yep. HarperCollins, 1991.

The Ugly Princess by Nancy Luenn. Little, Brown, 1981.

Wand: The Return to Mesmera by Alan Eckert. Little, Brown, 1985.

Wordless Books by the Author

Free Fall. Lothrop, Lee & Shepard, 1988.

Tuesday. Houghton Mifflin, 1991.

Media from Books by the Author

Free Fall. Video/sound filmstrip. American School Publishers.

Tuesday. Video. Troll Associates, 1992.

ABOUT WIESNER'S WORDLESS BOOKS

The first page of *Free Fall* suggests one of the themes of David Wiesner's works—that of charting unexplored land. On this page, a bedspread ripples and transforms into a map. On the following page, a second theme is introduced as the map flies away with white birds flying above it. These themes of the unexpected landscape of imagination and unusual flight flow through both *Free Fall* and *Tuesday*. Unusual perspectives in luminous watercolors give form to invented landscapes and convey the floating quality of flight. Mystery and wonder predominate in *Free Fall*, while humor and magic prevail in *Tuesday*.

As the map floats away in *Free Fall*, a sleeping child follows it through a dream world reminiscent of Alice's looking glass world. Here, sizes change oddly as one scene transforms into the next, and fantastic characters welcome the dreamer and assist his quest. As the boy begins his final journey across a tossing sea to his own bed, his three mysterious companions are revealed as a salt cellar and two chess pawns. When the boy awakes, all the elements of dream and mystery are revealed as objects in his sunlit bedroom.

Tuesday makes the ordinary world an unexpected land by showing improbable events in an everyday setting. One Tuesday evening, frogs take flight on their lily pads and invade a sleeping small town. The airborne frogs chase sleeping pigeons—and then a dog, which becomes entangled in wash hanging on a line; they discover television as they fly through a living room where the inhabitant is asleep. The frogs' humorous adventures come to an abrupt end at dawn. In the early morning, the television news crew and puzzled police search for an explanation of the strange events as related by one lone man who viewed them. The final pages of the book set the stage for the story to continue on the following Tuesday, as pigs with wings begin to leave a barn.

ACTIVITIES

Arts/Crafts

1. After sharing *Free Fall* and *Tuesday* with the class, discuss works that might have influenced the author. Include books, films, games, poetry, and other resources.

2. After sharing these two books, discuss perspective, noting different perspectives shown in the books. Where might the artist have imagined himself as he was drawing? Have students take an object and look at it from a variety of perspectives; then have them imagine their object from above, from the side, from below, and so forth.

3. In *Free Fall* the leaves turn into swans. Using a variety of leaf shapes, have students trace a leaf and then change it into something else.

4. Discuss mazes and show students the maze in *Free Fall*. Have them draw their own intricate mazes.

5. While sharing *Tuesday*, have students note the expressive faces of the frogs. What do the expressions tell the reader? Students can draw their own frog pictures with interesting expressions.

6. David Wiesner has been interested in wordless cartoons and wordless picture books for quite some time. Invite students to create a wordless cartoon or a wordless panel story.

Bulletin Board/Display

7. Make a display of books written and/or illustrated by David Wiesner. Use a photocopier to enlarge his photograph, and use it as the center of the display.

8. Have students make a class map mural of the boy's dream journey in *Free Fall*.

9. On the back cover of *Free Fall* is a picture of a dragon coming out of a book. Use an enlargement of this picture as the center of a display of characters that might come out of other books students read. Make a pattern of the front cover of a book that students can trace around on construction paper, and cut it out. Each student can label his or her cutout book with the title and author of a favorite book he or she has read and thinks other students would enjoy. A character from the book can be drawn, cut out, and placed as though it is coming out of the book to greet the reader.

Geography

10. David Wiesner was born in Bridgewater, New Jersey. He went to school in Rhode Island and now lives in Brooklyn, New York. Have students locate these three states on a map of the United States. Divide the class into three groups and have each group learn about using library resources by researching one of the states. Each group can share its information with the whole class. What do the states have in common? How do they differ?

Language Arts

11. Before sharing these books with the class, have students predict the contents based on the covers. After sharing the books, discuss how accurate the predictions were. What clues did the author give the reader about the contents of the book through the cover illustration?

12. As you share the book *Free Fall* with the class, stop before the identities of the three companions are shown. Invite students to speculate about the identities of these three mysterious creatures and why they are with the boy. Upon completion of the book, have students write an imaginary adventure incorporating objects from their bedrooms.

13. After sharing *Free Fall*, have students write the story from the boy's point of view.

14. The boy encounters many characters on his nighttime journey in *Free Fall*, including a dragon and a band of pigs. Have students select one of the characters and continue that character's story after the boy returns to his own bed.

15. After reading *Tuesday*, have students write about the occurrences of Tuesday night from the perspective of one of the characters: the turtle, one of the frogs, the dog, the cat, the man eating a late-night snack.

16. Discuss good interviewing skills and the five W's of journalism (who, what, when, where, why). Share the book *Tuesday* with the class. Divide the class into two groups, one representing the man who saw the strange happenings on Tuesday night, and the other the media reporters who interviewed him the next day. Allow time for students to write down notes on what they are going to say and questions reporters might ask, then role-play the interviews in front of the class.

17. Bring in newspapers and discuss the writing of news articles. Have students pretend they are newspaper reporters and write an article about what really happened on Tuesday night. Newspaper headlines are not written by the writer of the article. When the writing is complete, collect the articles and redistribute them so that no one has her or his own article. Have students, after reading an article that someone else has written, write a catchy headline to go with it. Display articles or make a class newspaper.

18. After sharing *Tuesday*, divide the class into seven groups. Give each group a day of the week with instructions to create an imaginary story about what very unusual event might happen on that night. Allow time for brainstorming and discussion of plot, character(s), setting, action, and so forth; one person may be the recorder. Groups can decide how they want to share their story with the rest of the class. They could make an illustrated book, tell the story aloud, dramatize the story, create a puppet play, or other. After all groups have completed their stories and had time to practice, they can present this week of unusual happenings to another class or as a parents' or assembly program.

19. Following the Tuesday night disturbance, the police and detectives interviewed the man who saw the strange events. Have students imagine they are detectives—how are they going to investigate this unusual situation? Have students write a police or detective report of the events and describe how they will proceed with their investigation.

Library Research

20. Have students use the author catalog to locate other books by David Wiesner.

21. David Wiesner has included dragons in three books he has illustrated: *Free Fall, The Loathsome Dragon*, and *Kite Flyer*. Many other books also have dragons as characters. Have students use the subject catalog and booklists to locate other books with dragons in them.

22. In one illustration in *Free Fall*, two knights in armor are standing on the castle wall. Have students research knights and castles using reference and nonfiction resources.

23. The frogs in *Tuesday* are memorable characters. Have students locate and read other picture books and fiction titles that include frogs as characters.

Math

24. A chess set is shown in *Free Fall*. The game of chess helps develop logic skills. Teach students how to play chess and how to express chess moves mathematically.

25. The large clock on the front of *Tuesday* indicates the time, which becomes important in the book. Discuss how time is measured to introduce learning to tell time, or to practice telling time. Make a class list of times (both day and night) that are important to class members.

26. Cut out paper frogs and lily pads to be used as manipulatives for simple addition and subtraction problems.

Music

27. Each of these books creates a mood. *Free Fall* is dreamy, while *Tuesday* is fast-paced and humorous. Play several pieces of mood music for each book and have students decide which music they prefer to set the mood for each title.

28. Use each of these books to begin a lesson on movement. Then play music that fits with the book and have students move to it. Students might float like the leaves in *Free Fall*, then increase their pace as the lily pads fly through the air in *Tuesday*.

Science

29. Flight is portrayed in both *Free Fall* and *Tuesday*. Share these books and have students discuss which things in the books could really fly. Study natural flight and why it is possible.

30. Pigeons are depicted in both books. Use library resources to develop a study about pigeons.

31. At sunrise on Wednesday, the frogs are once again affected by the natural law of gravity. Discuss gravity and its effects.

32. In *Tuesday*, the frogs leave their pond on lily pads. Use library resources to learn about lily pads. Where do they grow? Would it be possible for them to become airborne, or would their long roots keep them in the water? Do water lily plants have flowers?

Social Studies

33. The title page of *Free Fall* includes a map that plays a major part in the story. Maps have been important to explorers for centuries, and today they play a role in almost everyone's life. Discuss maps and mapmaking as well as the skills required to read a map.

34. The cover of *Tuesday* shows a large, public clock. What is the purpose of public clocks? Where are public clocks in your community? Locate information on famous public clocks such as Big Ben in England.

Group Activities

35. As you share these books, invite students to make observations about the illustrations and discuss their observations. For example, in *Free Fall* the map from the title page can be found in every picture—what is its significance? Look at the last picture, where the boy is waking up in his bed, and go back through the book identifying the objects from his room and how they are portrayed in his fantasy adventure.

36. The frogs in *Tuesday* are jubilant as they fly through the air. Teach the students to play a jubilant game of leapfrog.

37. Pigs are portrayed in both books. Select one of the books and have students pay particular attention to the pigs, then create a class story about the pigs' further adventures. After beginning the story, say "oink" and point to a student who continues the story until you say "oink" again. The student then points to another student to continue the story until all students have had a chance to participate.

Other

38. After sharing these books, invite a school librarian or a children's librarian from a public library to present to the class a booktalk on other dream or nighttime fantasy adventures.

39. As a class, learn about the Randolph Caldecott Award. Who was Randolph Caldecott? Why is it such an honor for David Wiesner to be awarded the Randolph Caldecott Medal for *Tuesday*, and for *Free Fall* to be a Randolph Caldecott Honor Book? Invite students to look at other Caldecott Award and Honor books.

Ways to Use Activities

For an author study. *See* 6, 7, 10, 20, 21

For *Free Fall*. *See* 3, 4, 8, 9, 12, 13, 14, 22, 24, 33

For *Tuesday*. *See* 5, 15, 16, 17, 18, 19, 23, 25, 26, 29, 31, 32, 34, 36

For all titles by Wiesner. *See* 1, 2, 11, 27, 28, 30, 35, 37, 38, 39

Section 2

Individual Title Studies

Baker, Jeannie

Window
Greenwillow, 1991.
ISBN 0-688-08917-8; 0-688-08918-6 (lib); LC 90-3922

ABOUT THE AUTHOR AND HER BOOKS

Jeannie Baker was born in England on November 2, 1950. She attended Croydon College of Art in Surrey and received a B.S. degree from Brighton College of Art in Sussex, England. She has worked on collage constructions as a freelance artist and illustrator since 1972. She uses natural materials such as grass, leaves, stones, and real hair for her finely detailed collages. Although her writings are mainly for children and many of her collages are designed to illustrate picture books, she has also worked as a freelance illustrator for publications such as *NOVA*, the *London Times*, the *Sunday Times*, the *Sunday Observer*, and the *New Scientist*. Her collages have been exhibited in London and New York, and in Australia, where they are part of permanent collections at the Australian National Gallery, the State Gallery of Queensland, and the Droomkeen Museum of Children's Literature. Jeannie Baker lives in Sydney, Australia.

Selected Books by the Author

Grandfather. Dutton, 1980.

Grandmother. Dutton, 1980.

Home in the Sky. Greenwillow, 1984.

Millicent. Dutton, 1980.

One Hungry Spider. André Deutsch, 1982.

Where the Forest Meets the Sea. Greenwillow, 1988.

Selected Media from the Author's Books

Where the Forest Meets the Sea. Video. Films Inc., 1988.

Other Books Illustrated by the Author

Polar by Elaine Moss. Dutton, 1979.

ABOUT WINDOW

The same adjectives can be used to describe both the illustration and the content of this book: richly layered, multidimensional, and complex.

The cover art places the window of the title in a house on a newly cleared spot in the Australian woods. A young mother holding a baby looks out of the new window onto a wilderness teeming with animal life. Birthday cards and artifacts on the windowsill, and the altering exterior scene, show the passage of time as the view from the same window is pictured every other year, until the baby has become a 22-year-old man. The final window is a new one, in a newly built house, with the former child now a father himself, holding his infant and looking out as the cycle begins again.

The change from wilderness to city is chronicled in slow stages as the neighborhood is first rural, then suburban, then urban, with only one tree remaining from the original forest. The child's changing experience is also chronicled with his development at each birthday. Touches of irony point to the environmental theme. For example, the beautiful bird flying on the cover has disappeared from the landscape by the time a paper model of it appears hanging above the window 22 years later.

The multimedia collage is textured and effective in conveying the messages of the book. The use of an unchanging frame adds to the impact of the changes seen from outside the window. Following a single child from birth to maturity gives emotional power to the ideas of an individual's impact on the environment and the impact of the environment on the individual.

The fine details in each picture make the illustrations difficult to share with a large group, but rewarding to discuss with a small group. Pointing out changes in each scene engages younger children, and often one needs to go back to a prior page to confirm what has altered. Older children go beyond identifying the changes to discussing and amplifying the boy's life and the reasons for each change.

In the Library (or In the Classroom)

BOOKTALK PROGRAM

The book traces changes from forest to city. Display and booktalk this and other similar titles. Invite children to find out what might have preceded the current appearance of their house, library, or school. What was the original environment of their area? Are there any clues left to the changes that have occurred over the years? City directories, local histories, old photographs, and early maps can be introduced and used in the program.

RELATED MATERIALS

Beekman, Dan. *Forest, Village, Town, City*. Crowell, 1982.

Dragonwagon, Crescent. *Home Place*. Macmillan, 1990.

Goodall, John S. *The Story of a Farm*. McElderry, 1989.

_____. *The Story of a Main Street*. McElderry, 1987.

_____. *The Story of an English Village*. Atheneum, 1978.

Provensen, Alice. *Shaker Lane*. Viking, 1987.

Pryor, Bonnie. *House on Maple Street*. Illustrated by Beth Peck. Morrow, 1987.

von Tscharner, Renata. *New Providence: A Changing Cityscape*. Illustrated by Denis Orloff. Harcourt Brace Jovanovich, 1987.

CRAFT PROGRAM

Begin with a discussion of the types of places in which people live. If you have a window in the room, children can look outside to find clues to the setting they are in. Introduce this book with the idea that looking outside the window tells a lot about people and where they live.

After sharing the book, invite children to create their own window scenes by folding a sheet of dark construction paper in half and cutting out the center. Have scraps of various papers, wallpaper samples, fabric scraps, and natural objects such as leaves and feathers available for the creation of a collage on a light-colored sheet of paper. When the scene is completed, glue the window frame in place. Encourage children to think about the environment they are creating—is it rural, suburban, or urban? What sort of things do the people in the scene do? What is the story in their picture?

RELATED MATERIALS

Bozzo, Maxine Zohn. *Toby in the Country, Toby in the City*. Illustrated by Frank Modell. Greenwillow, 1982.

Chwast, Seymour. *Tall City, Wide Country: A Book to Read Forward and Backward*. Viking, 1983.

LeSieg, Theo. *Come Over to My House*. Illustrated by Richard Erdoes. Random House, 1966.

Provensen, Alice. *Town and Country*. Illustrated by Alice Provensen and Martin Provensen. Crown, 1984.

Spier, Peter. *People*. Doubleday, 1980.

BOOKTALK AND DIARY WRITING PROGRAM

Each of the illustrations in this book encapsulates a day/stage/time period in the same way that a diary entry does. This book can be a dramatic introduction to a booktalking program on books written in diary format, as well as a springboard to writing in diary entry format for older children. As a group, the children can decide who will be the speaker in the diary and compose entries for each page. Individually, children can write an entry for one page of the book and then compare their entries. Notice what details convey meaning for different people, and point out the way in which diaries give information about both the personality of the writer and the time in which the writer lives.

RELATED MATERIALS

Anderson, Joan. *Joshua's Westward Journal*. Photographs by George Ancona. Morrow, 1987.

Blos, Joan W. *Gathering of Days: A New England Girl's Journal, 1830-32: A Novel*. Scribner, 1979.

Bradford, William, and others of the Mayflower Company. *Homes in the Wilderness: A Pilgrim's Journal of Plymouth Plantation in 1620*. Linnet/Shoe String, 1988.

Cleary, Beverly. *Dear Mr. Henshaw*. Illustrated by Paul O. Zelinsky. Morrow, 1983.

_____. *Strider*. Illustrated by Paul O. Zelinsky. Morrow, 1991.

Fritz, Jean. *The Cabin Faced West*. Illustrated by Feodor Rojankovsky. Coward, 1958.

McPhail, David. *Farm Boy's Year*. Atheneum, 1992.

Oakley, Graham. *The Diary of a Church Mouse*. Atheneum, 1987.

Wilder, Laura Ingalls. *On the Way Home; The Diary of a Trip from South Dakota to Mansfield, Missouri, in 1894*. Harper & Row, 1962.

MAKING A DISPLAY

In the first scene in this book, there are many native wild creatures—birds, mammals, and reptiles. By the time the boy is grown and has his own child, only domesticated animals can be seen. Create a display in the library of animals formerly found in your area that might have been seen outside a window in an earlier time. To frame your display, either cut a window frame of dark poster board or borrow a real window frame from a local contractor. Animals for the display can be created by the children, or they can be represented with models or plush toy animals. Outline figures can be cut out and painted, or children can make animals from brown paper bags, molded around wadded-up newspaper with features glued on. Position the animals against a backdrop representing the original habitat of your area.

Include in the exhibit books that highlight the original environment of your area, or that go along with the environmental theme of the book *Window*. The author's note at the end of the book can be typed and set by the display.

RELATED MATERIALS

Carrick, Carol, and Donald Carrick. *A Clearing in the Forest*. Dial, 1970.

Peet, Bill. *Farewell to Shady Glade*. Houghton Mifflin, 1966.

Thiele, Colin. *Farmer Schulz's Ducks*. Illustrated by Mary Milton. Harper & Row, 1988.

Turner, Ann Warren. *Heron Street*. Illustrated by Lisa Desimini. Harper & Row, 1988.

Wegen, Ron. *Where Can the Animals Go?* Greenwillow, 1978.

COLLECTION DEVELOPMENT

Jeannie Baker lives in Sydney, Australia. Use her books and those of other Australian writers for displays, text sets, or thematic units to explore the point of view from "down under." Include a map of Australia and nonfiction materials.

RELATED MATERIALS

Cox, David. *Bossyboots*. Crown, 1987.

_____. *Tin Lizzie and Little Nell*. Bodley Head, 1982.

Fox, Mem. *Koala Lou*. Illustrated by Pamela Lofts. Harcourt Brace Jovanovich, 1989.

_____. *Possum Magic*. Illustrated by Julie Vivas. Harcourt Brace Jovanovich, 1983.

Pender, Lydia. *Barnaby and the Horses*. Illustrated by Inga Moore. Abelard-Schuman, 1961.

Thiele, Colin. *Farmer Schulz's Ducks*. Illustrated by Mary Milton. Harper & Row, 1988.

_____. *Storm Boy*. Illustrated by John Schoenherr. Harper & Row, 1978.

Vaughan, Marsha K. *Wombat Stew*. Illustrated by Pamela Lofts. Silver Burdett, 1984.

Wagner, Jenny. *The Bunyip of Berkeley's Creek*. Illustrated by Ron Brooks. Bradbury, 1977.

In the Classroom (or In the Library)

VISUAL DISCRIMINATION AND LIST MAKING

Have students work in pairs to look carefully at this book. As they look at each two-page spread, have them make a list of what they see in the picture. How does the scene change from picture to picture? What things stay the same? What things change? When the class has completed this task, have two pairs work together and compare their lists.

LANGUAGE ARTS AND ART

Many changes take place in the environment shown in *Window* over a 20-year time period. Have students discover how their neighborhood has changed in the past 20 years. Students can interview people that have lived in the neighborhood for at least 20 years to find out what types of changes they have noticed. Students should take notes on what they learn. Students can also look at back issues of a local newspaper on file in the newspaper's library to find out how the area has changed.

When students have completed gathering information about the past, they can make a list and discuss what they have learned about what the neighborhood was like 20 years ago, as compared to the present. After a discussion of the present, have students make predictions about what the neighborhood will be like in another 20 years.

Students can make a class mural of their neighborhood. It should be divided into three parts—past, present, and future—and illustrate what they have learned in their research and discussions.

RELATED MATERIALS

Coats, Laura Jane. *The Almond Orchard*. Macmillan, 1991.

Pease, Robert. *When Grandfather Was a Boy*. Illustrated by William Dugan. McGraw-Hill, 1973.

Pryor, Bonnie. *House on Maple Street*. Illustrated by Beth Peck. Morrow, 1987.

RELATED NONFICTION MATERIALS

Mabery, D. L. *Tell Me About Yourself: How to Interview Anyone from Your Friends to Famous People*. Lerner, 1985.

Royston, Robert. *Cities 2,000*. Facts on File, 1985.

Weitzman, David. *My Backyard History Book*. Illustrated by James Robertson. Little, Brown, 1975.

LANGUAGE ARTS

The passage of time is shown in the book as the boy celebrates his birthday. Have students think about their own birthdays and the changes that occur from year to year in their own lives. Students can make a web with their current age in the center and previous ages going out from the center. Information about each birthday can be added to the web in brief form. Students may need to talk with family members and look at family photo albums to gain information.

When students have information about each of their birthdays, they can make individual birthday books. For each birthday, students can draw an illustration incorporating information that they have about that birthday. Or, they can write about each birthday: What did they do on their birthday? Where did they live? Who was with them on their birthday?

VISUAL PERCEPTION AND LANGUAGE ARTS I

Windows give us a view of our world. Have students look out the classroom window and describe what they see in oral, visual, or written form. Have the class share their descriptions and discuss whether students saw the same things or different things.

As a class, discuss what someone outside might see by looking in the window.

Share one or more of Roxie Munro's books that show inside and outside views of the same place. Then share the book *Window* and have students write about what someone might see by either looking out the window or looking in the window, using one two-page spread from the book.

RELATED MATERIALS

Mendoza, George. *The World from My Window: Poems and Drawings*. Designed by Alan Peckolick. Hawthorne, 1969.

Munro, Roxie. *The Inside-Outside Book of London*. Dutton, 1989.

_____. *The Inside-Outside Book of New York City*. Dodd, Mead, 1985.

_____. *The Inside-Outside Book of Paris*. Dutton, 1992.

_____. *The Inside-Outside Book of Washington, D.C.* Dutton, 1987.

VISUAL PERCEPTION AND LANGUAGE ARTS II

Take students on a walking field trip of the neighborhood, or a downtown area, and have them pay attention to the different types of windows they see. Take pictures of many different types of windows that students point out, including plain windows, store windows, stained glass, and so forth. Use the pictures to stimulate discussion, research, and writing about windows.

RELATED NONFICTION MATERIALS

Giblin, James Cross. *Let There Be Light: A Book About Windows*. Crowell, 1988.

Bonners, Susan

Just in Passing
Lothrop, Lee & Shepard, 1989.
ISBN 0-688-07711-0; 0-688-07712-9 (lib); LC 88-22021

ABOUT THE AUTHOR AND HER BOOKS

Susan Bonners was born on April 8, 1947, in Chicago, Illinois. Her mother, a commercial artist, taught Susan to draw when she was young. After attending Fordham University and earning a B.A. degree in English, Susan Bonners studied illustration at the New York-Phoenix School of Design in New York City. *Panda* was the first book she wrote and illustrated. Her book *A Penguin Year* received the American Book Award in 1982. Susan Bonners is married and lives in Providence, Rhode Island.

Selected Books by the Author

Panda. Delacorte, 1978.

A Penguin Year. Delacorte, 1981.

Books Illustrated by the Author

Animals in Your Neighborhood by Seymour Simon. Walker, 1976.

Cold Stars and Fireflies: Poems of the Four Seasons by Barbara Esbensen. Crowell, 1984.

A Forest Is Reborn by James Newton. Crowell, 1982.

I Am Four by Louise Fitzhugh. Delacorte, 1982.

Inside Turtle's Shell and Other Poems of the Field by Joanne Ryder. Macmillan, 1985.

Rain Shadow by James Newton. Crowell, 1983.

Sarah's Questions by Harriet Ziefert. Lothrop, Lee & Shepard, 1986.

ABOUT JUST IN PASSING

A baby's yawn begins a sequence of yawns that traverse city and countryside until finally returning to the baby. Based on the idea that yawning is contagious, the sequence can be used as a metaphor for the ways in which people unknowingly influence each other.

The outside cover of the book sets the scene with a mother holding a baby on her shoulder as she tests melons at a fruit stand. As an older woman approaches, the sleeping baby rouses to begin the real action of the book. The importance of this initial yawn is emphasized by a double-page spread showing the mother's back with the yawning baby over her shoulder on the left, and the face of the older woman isolated on the right. The positioning indicates that the action will move from the baby to the older woman, with the surrounding white space isolating and emphasizing the event.

The yawn is a little more difficult to follow in the next sequence as the older woman buys a newspaper, covering her yawn with one hand. As the yawn is passed from person to person, various devices are used to carry it across wider distances. Included are a surveyor who views the yawn through his telescope and a bird watcher using binoculars who sees a telephone lineman yawning.

Once the reader catches the premise of the yawn being passed from person to person, the action becomes easier to follow, although readers may need to review the first two sequences in which the yawns are suggested but not clearly depicted. When the initial premise is understood, the book is easily read, which makes it very appropriate for the less able student, or for the illiterate adult. The panel format assists these readers in sequencing and in following left-to-right, top-to-bottom structure.

The illustrations create a light and airy effect. Summer clothing and outdoor activities set the book in a warm climate, although the cool greens and grays of the artist's pallet keep the sunny day from becoming hot. Illustrations are watercolor and colored pencil in muted shades that fill in simple pen-and-ink outline drawings.

The small size of many of the illustrations and the lack of sharp contrast in the colors make the illustrations difficult to view from a distance and the yawns impossible to pick out. This makes the book difficult to share with a larger group.

In the Library (or In the Classroom)

BOOKTALK PROGRAM

Bedtime tales frequently use a yawn to indicate sleepiness. Booktalk *Just in Passing* using the cover, title page, dedication page, and first yawn to set the scene and to introduce the idea. Close the book and inform the audience that the older woman now feels an irresistible urge to yawn and that someone is going to see her. Invite the group to predict the action that will follow. Then use the section on yawning in Melvin Berger's book *Why I Cough, Sneeze, Shiver, Hiccup and Yawn* and the title of the book to make a transition to other related stories.

RELATED MATERIALS

Brown, Ruth. *The Big Sneeze.* Lothrop, Lee & Shepard, 1985.

Mayer, Mercer. *AH-CHOO.* Dial, 1976.

_____. *Hiccup.* Dial, 1976.

Mueller, Virginia. *Monster's Birthday Hiccups.* Illustrated by Lynn Munsinger. Whitman, 1991.

Saltzberg, Barney. *The Yawn.* Atheneum, 1985.

Thomas, Patricia. *"Stand Back," Said the Elephant, "I'm Going to Sneeze!"* Illustrated by Wallace Tripp. Lothrop, Lee & Shepard, 1971.

Wood, Audrey. *The Napping House.* Illustrated by Don Wood. Harcourt Brace Jovanovich, 1984.

RELATED NONFICTION MATERIALS

Berger, Melvin. *Why I Cough, Sneeze, Shiver, Hiccup and Yawn.* Illustrated by Holly Keller. Crowell, 1983.

STORYTELLING AND PARTICIPATION PROGRAM

This book begins and ends with the same baby yawning, indicating that the story is about to begin again. Introduce this genre of stories with either "The Snooks Family" or *If You Give a Mouse a Cookie*.

With the group of children seated in a circle, introduce *Just in Passing* and share the opening. Then pass the book to the child beside you who "reads" aloud the sequence through the next yawn before passing the book to the next child. Continue until the book is completed and discuss what will happen next. The story can be continued once more around the circle, with each child creating a sequence.

A similar book, *The Yawn*, can be used to incorporate the addition of strange creatures to the sequence.

Prepare a display of books containing other circular stories that children might like.

RELATED MATERIALS

Barton, Byron. *Buzz, Buzz, Buzz*. Macmillan, 1973.

Numeroff, Laura. *If You Give a Mouse a Cookie*. Illustrated by Felicia Bond. Harper & Row, 1985.

Saltzberg, Barney. *The Yawn*. Atheneum, 1985.

"The Snooks Family" in *The Diane Goode Book of American Folk Tales and Songs*. Collected by Ann Durrell. Dutton, 1989.

Testa, Fulvio. *The Paper Airplane*. North-South, 1981.

GAME PROGRAM

Share this book and discuss the way the yawn is passed from one person to the next throughout the story. Have children think of other things we pass from one person to another and share them aloud (smiles, saying "hello," and so forth). Share the book *Surprise Party*, in which a rabbit's news about a party is whispered from animal to animal with resulting changes each time the news is repeated.

Tell the children that the class is going to play a listening game. Think up a short story or bit of information and write it down to share with the group when the game is completed. Begin by saying "Just in passing I want you to know ...," and whisper the written information to one child. The first child then whispers the information to the second child, and so forth until all the children have heard it. The last child tells the group what he or she has heard. Follow by reading the original words and discuss how they stayed the same and how they changed during the passage from one person to the next.

RELATED MATERIALS

Hutchins, Pat. *Surprise Party*. Macmillan, 1986.

MAKING A DISPLAY

Collect pictures from magazines and posters of people and animals yawning. Yawns have different meanings for different animals. Canines yawn to communicate, while crocodiles and hippos yawn for temperature control. Create a bulletin board with the pictures you have located and pose questions near the pictures inviting children to find the answers in related science books. Questions might include: What does yawning signify to wolves? Under what circumstances do you yawn? Do you yawn in the morning? Do you feel like yawning when you look at these pictures? What manners and customs have arisen about yawning?

RELATED NONFICTION MATERIALS

Arnold, Caroline. *Hippo*. Photographs by Richard Hewett. Morrow, 1989.

Rockwell, Jane. *Wolves*. Watts, 1977.

Schlein, Miriam. *Hippos*. Photographs by Leonard Lee Rue III and Len Rue, Jr. Atheneum, 1989. (Jane Goodall's Animal World Series)

Trevisick, Charles. *Hippos*. Raintree, 1980.

LITERATURE SHARING

Invite each child in the group to smile at another child. What is the effect of their smiling? Invite the group to join you in a song in which they follow your actions, such as "If you're happy and you know it...." End by singing, "If you're sleepy and you know it, yawn and stretch," and have everyone yawn and stretch.

Discuss yawning and how people sometimes yawn when they aren't sleepy. Share the book *Just in Passing*. Point out that the baby influenced the woman to yawn. Encourage conversation about different experiences in which children in the group have been influenced by people, possibly strangers, when they saw them doing something (such as wanting ice cream when they saw someone eating an ice cream cone).

Read aloud the book *Maxie*, in which a lonely old woman unknowingly influences her neighbors and is an important member of the neighborhood. Encourage children to think about who they might influence, and how. Whom are they influenced by?

RELATED MATERIALS

Kantrowitz, Mildred. *Maxie*. Illustrated by Emily A. McCully. Parents Magazine Press, 1970.

In the Classroom (or In the Library)

MAPMAKING

Six of the people who participate in the yawn are shown in the two-page spread in the middle of this book. Use this two-page spread to create a map of the book's action. As children puzzle out the relative location of each of the people, draw a map on a large mural-size piece of paper. Work backward to the beginning of the book and forward to the end of the book using this illustration. Be sure to include roads, parks, zoos, and bodies of water. Locate each person in the book on the map. Where do you think the baby and mother live? Small groups can map out the movement of the yawn and decorate the map with drawings of the city as they envision it. When the map is completed, have students discuss how the yawn was able to travel in ways that a person could not.

Follow a route in another book such as *Good Morning, Maxine!* or *The City*.

RELATED MATERIALS

Cazet, Denys. *Good Morning, Maxine!* Bradbury, 1989.

Florian, Douglas. *The City*. Crowell, 1982.

RELATED NONFICTION MATERIALS

Broekel, Ray. *Maps and Globes*. Childrens, 1983.

McVeye, Vicki. *The Sierra Club Wayfinding Book*. Illustrated by Martha Weston. Sierra Club Books/Little, Brown, 1988.

HEALTH, LANGUAGE ARTS, AND LIBRARY RESEARCH

When the baby in this book yawns, the yawn passes from person to person. Discuss yawns and why they seem to be contagious. As a class, brainstorm other things that are, or seem to be, contagious. When the list is complete, discuss which things are really contagious (diseases) and which ones aren't (such as feeling your skin itch when you see someone else scratching).

Form teams to research, take notes, and report on something that is contagious. What is it? How is it transmitted? What are the symptoms? How can it be prevented? How can it be treated? Teams can make informal oral reports to the class. After the reports are completed, have a class discussion on the similarities in what the different teams have found.

RELATED NONFICTION MATERIALS

Berger, Melvin. *Germs Make Me Sick!* Illustrated by Marylin Hafner. Crowell, 1985.

Parker, Steve. *Catching a Cold: How You Get Ill, Suffer and Recover*. Watts, 1992.

Patent, Dorothy Hinshaw. *Germs!* Holiday House, 1983.

RELATED NONPRINT MATERIALS

Sniffles, Sneezes, and Contagious Diseases. 16mm/video. Coronet, 1982.

CAREER EDUCATION AND LANGUAGE ARTS

After sharing this story, have students go back and classify the people in the book according to the work they are doing (shopper, newsdealer, housecleaner, telephone lineman, zookeeper, office worker, construction worker, mail room clerk, and so forth). As a class, discuss the different jobs and the skills needed for those jobs.

As a homework assignment, have students interview someone in their household about the type of work they do. (You may want to prepare a form for students to take home and fill out as they gather their information.) Information to be included: What is their job? Where do they work? When do they go to work? What do they do on their job? What skills do they use on their job? Where did they learn those skills? Students can share this information with the class and make individual or class books about different jobs.

RELATED NONFICTION MATERIALS

Civardi, Anne. *Things People Do*. Illustrated by Stephen Cartwright. EDC, 1986.

Florian, Douglas. *People Working*. Crowell, 1983.

Mabery, D. L. *Tell Me About Yourself: How to Interview Anyone from Your Friends to Famous People*. Lerner, 1985.

Merriam, Eve. *Daddies at Work*. Illustrated by Eugenie Fernandes. Simon & Schuster, 1989.

_____. *Mommies at Work*. Illustrated by Eugenie Fernandes. Simon & Schuster, 1989.

LANGUAGE ARTS

In this book there are many people in each scene, all busily pursuing something as the yawn travels from one person to another, from the city to the countryside. Each of these characters has her or his own story to tell. As a class, make a list of all the people that have been illustrated, checking the book to be certain that the list is complete. Have each student select a character and write a character sketch that will include the person's name, why he or she is in the scene, what the person does the rest of the time, and so forth. When students have completed their sketches, they can share them orally with the rest of the class.

SCIENCE AND LIBRARY RESEARCH

When each character in the book sees another character yawn, he or she begins to yawn. Yawning is a reflex action. As a class, discuss reflex actions and make a class list of other reflex actions (goose bumps, eye twitches, self-protective actions, and so forth). Have students use library resources to learn about reflex actions.

RELATED NONFICTION MATERIALS

Berger, Melvin. *Why I Cough, Sneeze, Shiver, Hiccup and Yawn*. Illustrated by Holly Keller. Crowell, 1983.

Settel, Joanne. *Why Does My Nose Run? (And Other Questions Kids Ask About Their Bodies)*. Illustrated by Linda Tunney. Atheneum, 1985.

Briggs, Raymond

The Snowman
Random House, 1978.
ISBN 0-394-83973-0; 0-394-93973-5 (lib); LC 78-55904

ABOUT THE AUTHOR AND HIS BOOKS

Raymond Briggs was born January 18, 1934, in London, England. He became interested in becoming a cartoonist when he was 15 years old. He attended both the Wimbledon School of Art and the Slade School of Fine Art and started working as a freelance illustrator while he was still in school. He served in the British army for two years. He also taught at the Brighton College of Art. Raymond Briggs lives in Sussex, England, where he teaches art part-time and enjoys working in his vegetable garden.

Selected Books by the Author

Father Christmas. Coward-McCann, 1973.

Father Christmas Goes on Holiday. Coward, 1975.

Fungus the Bogeyman. Hamish Hamilton, 1977.

Gentleman Jim. Hamish Hamilton, 1980.

Jim and the Beanstalk. Coward, 1970.

Midnight Adventure. Hamish Hamilton, 1961.

The Mother Goose Treasury. Coward, 1966.

Ring-a-Ring O' Roses. Coward, 1962.

The Strange House. Hamish Hamilton, 1961.

When the Wind Blows. Schocken Books, 1982.

The White Land: A Picture Book of Traditional Rhymes and Verses. Coward, 1963.

Selected Books Illustrated by the Author

A Book of Magical Beasts by Ruth Manning-Sanders. Thomas Nelson, 1970.

The Elephant and the Bad Baby by Elfrida Vipont. Coward, 1969.

The Fairy Tale Treasury. Edited by Virginia Haviland. Coward, 1972.

Festivals. Edited by Ruth Manning-Sanders. Heinemann, 1972.

Richthofen, the Red Baron by Nicholas Fisk. Coward-McCann, 1968.

Shackleton's Epic Voyage by Michael Brown. Coward-McCann, 1969.

ABOUT THE SNOWMAN

A genial, slightly stooped snowman smiles from the cover and title page. Inside, softly colored pencil drawings tell a magical story through panels in a variety of sizes.

Delighted by a yard filled with snow, a boy rushes outside to build a snowman, placing an old hat on its head and a scarf around its neck. The boy reluctantly goes into the house for dinner and bedtime. During the night the boy opens the door to invite the snowman inside. After showing the snowman around the house, the boy serves him a frozen food dinner. The snowman returns the favor, taking the boy outside and flying off into the snowy sky with him in tow. They fly over a seaside town and look over the sea from a promenade. When the sky begins to lighten, they hurry home again, hug, and the boy runs inside to his bed. The morning finds the snowman melted and the boy unsure whether he dreamed the whole adventure, or whether it was real.

Many of the panels in the original version of the book are small, and details are difficult to see; however, each sequence is well developed and easy to follow. Light pastel colors reinforce the whimsical nature of the plot. Humorous elements are balanced with magical ones, and the book conveys a feeling of wonder at both everyday and extraordinary occurrences.

The book has been made into a popular film and a video in which the story changes somewhat. Details of the exploration of the house differ, and the flying trip is much longer, taking the boy and snowman to the far north and a party with Santa Claus and many snowpeople. Board books have been made from the movie version of the story. The book has also been released with words as *The Snowman Storybook*.

In the Library (or In the Classroom)

MAKING A DISPLAY

The figure of the snowman from this book is available as a stuffed toy and can be used as the center of a display on snowpeople. If the toy is not used, the figure can be drawn on poster board and cut out. A white sheet makes an easy background, or poster board can be used with blue, gray-green, and turquoise crayon rubbed across it. Snowflakes cut from white paper can be hung about the display.

RELATED MATERIALS

Bauer, Caroline Feller. *Midnight Snowman*. Illustrated by Catherine Stock. Atheneum, 1987.

Croll, Carolyn. *The Little Snowgirl*. Putnam, 1989.

Erskine, Jim. *The Snowman*. Crown, 1978.

Goffstein, M. B. *Our Snowman*. Harper & Row, 1986.

Hoban, Julia. *Amy Loves the Snow*. Illustrated by Lillian Hoban. Harper & Row, 1989.

Hol, Coby. *Lisa and the Snowman*. North-South, 1989.

McKee, David. *Snow Woman*. Lothrop, Lee & Shepard, 1988.

Mendez, Phil. *The Black Snowman*. Illustrated by Carole Byard. Scholastic, 1989.

RELATED NONPRINT MATERIALS

Snowman doll. 7 inches, 11 inches, or 4 feet. Available from Listening Library.

LITERATURE SHARING I

The snowman in this title takes the boy flying above the countryside. Use the video of *The Snowman* to introduce books about fantastic journeys. The video animates the flight over ocean and land to a place where snowpeople gather for a party with Santa Claus. Another nighttime journey takes a child to see Santa Claus in *The Polar Express*. In the first title, the snowman takes the boy flying, and in the second the boy is taken to the North Pole on a train. In a third book, *Mistletoe*, an ordinary rocking horse takes a child on a magical journey. While all three of these books happen at Christmastime, some journeys might happen any winter night.

A cat introduces the wonders of a snowy winter woods in *Winter Magic*. The sandman takes someone on a trip to the moon in *Midnight Moon*, and Max sets sail from his room at night for a place "where the wild things are." Not all journeys take place at night. Maggie makes a wish that comes true in *The Maggie B*. and finds herself on the ocean in a boat named for her. The small girl in *Little Pickle* also has an unexpected ocean journey. Encourage children to explore these and other books about fantastic journeys.

Make a booklist of titles on this topic and stamp it with the snowman stamp.

RELATED MATERIALS

Collington, Peter. *Little Pickle*. Dutton, 1986.

Haas, Irene. *The Maggie B*. McElderry, 1975.

Hasler, Eveline. *Winter Magic*. Illustrated by Michèle Lemieux. Morrow, 1984.

McPhail, David. *Mistletoe*. Dutton, 1978.

Root, Phyllis. *Moon Tiger*. Illustrated by Ed Young. Holt, Rinehart & Winston, 1985.

Sendak, Maurice. *Where the Wild Things Are*. Harper & Row, 1963.

Van Allsburg, Chris. *The Polar Express*. Houghton Mifflin, 1985.

Ward, Lynd. *Silver Pony: A Story in Pictures*. Houghton Mifflin, 1973.

Watson, Clyde. *Midnight Moon*. Illustrated by Susanna Natti. Collins, 1979.

RELATED NONPRINT MATERIALS

The Snowman regular or mini-stamp. Kidstamps.

The Snowman. Video. Weston Woods, 1983.

INTEREST CENTER I

The story of *The Snowman* is told in panels, small and large, in the manner of comic strips or comic books. This method of pictorial storytelling organizes the action in sequence from left to right, top to bottom. The artist has to decide how much time can elapse between each panel without the story losing its sense. Close-up pictures alternate with pictures from varying points of view to provide visual interest. This art is similar to good prose writing, and it is a challenge for youngsters to try.

An interest center can feature *The Snowman* and several other books that use the panel format, such as those listed. Reproduce many sheets of paper with blank panels outlined in the patterns used in *The Snowman*. Suggest some ideas to get young authors and artists started, and have each reader try to create a panel sequence that tells a brief story. Ideas can come from *The Snowman*: How would you build an unusual snowman? What else could the snowman explore inside a building? Show the snowman taking you somewhere special.

RELATED MATERIALS

Collington, Peter. *The Angel and the Soldier Boy*. Knopf, 1987.

Dupasquier, Philippe. *The Great Escape*. Houghton Mifflin, 1988.

Prater, John. *The Gift*. Viking Kestrel, 1985.

Spier, Peter. *Peter Spier's Rain*. Doubleday, 1982.

Stevenson, James. *Could Be Worse*. Greenwillow, 1977.

Wright, Cliff. *When the World Sleeps*. Ideals Children's Books, 1989.

RELATED NONFICTION MATERIALS

Aliki. *How a Book Is Made*. Harper & Row, 1986.

Cummings, Richard. *Make Your Own Comics for Fun and Profit*. Walck, 1976.

LITERATURE SHARING II

It seems to be human nature to create figures that resemble people from whatever materials are available, and it seems easy for the imaginative writer to imagine these characters coming to life. Because *The Snowman* is such a well-known book, it can be used to begin a discussion of such figures. Children may suggest other well-known figures from popular culture, such as "Frosty the Snowman" and the scarecrow from *The Wonderful Wizard of Oz*. Nonfiction books such as *Ephemeral Folk Figures* and magazine articles on snow or ice sculpture will enable the group to appreciate the range of creativity involved in making these figures. Chapter 7 in *The Enchanted Castle* shows a sinister side of this theme when the Ugly-Wuglies—figures created by children to be a pretend audience for a play—come to life. Picture books show a more upbeat image of this theme.

RELATED MATERIALS

Baum, L. Frank. *The Wonderful Wizard of Oz*. Morrow, 1987. (Reissue of 1900 edition)

Carlson, Natalie. *The Night the Scarecrow Walked*. Illustrated by Charles Robinson. Scribner, 1979.

Littledale, Freya. *The Snow Child*. Scholastic, 1978.

Lobe, Mira. *The Snowman Who Went for a Walk*. Illustrated by Winfried Opgenoorth. Morrow, 1984.

Nesbit, Edith. *The Enchanted Castle*. Illustrated by Betty Fraser. Platt & Munk, 1966.

Schertle, Alice. *Witch Hazel*. Illustrated by Margo Tomes. HarperCollins, 1991.

Stolz, Mary. *The Scarecrows and Their Child*. Illustrated by Amy Schwartz. Harper, 1987.

Ziefert, Harriet. *Snow Magic*. Illustrated by Claire Schumacher. Viking, 1988.

RELATED NONFICTION MATERIALS

Giblin, James, and Dale Ferguson. *The Scarecrow Book*. Crown, 1980.

Neal, Avon. *Ephemeral Folk Figures: Scarecrows, Harvest Figures, and Snowmen*. Crown, 1969.

INTEREST CENTER II

When the boy shows the snowman around the house in this book, many ordinary things seem marvelous to the snowman. For example, he delights in clicking the lights on and off. Set up a writing interest center that encourages children to think about ordinary things as wonders. Display the spreads from the book in which the boy is showing the snowman around the house. Make copies of a sheet of paper with a heading such as, "If the snowman came to my house, I would show him...." Collect these papers in a looseleaf binder for others to read.

In the Classroom (or In the Library)

LANGUAGE ARTS

Discuss dialogue with students, including inner dialogue. Working individually or in small groups, have students read *The Snowman* and then write dialogue for one page. You may want to number the 29 pages in the book to make it easier for students to find their section. Have students number their pages to correspond with the number in the book. When all students have completed their writing, they can stand in order one at a time to read their dialogue as the rest of the class envisions the story. Student writing can then be arranged in numerical order and put into book form to be read aloud by one student while another is looking at a copy of *The Snowman*.

LITERATURE SHARING

The Snowman is available in many formats, including sound filmstrip, video, board books, and miniature book. Provide as many formats as possible and share them with students. Encourage students to evaluate the different formats and to decide which one they like best, providing thoughtful reasons for their choices.

RELATED MATERIALS

The Snowman. Miniature edition. Random House, 1990.

The Snowman. Paperback. Random House, 1986.

The Snowman Advent Calendar. WJ Fantasy, 1992.

The Snowman Flap Book. Illustrated by Sara Silwinska. Random House, 1991.

The Snowman Game. PIC Games. Distributed by WJ Fantasy.

RELATED NONPRINT MATERIALS

The Snowman. Book/cassette. Weston Woods.

The Snowman. Sound filmstrip. Weston Woods, 1984.

The Snowman. Video. Weston Woods, 1983.

GEOGRAPHY, SCIENCE, AND LANGUAGE ARTS

There are people in many parts of the world who have never seen snow. Using a world globe, discuss areas of the world that would have snow and those that would not have snow. Discuss snow and what causes it to fall.

Have students imagine that they are exchange students visiting a classroom in the African desert, or in another hot climate where no one has ever seen snow. Have them write about how they would explain snow and making a snowman to students in their exchange classroom. Invite students to share their responses orally, or use them for a bulletin board display.

RELATED NONFICTION MATERIALS

Branley, Franklyn M. *It's Raining Cats and Dogs: All Kinds of Weather and Why We Have It*. Illustrated by True Kelley. Houghton Mifflin, 1987.

_____. *Snow Is Falling*. Illustrated by Holly Keller. Crowell, 1986.

Cosgrove, Margaret. *It's Snowing!* Dodd, Mead, 1980.

Sugarman, Joan. *Snowflakes*. Little, Brown, 1986.

Webster, David. *Snow Stumpers*. Natural History Press, 1968.

Williams, Terry Tempest, and Ted Major. *The Secret Language of Snow*. Illustrated by Jennifer Dewey. Sierra Club/Pantheon, 1984.

LANGUAGE ARTS

Have students make individual books shaped like a snowperson, or prepare books in advance for each student and have them decorate the cover to reflect their snowperson. Students can write stories to go in their books about actual incidents that they have had with a snowperson (making one, seeing an unusual one, and so forth), or an imaginary incident.

ART

Using a piece of white candle, students can draw a picture of the outside of their house with the snowman in the yard, or inside one of the rooms in their house. Then have them paint over the entire sheet of paper using a thin tempera paint. The paint will not cover the waxed area and their house will appear.

Brown, Craig

The Patchwork Farmer
Greenwillow, 1989.
ISBN 0-688-07735-9; 0-688-07736-6 (lib); LC 88-29229

ABOUT THE AUTHOR AND HIS BOOKS

Craig Brown was born on September 4, 1947, in Tama, Iowa, and grew up there. He graduated from the Layton School of Art in Milwaukee, Wisconsin, and has worked as an illustrator and a graphic designer. Currently living in Colorado Springs, Colorado, he has two children, Heather and Cory. *The Patchwork Farmer* was the first book Craig Brown both wrote and illustrated.

Selected Books by the Author

City Sounds. Greenwillow, 1992.

My Barn. Greenwillow, 1991.

Selected Books Illustrated by the Author

Big Thunder Magic by Craig Kee Strete. Greenwillow, 1990.

The Gossamer Tree: A Christmas Fable by Toni Knapp. Rockrimmon Press, 1988.

The Six Bridges of Humphrey the Whale by Toni Knapp. Rockrimmon Press, 1989.

Snips the Tinker by Connie Roop and Peter Roop. Milliken, 1990.

The Talking Bird and the Story Pouch by Amy Lawson. HarperCollins, 1987.

ABOUT THE PATCHWORK FARMER

As morning light breaks over uniformly green fields, the farmer rises and dons his blue overalls. He goes about the work of the farm with an assortment of tools and in performing each task manages to rip a new hole in his overalls. Each evening he sews a new patch over the torn spot. Finally his overalls are more patchwork than original fabric, and he wears them to admire his fields, which are now various colors as the crops have grown and ripened. His satisfied look invites the viewer to enjoy the implied relationship between the patchwork fields and patchwork clothing.

The artwork is pointillistic, and the colors are muted. Each illustration is a full page and large enough to share with a small group. The farmer's eyes are hidden in each picture by his hat or the position of his head. The use of various tools and the ease with which the farmer plies the needle to patch his overalls demonstrate a cheerful self-reliance. This appears to be a farm without animals, unlike most picture book farms, and the farmer is an adult living alone. The passage of time is shown in evening and morning scenes and in the comparison of the original view of the farm with the final one.

The repetitive plot makes this book one in which groups can easily predict what will happen. Looking for detail and discussing what the farmer will do with each tool will not detract from the flow of the story as it might in a book with more plot. The mood of the ending is that of satisfaction in accomplishment, and young children may need help understanding or articulating this type of plot resolution.

In the Library (or In the Classroom)

MAKING A DISPLAY

Each time the farmer goes out to work he carries a different tool. The needle that he uses to sew on patches is another tool. A display can draw attention to these tools. Put a patchwork quilt in the background. Collect such tools as the ones the farmer uses in the book (hoe, rake, clippers) and others he might use and arrange them around the book. Write questions about the uses and names of each tool on index cards, using colored markers to match the quilt colors. Display related books for checkout. Young children can be challenged to look through the book and count the number of tools in each book, or to name each tool and tell what it is used for. Older children can be challenged to name the kind of work each tool makes easier. What other ways are there to do this work? Some tools use physical principles such as levers to make work easier. Invite children to explain how each tool works.

RELATED MATERIALS

Adkins, Jan. *Toolchest: A Primer of Woodcraft*. Walker, 1973.

Gibbons, Gail. *Tool Book*. Holiday House, 1982.

Rockwell, Anne F., and Harlow Rockwell. *The Toolbox*. Macmillan, 1971.

Shone, Venice. *Tools*. Scholastic, 1990.

MUSIC AND GAME PROGRAM

Illustrations in *The Patchwork Farmer* show the farmer whistling as he goes to work. Share the book to begin a program of farm songs and games. Invite children to suggest songs the farmer might whistle and have them whistle one along with you.

A well-known song such as "Old MacDonald" can be used to get the group singing; the illustrated version by Glen Rounds is easy to use with a group. Follow with songs that children may not know as well, such as "Oats, Peas, Beans, and Barley Grow." Many songs are available as individually illustrated picture books, which can be shared and displayed with the program. The video *A Day at Old MacDonald's Farm* might be used as part of a sing-along. Instructions for song games can be found in *The Fireside Book of Children's Songs* and other compilations.

RELATED MATERIALS

Aliki. *Aunt Rhody*. Macmillan, 1974.

Brand, Oscar. *When I First Came to This Land*. Illustrated by Doris Burn. Putnam, 1974.

The Farmer in the Dell. Illustrated by Diane Zuromskis. Little, Brown, 1978.

Old MacDonald Had a Farm. Illustrated by Tracey Campbell Pearson. Dial, 1984.

Rae, Mary Maki. *The Farmer in the Dell*. Viking, 1988.

Rounds, Glen. *Old MacDonald Had a Farm*. Holiday House, 1989.

Winn, Marie, editor. *The Fireside Book of Children's Songs*. Illustrated by John Alcorn. Simon & Schuster, 1966.

RELATED NONPRINT MATERIALS

A Day at Old MacDonald's Farm. Video. View-Master Video, 1985. (Kidsongs Series)

STORY AND CRAFT PROGRAM

The farmer is cheerfully self-reliant in sewing his patches on his overalls. Begin this program on sewing things with the film *Corduroy*. The little girl sews the button on Corduroy's strap to fit it. Explain that sewing is one way of fixing things. Share the book *The Patchwork Farmer* and talk about how he fixes his rips.

For each of the children, cut a square from plastic mesh bags. (Onion bags also work well.) Using several short lengths of thick yarn, have the children sew multicolored squares. Using blunt plastic needles, show children how to sew in and out, and how to stop the yarn from pulling all the way through the bags. If needles are not available, wrap tape around one end of the yarn and twist it to a point. This will stiffen the end of the yarn so that it can be pushed through the mesh openings.

RELATED MATERIALS

Fair, Sylvia. *The Bedspread*. Morrow, 1982.

Freeman, Don. *Corduroy*. Viking, 1968.

Potter, Beatrix. *The Tailor of Gloucester*. Warne, 1987.

RELATED NONPRINT MATERIALS

Corduroy and Other Bear Stories. 16mm film/video. Weston Woods, 1984.

STORYHOUR

The patchwork farmer wears the same pair of overalls every day. Use this book to begin a program on clothing, old and new. Follow *The Patchwork Farmer* with a book about someone who needs something new, such as Pelle in *Pelle's New Suit* or Charlie in *Charlie Needs a Cloak*. Talk about clothes that are handed down, using *You'll Soon Grow into Them, Titch* and *I Like Old Clothes*.

RELATED MATERIALS

Beskow, Elsa. *Pelle's New Suit*. Harper, 1919; 1929.

Cobb, Vicki. *Getting Dressed*. Illustrated by Marylin Hafner. Lippincott, 1989.

dePaola, Tomie. *Charlie Needs a Cloak*. Prentice-Hall, 1973.

Hoberman, Mary Ann. *I Like Old Clothes*. Illustrated by Jacqueline Chwast. Knopf, 1976.

Hutchins, Pat. *You'll Soon Grow into Them, Titch*. Greenwillow, 1983.

Keats, Ezra Jack. *Jennie's Hat*. Harper, 1966.

Ziefert, Harriet. *A New Coat for Anna*. Illustrated by Anita Lobel. Knopf, 1986.

COLLECTION DEVELOPMENT

Include *The Patchwork Farmer* in displays, booklists, text sets, and programs on farms and farmers. Note that this farm has no animals, which makes the book somewhat different from most farm titles. Compare the tasks of this farmer with those in such books as *Eddy B. Pigboy*. The "P" and "Q" pages of Mary Azarian's *A Farmer's Alphabet* go well with this book.

RELATED MATERIALS

Allen, Tom. *On Grandaddy's Farm*. Knopf, 1989.

Azarian, Mary. *A Farmer's Alphabet*. Godine, 1981.

Bellville, Cheryl W. *Farming Today Yesterday's Way*. Carolrhoda, 1984.

Dunrea, Olivier. *Eddy B. Pigboy*. Atheneum, 1983.

Gibbons, Gail. *Farming*. Holiday House, 1988.

Miller, Jane. *Farm Alphabet Book*. Prentice-Hall, 1984.

_____. *Farm Counting Book*. Prentice-Hall, 1983.

_____. *Farm Noises*. Simon & Schuster, 1989.

_____. *Seasons on the Farm*. Prentice-Hall, 1986.

In the Classroom (or In the Library)

LANGUAGE ARTS I

As a class, discuss daily schedules: When do students get up? What do they do during the day and why? What chores do they do? Share *The Patchwork Farmer* and discuss the patchwork farmer's daily schedule. What type of farm does the farmer have? What crops might the farmer raise? How would the type of farm affect the farmer's schedule? What might be the schedules and chores of other farmers that raise animals or have animals on their farm? Compare student schedules and chores with the schedules and chores of farmers; are they alike or different?

Have students pretend they live on a farm and write a diary entry about a day in their life; or have them draw a picture of themselves on a farm.

RELATED MATERIALS

Demuth, Patricia. *Joel: Growing Up a Farm Man*. Photographs by Jack Demuth. Dodd, Mead, 1982.

Gibbons, Gail. *Farming*. Holiday House, 1988.

Henley, Claire. *Farm Day*. Dial, 1991.

McPhail, David. *Farm Boy's Year*. Atheneum, 1992.

————. *Farm Morning*. Harcourt Brace Jovanovich, 1985.

RELATED NONPRINT RESOURCES

Life on a Farm. Filmstrip. Encyclopaedia Britannica, 1977.

ART

Have students make patchwork pictures by gluing fabric scraps onto cardboard. Provide a variety of fabric scraps and let students rip the scraps to make shapes. How does the fabric sound when it rips? Which ways will it rip? Are some fabrics easier to rip than others?

SCIENCE

As a class, discuss farm fields as they are shown in *The Patchwork Farmer* and as they are seen in the countryside. What makes the fields look like patchwork? Have students make their own patchwork plantings. Fill square or rectangular cake pans with dirt or potting soil. Mark off sections or squares by taping string across the top of the pan. Plant every other section with grass seed. Use moss, rye, or wheat seed for the alternate sections. As the plants grow, have students observe the differences between the sections.

RELATED NONFICTION MATERIALS

Brown, Marc. *Your First Garden Book*. Little, Brown, 1981.

Krementz, Jill. *A Very Young Gardener*. Dial, 1991.

McMillan, Bruce. *Growing Colors*. Lothrop, Lee & Shepard, 1988.

Miller, Susanna. *Beans and Peas*. Carolrhoda, 1990.

Oechsli, Helen, and Kelly Oechsli. *In My Garden: A Child's Gardening Book*. Macmillan, 1985.

Wilner, Isabel. *Garden Alphabet*. Illustrated by Ashley Wolff. Dutton, 1991.

LANGUAGE ARTS II

Draw a life-size picture of the patchwork farmer as he appears at the beginning of the book, and hang the cutout on a wall with plenty of space around it.

Share *The Patchwork Farmer*, paying particular attention to the different patches that the farmer uses to mend his overalls. Then read aloud *The Rag Coat*, in which a young girl can tell a story about each of the pieces of fabric on her patchwork coat. Or, read aloud *Apricots at Midnight* in which an elderly dressmaker tells marvelous stories from the patches on her quilt.

Ask students to bring fabric scraps (2 by 2 inches or 3 by 3 inches) from home and be prepared to write the story behind the fabric scrap. Give each student a number to put on both their fabric scrap and on their paper. After writing their stories about their fabric scraps, the children can glue them to the farmer's overalls and hang their stories nearby. The numbers will help viewers read the story that goes with each patch. You might ask students to share their stories orally with the rest of the class before gluing their patches to the overalls.

RELATED MATERIALS

Coerr, Eleanor. *The Josefina Story Quilt*. Illustrated by Bruce Degen. Harper & Row, 1986.

Flournoy, Valerie. *The Patchwork Quilt*. Illustrated by Jerry Pinkney. Dial, 1985.

Geras, Adele. *Apricots at Midnight: And Other Stories from a Patchwork Quilt*. Illustrated by Doreen Caldwell. Atheneum, 1977.

Mills, Lauren. *The Rag Coat*. Little, Brown, 1991.

Paul, Ann Whitford. *Eight Hands Round: A Patchwork Alphabet*. Illustrated by Jeanette Winter. Harper-Collins, 1991.

ECONOMICS

As a class, discuss how farmers earn their income and when they get their earnings. Farmers do not get weekly or monthly paychecks like most workers; they get money when they sell their livestock or crops once or twice a year. How might the patchwork farmer earn his money? When would he get money? Tie economic realities in with the patchwork farmer's decision to mend his overalls instead of throwing them away and buying new ones. Discuss the concept of "making do" with what you have, and have students share incidents when they have had to "make do" until they earned money. Discuss ways that the patchwork farmer and other farm families would have to budget their money to make it last until the next season. Discuss farm country and shopping opportunities. Could this impact the patchwork farmer's decision to mend his overalls instead of going to buy a new pair?

RELATED MATERIALS

Andrews, Jan. *The Auction*. Illustrated by Karen Reczuch. Macmillan, 1991.

Locker, Thomas. *Family Farm*. Dial, 1988.

TEXT SET AND THEME UNIT

The patchwork farmer mends his own clothing. There are many men who sew for themselves or for others. Have students brainstorm a list of men who might sew (sailors, fishermen repairing nets, tailors, cobblers, upholsterers, and so forth). Develop a set of materials about men who sew. Students may bring to class family anecdotes about men who sew.

RELATED MATERIALS

Knitting

Lewis, Marjorie. *Ernie and the Mile-Long Muffler*. Illustrated by Margot Apple. Coward, McCann & Geoghegan, 1982.

Wild, Margaret, and Dee Huxley. *Mr. Nick's Knitting*. Harcourt Brace Jovanovich, 1989.

Sewing

Bunting, Eve. *Clancy's Coat*. Illustrated by Lorinda Bryan Cauley. Warne, 1984.

Ernst, Lisa Campbell. *Sam Johnson and the Blue Ribbon Quilt*. Lothrop, Lee & Shepard, 1983.

Siegel, Beatrice. *Sewing Machine*. Walker, 1984.

Van Steenwyk, Elizabeth. *Levi Strauss: The Blue Jeans Man*. Walker, 1988.

Shoes and Cobblers

Grimm, Jacob. *The Shoemaker and the Elves*. Retold and illustrated by Cynthia Birrer and William Birrer. Lothrop, Lee & Shepard, 1983.

Grimm, Jacob. *The Elves and the Shoemaker*. Retold by Bernadette Watts. Holt, 1986.

Mitchell, Barbara. *Shoes for Everyone: A Story About Jan Matzeliger*. Carolrhoda, 1986.

Tailors

Ackerman, Karen. *Just Like Max*. Illustrated by George Schmidt. Knopf, 1989.

dePaola, Tomie. *Charlie Needs a Cloak*. Prentice-Hall, 1973.

Galdone, Paul. *The Monster and the Tailor*. Clarion, 1982.

Hest, Amy. *The Purple Coat*. Illustrated by Amy Schwartz. Four Winds, 1986.

Ziefert, Harriet. *A New Coat for Anna*. Illustrated by Anita Lobel. Knopf, 1986.

RELATED NONPRINT MATERIALS

dePaola, Tomie. *Charlie Needs a Cloak*. Filmstrip/video. Weston Woods, 1977.

Bullock, Kathleen

The Rabbits Are Coming!
Simon & Schuster, 1991.
ISBN 0-671-72963-2; LC 90-49830

ABOUT THE AUTHOR AND HER BOOKS

Kathleen Bullock was born in San Francisco in 1946. She attended the College of San Mateo in California. She has worked as a calligrapher, photographer, art teacher, and magazine writer. She is the mother of three children and lives in Ashland, Oregon.

Selected Books by the Author

A Friend for Mitzi Mouse. Simon & Schuster, 1990.

It Chanced to Rain. Simon & Schuster, 1989.

A Surprise for Mitzi Mouse. Simon & Schuster, 1989.

Selected Books Illustrated by the Author

Composition and Creative Writing for the Middle Grades by Imogene Forte and Joy MacKenzie. Incentive Publications, 1991.

Games Teachers Make by Joyce Gallagher. Incentive Publications, 1991.

Hey Diddle Rock by David Zaslow and Lawson Inada. Kids Matter, 1986.

Hickory Dickory Rock by David Zaslow and Lawson Inada. Kids Matter, 1986.

Rock-a-Doodle-Doo by David Zaslow and Lawson Inada. Kids Matter, 1986.

Shakin' Loose with Mother Goose by Steve Allen and Jayne Meadows. Kids Matter, 1987.

ABOUT THE RABBITS ARE COMING!

Twenty little rabbits each get a helium balloon from their mother and hop off down a path, across a garden, through an open window, and into a human family's house. In each part of the house, a member of the family is astonished as the area is invaded with the frolicking bunnies and their balloons. The bunnies bounce over a boy who is reading by the window, taste the muffin dough in the kitchen where the father is cooking, and stream up the stairs. A girl and her cat watch in amazement as the bunnies invade the bathroom where Grandfather is getting ready for his bath. The humans and their pets accumulate in the doorway to watch as bunnies try the toys in the playroom; then the humans follow the bunnies down the stairs. Mother and Grandmother join the astonished group in staring out the window as the rabbits depart. The rabbits complete their trip by floating over a lake and back to their tree home, where mother is waiting to put them into their beds at the end of a long day.

Watercolors in jellybean hues, along with pink endpapers and the joyful bunny characters, emphasize the springtime feeling of the book. An exuberant, bouncy feeling is expressed in ingenuous drawings. The simple storyline is full of good humor, with appeal to those young enough to giggle over Grandfather in a towel and to appreciate bouncing on the bed and poking paws in dough.

In the Library (or In the Classroom)

COLLECTION DEVELOPMENT

Include *The Rabbits Are Coming!* in displays, booklists, text sets, thematic units, and programs in which animals cause commotion in human houses.

RELATED MATERIALS

Alexander, Martha. *Out! Out! Out!* Dial, 1968.

Banchek, Linda. *Snake In, Snake Out*. Illustrated by Elaine Arnold. Crowell, 1978.

Christelow, Eileen. *Five Little Monkeys Jumping on the Bed*. Clarion, 1989.

Day, Alexandra. *Good Dog, Carl*. Farrar, Straus & Giroux, 1985.

Kellogg, Steven. *A Rose for Pinkerton*. Dial, 1981.

Noble, Trinka Hakes. *Jimmy's Boa Bounces Back*. Illustrated by Steven Kellogg. Dial, 1984.

Winter, Paula. *The Bear and the Fly*. Crown, 1976.

MAKING A DISPLAY

Use *The Rabbits Are Coming!* as the center of a display of picture books with rabbit characters. Use pink paper or cloth for the backdrop. (Hint: Paper tablecloths found during the springtime sometimes come in the right shade of pink.) Open *The Rabbits Are Coming!* to the scene in which the young rabbits are bounding over the garden. Make a large label with the caption, "Watch Out! The Rabbits Are Coming!" Surround the book with inflated balloons in various colors. Place other rabbit picture books nearby for reading or checkout.

RELATED MATERIALS

Balian, Lorna. *Humbug Rabbit*. Abingdon, 1974.

Becker, John. *Seven Little Rabbits*. Illustrated by Barbara Cooney. Walker, 1973.

Brown, Margaret Wise. *The Golden Egg Book*. Illustrated by Leonard Weisgard. Golden, 1976.

_____. *Goodnight Moon*. Illustrated by Clement Hurd. Harper & Row, 1947.

_____. *The Runaway Bunny*. Illustrated by Clement Hurd. Harper & Row, 1942.

Cooper, Helen. *Ella and the Rabbit*. Crocodile Books, 1990.

Dunn, Judy. *The Little Rabbit*. Illustrated by Phoebe Dunn. Random House, 1980.

Gág, Wanda. *The ABC Bunny*. Coward, 1978.

Maris, Ron. *Runaway Rabbit*. Delacorte, 1989.

Wahl, Jan. *Rabbits on Roller Skates*. Illustrated by David Allender. Crown, 1986.

STORYHOUR I

Welcome children with variously colored balloon-shaped nametags. Discuss the colors of the nametags that the children are wearing. Have a blue nametag for yourself and use it to introduce the story of the balloon that grows in *The Blue Balloon*. People aren't the only ones that like balloons; share *Curious George* as he is carried away by balloons. What if rabbits had balloons? Share the book *The Rabbits Are Coming!* Afterward, explain the game of follow the leader, then take a balloon walk like the bunnies — follow the leader and hop, bounce, and so forth. End the walk beside a shelf or display of stories about balloons.

RELATED MATERIALS

Alexander, Martha G. *The Story Grandmother Told*. Dial, 1969.

Bonsall, Crosby. *Mine's the Best*. HarperCollins, 1973.

Carrick, Carol. *The Highest Balloon on the Common*. Illustrated by Donald Carrick. Greenwillow, 1977.

Cuyler, Margery. *That's Good, That's Bad!* Holt, 1991.

Fenton, Edward. *The Big Yellow Balloon*. Doubleday, 1967.

Gray, Nigel. *A Balloon for Grandad*. Illustrated by Jane Ray. Orchard, 1988.

Inkpen, Mick. *The Blue Balloon*. Little, Brown, 1990.

Matthias, Catherine. *Too Many Balloons*. Illustrated by Gene Sharp. Childrens, 1982.

Ray, H. A. *Curious George*. Houghton Mifflin, 1973.

Willard, Nancy. *The Well-Mannered Balloon*. Illustrated by Regina Shekerjian and Hiag Shekerjian. Harcourt Brace Jovanovich, 1991.

Wood, Audrey. *Balloonia*. Child's Play, 1989.

WORKSHOP

Prepare an outline drawing of a room from the book *The Rabbits Are Coming!* and make a copy for each child. Cut bunny shapes and balloon shapes from thin sponges. Use flat pie pans or trays to hold poster paint in various colors. After sharing *The Rabbits Are Coming!* have children look at the bunnies and the balloons in the book. Then, they can stamp bunnies and balloons on their copies of the room, being sure to stamp the same number of rabbits and balloons. When the paint is dry, details such as balloon strings and facial features can be added with pens or markers. Encourage children to describe the scene as they work on it. Where are they placing the rabbits? What are the rabbits doing? How many rabbits or balloons have they stamped?

STORYHOUR II

Rabbits and gardens seem to go together. Plan a storyhour that combines these two themes. Peter Rabbit gets into Farmer McGregor's garden in *The Tale of Peter Rabbit*, while the bunnies in *The Rabbits Are Coming!* hop through the garden on their way to the humans' house. In *Rabbit Seeds*, a rabbit is kept busy preparing, planting, and tending his garden. The rabbit in *Hired Help for Rabbit* becomes so tired from working in his garden that he gets other animals, which are unprepared for their jobs, to help him with his chores, with humorous results.

Before leaving, children can make bookmarks using a rabbit stamp and stamp pad on precut paper strips.

RELATED MATERIALS

Cooper, Helen. *Ella and the Rabbit*. Crocodile Books, 1990.

Delton, Judy. *Hired Help for Rabbit*. Illustrated by Lisa McCue. Macmillan, 1988.

Le Tord, Bijou. *Rabbit Seeds*. Four Winds/Macmillan, 1984.

Miles, Miska. *Rabbit Garden*. Illustrated by John Schoenherr. Little, Brown, 1967.

Modesitt, Jeanne. *Vegetable Soup*. Illustrated by Robin Spowart. Macmillan, 1988.

Potter, Beatrix. *The Tale of Peter Rabbit*. Warne, 1985.

_____. *The Tale of the Flopsy Bunnies*. Warne, 1987.

Schotter, Roni. *Bunny's Night Out*. Illustrated by Margot Apple. Little, Brown, 1989.

Simont, Marc. *Lovely Summer*. Bantam, 1992.

RELATED NONPRINT MATERIALS

"Peter Rabbit" or "Real Rabbit" rubber stamp from Kidstamps.

In the Classroom (or In the Library)

BOOK REPORT

Use this book to initiate a reading recognition activity with a group of younger children. After sharing the story of *The Rabbits Are Coming!* invite children to be little rabbits like the ones in the book. Have a large outline of the tree trunk house drawn and posted on a blank wall or bulletin board. Pretend to be the mother rabbit and tell the students, "I will give you a balloon each time you read a book, or share a book with your mom or dad. Here's our tree. Draw a picture of yourself as a bunny and we'll cut out your picture and put it in one of the windows of our tree house. Each time you get a balloon, write your name and the title of the book on it, and put the balloon under the branches of the tree, just like the balloons at the end of the book."

SENSES

Rabbits are very quiet animals. As the bunnies hopped along on their daytime outing in *The Rabbits Are Coming!* they were able to hear many different sounds. As you share the book a second time, discuss each two-page spread and the sounds the little rabbits might hear on that page (forest sounds, the dog, the boy, kitchen sounds such as the teakettle, pan, toaster, radio, cupboard door, and so forth). Invite children to make the sounds that are mentioned. You may want to make a list of those sounds.

RELATED NONFICTION MATERIALS

Aliki. *My Five Senses*. Crowell, 1989.

Branley, Franklyn. *High Sounds, Low Sounds*. Illustrated by Paul Galdone. Crowell, 1967.

Broekel, Ray. *Sound Experiments*. Childrens, 1983.

Parramon, J. M. *Hearing*. Illustrated by Maria Rius. Barron's, 1985.

Webb, Angela. *Sound*. Watts, 1988. (Talkabout Series)

LIBRARY RESEARCH

After sharing *The Rabbits Are Coming!* ask students whether real rabbits could do the things the young rabbits in this book do. Can real rabbits hop? Can they hold balloons? Do rabbits have large families? Do rabbits live in trees? Do rabbit mothers wear aprons? Do rabbits hop into human houses? Use library resources to learn more about real rabbits, including their care and the difference between rabbits and hares.

RELATED NONFICTION MATERIALS

Bare, Colleen Stanley. *Rabbits and Hares*. Dodd, Mead, 1983.

Coldrey, Jennifer. *The Rabbit in the Fields*. Gareth Stevens, 1987.

Hess, Lilo. *Diary of a Rabbit*. Scribner, 1982.

Porter, Keith. *Discovering Rabbits and Hares*. Illustrated by Wendy Meadway. Watts, 1986. (Discovering Nature Series)

Tarrant, Graham. *Rabbits*. Putnam, 1984.

Watts, Barrie. *Rabbit*. Lodestar, 1992. (See How They Grow Series)

THEME UNIT

Use *The Rabbits Are Coming!* as one of the books to begin a discussion on the need for sleep. After a busy day, the young rabbits return home and go to bed in their tree house. Have a display of both picture books and nonfiction books about sleeping. Students can read stories about people and animals that take naps or go to bed after a long day, and they can learn why sleep is necessary for all animals. As a class, discuss why sleep is important and how much sleep is necessary for different animals. How much sleep is necessary for young children? How much sleep should children in the class get? Think of ways that the class can get the sleep they need. What are the results if they don't get enough sleep?

Children can make their own sleep books with stories and poems they have written about their sleeping habits; they can include pictures of themselves in their own beds taking a nap or going to sleep for the night. Included in sleep books might be stories of the students' pets or other animals telling when and where they sleep.

RELATED MATERIALS

Howard, Jane. *When I'm Sleepy*. Illustrated by Lynne Cherry. Dutton, 1985.

Hutchins, Pat. *Good-Night Owl*. Macmillan, 1972.

Murphy, Jill. *Peace at Last*. Dial, 1980.

Pfister, Marcus. *Sleepy Owl*. North-South, 1980.

Seuss, Dr. *I Am Not Going to Get Up Today!* Illustrated by James Stevenson. Random House, 1987.

Wood, Audrey. *Napping House*. Illustrated by Don Wood. Harcourt Brace Jovanovich, 1984.

RELATED NONFICTION MATERIALS

Showers, Paul. *Sleep Is for Everyone*. Illustrated by Wendy Watson. Crowell, 1974.

Silverstein, Alvin. *The Mystery of Sleep*. Illustrated by Nelle Davis. Little, Brown, 1987.

_____. *Sleep and Dreams*. Lippincott, 1974.

RELATED NONPRINT MATERIALS

Natural Cycles: Sleep and Dreams. Sound filmstrip. Guidance Associates, 1972.

LITERATURE SHARING

After sharing *The Rabbits Are Coming!* once, share it a second time and have students notice which characters are reading in the story. The boy is reading as the bunnies hop through the window; one bunny reads while sitting on a kitchen cupboard shelf; the mother is reading while sitting in the living room as the bunnies hop out of the window; the mother rabbit reads after the little bunnies go to bed. Have students make a list of books each character might be reading. Then have students compile a list of books they could recommend to the various characters. Recommendations might come from librarians, parents, or others. Share the lists as a class. Are there recommendations that the students would like to hear read aloud by their parents or teacher? Compile on the chalkboard a class list of books to read aloud. Have students copy the list in their best writing and take it home. Students could stamp their list with the "Rabbit Read" stamp and ink pad.

RELATED NONPRINT MATERIALS

"Rabbit Read" rubber stamp. Kidstamps.

Amanda's Butterfly
Delacorte, 1991.
ISBN 0-385-30433-1; 0-385-30434-X (pbk); LC 90-48741

ABOUT THE AUTHOR AND HIS BOOKS

Nick Butterworth has had a variety of jobs. He has worked as a television host, a cartoonist, and a graphic designer, as well as a writer and illustrator of books. He has written or illustrated over 30 books for children. He lives with his wife and two children, Ben and Amanda, in Suffolk, England.

Selected Books by the Author

Nick Butterworth's Book of Nursery Rhymes. Viking, 1990.

One Snowy Night. Little, Brown, 1990.

Selected Books by the Author and Mick Inkpen

Field Day. Delacorte, 1991.

Just Like Jasper. Little, Brown, 1989.

The Nativity Play. Little, Brown, 1985.

Nice or Nasty: A Book of Opposites. Little, Brown, 1987.

The School Trip. Delacorte, 1990.

ABOUT AMANDA'S BUTTERFLY

A summer morning finds Amanda in bed reading to her stuffed toys. Inspired by the butterfly catcher in her picture book, Amanda digs a fishing net out of the hall closet and sets out on her own expedition. The daisies and poppies are lovely, but Amanda can't find any butterflies—and then it begins to rain. She sadly watches the rain from the window inside the garden shed, when something moves on the work bench. A blue wing appears, but instead of a butterfly there is a tiny barefoot fairy with a rip in her gossamer wing. Amanda searches for a tool to mend the wing and finally comes up with just the right thing. When the sun comes out, the grateful fairy flies off while Amanda watches with satisfaction.

Light watercolor and simple line drawings are framed with a broad white margin, making it easy for children to focus on each picture. Amanda's bright red striped shirt helps her to stand out in each illustration, although her facial expressions, conveyed with a line for a mouth and two dots for eyes, are hard to see when the book is shared in a large group. Details of the delicately colored fairy are lost at a distance. The plot and characterization, elements of fantasy, and satisfying resolution draw out varied and rich language from youthful storytellers.

In the Library (or In the Classroom)

MAKING A DISPLAY

Amanda goes into the garden shed to escape the rain and makes a surprising discovery. Set up a display similar to what might be found inside such a shed; use old boards, wood shavings, garden pots, paint cans, and so forth. Draw and cut out the figure of the fairy on poster board, then hide it within the display, allowing the fairy's wings to be partially shown. Set up a sign near the display inviting children to guess what is hiding in the display—and to read *Amanda's Butterfly*.

BOOKTALK

Booktalk *Amanda's Butterfly* to introduce the idea of running across something magical in a very ordinary situation. Emphasize Amanda's typical behavior as she shares a book with her toys, goes outside to play, and feels sad when the rain interrupts her activities. Talk about the old garden shed and the things that accumulate there. Hint that there is something else, something not so ordinary, something magical hiding in there—and it is not a butterfly!

Just as Amanda found something unusual in her garden shed, other book characters have also found unusual things in their everyday lives. Books such as *Half Magic, Five Children and It, Tuck Everlasting, Seven-Day Magic*, and *The Witch's Buttons* show ordinary children discovering something magical.

RELATED MATERIALS

Babbitt, Natalie. *Tuck Everlasting*. Farrar, Straus & Giroux, 1975.

Chew, Ruth. *The Witch's Buttons*. Hastings House, 1974.

Eager, Edward. *Half Magic*. Illustrated by N. M. Bodecker. Harcourt Brace Jovanovich, 1954.

_____. *Seven-Day Magic*. Illustrated by N. M. Bodecker. Harcourt Brace Jovanovich, 1962.

Nesbitt, Edith. *Five Children and It*. Dodd, Mead, 1905.

STORYHOUR

Amanda is eager to help the fairy and succeeds in mending her torn wing. As you share the story, emphasize Amanda's desire to be helpful. She helped a creature smaller than herself and one most people have never seen. Could a child help a smaller, real creature? Share the story of *The Helping Day*, in which David helps ants, worms, a butterfly, and a rabbit. Both Amanda and David helped those smaller than themselves. Can someone small help someone larger? The book *Helping Out* shows children helping adults, and the Aesop fable of "The Lion and the Mouse" shows the tiny mouse helping a large lion.

RELATED MATERIALS

Ancona, George. *Helping Out*. Clarion, 1985.

Chevalier, Christa. *Spence Is Small*. Whitman, 1987.

Herold, Ann Bixby. *The Helping Day*. Illustrated by Victoria De Larrea. Coward-McCann, 1980.

Kraus, Robert. *Herman the Helper*. Illustrated by José Aruego and Ariane Dewey. Dutton, 1974.

Lasker, Joe. *The Do-Something Day*. Viking, 1982.

Mayer, Mercer. *Just for You*. Golden, 1975.

Rockwell, Anne, and Harlow Rockwell. *Can I Help?* Macmillan, 1982.

RELATED NONPRINT MATERIALS

The Lion and the Mouse. National Film Board of Canada.

BOOKSHARING

Amanda begins her day reading a book. The book gives her an idea for an activity that begins her adventure. After presenting this story, return to the opening scene in which Amanda is reading the book in bed. Discuss how books can give one ideas for something to do. Have a selection of easy-to-read activity books on display and invite children to choose a book.

RELATED NONFICTION MATERIALS

Blocksma, Mary. *Easy-to-Make Water Toys That Really Work*. Illustrated by Art Seiden. Prentice-Hall, 1985.

Broekel, Ray. *Sound Experiments*. Childrens, 1983.

Rockwell, Harlow. *I Did It*. Macmillan, 1987.

Sanders, Sandra. *Easy Cooking for Kids*. Scholastic, 1979.

Simon, Seymour. *Shadow Magic*. Illustrated by Stella Ormai. Lothrop, Lee & Shepard, 1985.

Wyler, Rose. *Science Fun with Mud and Dirt*. Illustrated by Pat Stewart. Messner, 1987.

COLLECTION DEVELOPMENT

Include *Amanda's Butterfly* in displays, booklists, thematic units, text sets, and programs on fairies, elves, and other magical little people.

RELATED MATERIALS

Allingham, William. *The Fairies*. Illustrated by Michael Hague. Holt, 1989.

Andersen, Hans Christian. *Thumbelina*. (Numerous editions available)

Barker, Cicely. *Flower Fairies of the Garden*. Viking, 1991. (Several other titles about the Flower Fairies available)

Beskow, Elsa. *Peter in Blueberry Land*. Gryphon House, 1988.

Christiana, David. *White Nineteens*. Farrar, Straus & Giroux, 1992.

Enright, Elizabeth. *Tatsinda*. Illustrated by Katie Treherne. Harcourt Brace Jovanovich, 1991.

Fish, Helen Dean. *When the Root Children Wake Up*. Illustrated by Sibylle von Olfers. Green Tiger, 1988.

Forest, Heather. *The Woman Who Flummoxed the Fairies*. Illustrated by Susan Gaber. Harcourt Brace Jovanovich, 1990.

Fujikawa, Gyo. *Come Follow Me ... to the Secret World of Elves & Fairies & Gnomes & Trolls*. Putnam, 1979.

Hopkins, Lee Bennett, selector. *Elves, Fairies, and Gnomes*. Illustrated by Rose Krans Hoffman. Knopf, 1981.

Tompert, Ann. *Grandfather Tang's Story*. Illustrated by Robert Andrew Parker. Crown, 1990.

Wallace, Daisy, editor. *Fairy Poems*. Illustrated by Trina Schart Hyman. Holiday House, 1980.

Wells, Rosemary. *Fritz and the Mess Fairy*. Dial, 1991.

Yolen, Jane. *Elfabet: An ABC of Elves*. Illustrated by Lauren Mills. Little, Brown, 1990.

In the Classroom (or In the Library)

LANGUAGE ARTS

In two places in this story viewers can anticipate and predict what might happen next. At one or both of these places ask students to predict what will happen next, either verbally or in writing.

As you are sharing the book with a small group of students, stop at page 10, where a small blue wing is showing from behind paint cans. What is behind the cans? What action might take place from that point in the story to the end?

Or, share the book to page 29, where Amanda, after looking in a drawer in the house, reenters the shed with something under her shirt. Have students work in small groups to decide what Amanda has hidden under her shirt and what will happen next. Each group can share its prediction with the rest of the class before continuing the story.

BOOK REPORT

The cover and endpages of this book are filled with the same daisies and poppies that appear in the garden where Amanda looks for a butterfly. Use this floral motif to create a garden of books that students have read. Using construction paper, have students cut out large daisies and poppies. Students can print the title of a recently read book, the author, and their own name across the center of their flowers(s). A garden of flowers can then be created on a bulletin board.

This garden can attract butterflies or fairies, and students can watch to see if their flower has attracted one. When students aren't in the room, place a butterfly or fairy on a few flowers at a time and see if students notice. Use stickers or a stamp and ink pad for the butterflies or fairies.

RELATED NONPRINT MATERIALS

"Butterflies" rubber stamp by Aliki. Kidstamps.

"Wand Fairy" rubber stamp by Trina Schart Hyman. Kidstamps.

LANGUAGE ARTS AND DISCUSSION

Amanda wanted to help the fairy when she saw its torn wing. Mending the wing required problem-solving skills, and Amanda looked at several different options before she found one that would work. As you share the book with small groups of students, have them discuss the tools that Amanda found and why they couldn't be used to repair the fairy's wing. What could those tools be used to repair?

Share the book *Handy Hank Will Fix It* and discuss the repairs Hank made and the tools he used. Have students share things they have repaired and the tools they used to make the repairs.

RELATED MATERIALS

Brown, Craig. *The Patchwork Farmer*. Greenwillow, 1989.

Rockwell, Anne. *Handy Hank Will Fix It*. Holt, 1988.

LANGUAGE ARTS AND WRITING

After reading this story, students understand how the fairy's problem was resolved, but they do not know how the fairy tore her wing or why she was in the garden shed. Have students write their own explanations or those the fairy might have given Amanda while she was repairing the wing. Students might share their writings with the class orally or by putting them on a bulletin board display.

ART AND MASK MAKING

After sharing *Amanda's Butterfly*, discuss where the fairy might be going when she flies off after Amanda repairs her wing. Then read the book *The Butterflies Ball*, in which fairy folk and small animals prepare for a dance. Could the fairy that Amanda helped be flying off to the Butterflies Ball?

Discuss balls and the types of music that might be played. Plan a classroom Butterflies Ball, perhaps inviting another class to join you. What type of music will you have? Games? Refreshments?

Have students make masks to wear to the Butterflies Ball. Masks might be based on characters from the book.

RELATED MATERIALS

Yolen, Jane. *An Invitation to the Butterfly Ball: A Counting Rhyme*. Illustrated by Jane Zalben. Boyds Mill, 1976.

RELATED NONPRINT MATERIALS

Beaton, Clare. *Make and Play: Masks*. Watts, 1990.

Carle, Eric

I See a Song
Crowell, 1973.
ISBN 0-690-43306-9; 0-690-43307-7 (lib); LC 72-9249

ABOUT THE AUTHOR AND HIS BOOKS

Eric Carle was born in Syracuse, New York, on June 25, 1929. His family moved to Stuttgart, Germany, when he was in first grade, and he went through school there, graduating from the Akademie der Bildenden Kuenste in Stuttgart in 1950. He worked as a poster designer for the U.S. Information Center in Stuttgart, and as a graphic designer for the *New York Times*; he was a designer and art director for 10 years before becoming a freelance writer, illustrator, and designer. He has received many honors and won numerous awards for his children's books. He has illustrated more than 40 of his own books and approximately 30 written by other people. Eric Carle has two children—a son and a daughter—and lives in Northhampton, Massachusetts.

Selected Books by the Author

All Around Us. Picture Book Studio, 1986.

Do You Want to Be My Friend? Crowell, 1971.

The Grouchy Ladybug. Crowell, 1977.

Have You Seen My Cat? Picture Book Studio, 1987.

A House for Hermit Crab. Picture Book Studio, 1988.

Twelve Tales from Aesop: Retold and Illustrated. Philomel, 1980.

The Very Busy Spider. Philomel, 1984.

The Very Hungry Caterpillar. Philomel, 1981.

The Very Quiet Cricket. Philomel, 1990.

Selected Books Illustrated by the Author

Brown Bear, Brown Bear, What Do You See? by Bill Martin, Jr. Holt, 1967.

The Foolish Tortoise by Richard Buckley. Picture Book Studio, 1985.

The Lamb and the Butterfly by Arnold Sundgaard. Orchard, 1988.

The Mountain That Loved a Bird by Alice McLerran. Picture Book Studio, 1985.

Otter Nonsense by Norton Juster. Philomel, 1982.

The Scarecrow Clock by George Mendoza. Holt, 1971.

ABOUT I SEE A SONG

This title is deceptively simple in concept and design. The large-format pages begin with a violinist; the solid black block print shows him dressed for a concert. He bows and briefly addresses the reader: "I see a song. I paint music. I hear color." As the musician begins to play, color blobs swirl up, scattering across the pages, then combine in curving patterns, separating into the sun and moon, becoming an ocean, a face, falling as a tear into the earth and growing into magnificent plants, bursting into colorful blobs again, and finally floating to an end. As the musician finishes playing and bows, he has become transformed into all the colors he created with his music.

The bright colors and large forms set off with a white background make this a book that can be shared with a group. The images evoked can represent many different kinds of music, depending on the experiences of the group.

In the Library (or In the Classroom)

MAKING A DISPLAY

Drape a length of colorful cloth over the display area. Open *I See a Song* to the title page and center the book in the display. Place a violin, a bow, an open violin case, and some sheets of music around the book. Cut shapes from brightly colored paper that pick up on the colors in the cloth, and position the shapes on the violin, case, and music. Invite onlookers to read books that feature violins by displaying related materials nearby.

RELATED MATERIALS

Arnold, Caroline. *Music Lessons for Alex*. Photographs by Richard Hewett. Clarion, 1985.

Berger, Melvin. *The Violin Book*. Lothrop, Lee & Shepard, 1972.

Greenwald, Sheila. *Give Us a Great Big Smile, Rosy Cole*. Little, Brown, 1981.

Hautzig, Deborah. *Big Bird Plays the Violin*. Illustrated by Joe Mathieu. Random House, 1991.

McCurdy, Michael. *The Old Man and the Fiddle*. Putnam, 1992.

Micucci, Charles. *A Little Night Music*. Morrow, 1989.

Schaaf, Peter. *The Violin Close Up*. Four Winds, 1980.

Vincent, Gabrielle. *Bravo, Ernest and Celestine!* Greenwillow, 1982.

LISTENING INTEREST CENTER

Attract attention to a listening center with a large picture of a violin cut from black paper and a label, "Come See a Song!" Use brightly colored paper to ask, "What do you see when you listen?" Place a copy of *I See a Song* with each headset at the center. Have either compact discs or audiocassettes of violin music available for children to listen to while they look at the book.

STORY AND CRAFT PROGRAM

Begin the program with a song that features several instruments, such as "I Am a Fine Musician." Tell participants that a person who makes music is a musician and then share the pictures of the musician in *I See a Song*. After looking at the book and talking about it, invite the group to be musicians.

Singing is one way of making music. "I'll Sing a Song and You Sing a Song" can be expanded after the first verse as children suggest ways to make music or instruments to play, and you include their ideas into the verses while they mime the actions of playing the instruments.

Two nursery rhymes that show musicians are "Old King Cole" and "Hey Diddle Diddle." The cat is an unusual musician since people are usually the music makers. In the picture book *Max, the Music-Maker*, a child is shown finding things that make music. After hearing the story, have participants make their own musical instruments by putting dry macaroni in a plastic milk jug. The jugs can be colored with crayons. The group can shake these music makers along with a final song.

RELATED MATERIALS

The Ella Jenkins Songbook for Children. Oak, 1966. ("I'll Sing a Song and You Sing a Song")

Hawkinson, John. *Music and Instruments for Children to Make*. Whitman, 1969.

Raffi. *The Raffi Singable Songbook*. Illustrated by Joyce Yamamoto. Crown, 1980.

Stecher, Miriam B. *Max, the Music-Maker*. Lothrop, Lee & Shepard, 1980.

Tashjian, Virginia A. *With a Deep Sea Smile; Story Hour Stretches for Large or Small Groups*. Illustrated by Rosemary Wells. Little, Brown, 1974.

Winn, Marie, editor. *The Fireside Book of Children's Songs*. Illustrated by John Alcorn. Simon & Schuster, 1966.

Wiseman, Ann. *Making Musical Things: Improvised Instruments*. Scribner, 1979.

BOOKTALK

There are many stories about the violin and its ability to sing like a person, or its magical ability to make people dance. Use *I See a Song* to introduce a booktalk about the unusual ideas people have had about the violin.

RELATED MATERIALS

Aiken, Joan. *The Moon's Revenge*. Illustrated by Alan Lee. Knopf, 1987.

Hampden, John. *The Gypsy Fiddle*. World, 1969.

Otsuka, Yuzo. *Suho and the White Horse; A Legend of Mongolia*. Illustrated by Suekichi Akaba. Viking, 1981.

Schwartz, Howard. *Elijah's Violin, and Other Jewish Fairy Tales*. Harper & Row, 1983.

CRAFT PROGRAM

Present *I See a Song* to a group, discussing the idea that music creates a visual image in the imagination of the listener. Talk about the colors used in the book and what might represent slow or fast passages of music. What might represent high or low notes? Point out the abstract nature of the illustration.

Show the group the technique of tissue paper collage, and how overlapping paper creates different hues and intensities of color. Play a recording of violin music as background while the participants make their own tissue paper collages. When completed, invite children to share their collages with one another.

In the Classroom (or In the Library)

ART AND MUSIC

Begin this week-long music and art project by sharing the book *I See a Song* and discussing how music is "seen" by the mind's eye and can be interpreted differently by listeners. Then share the portion of *Fantasia* where the sounds of different musical instruments are shown in colors.

Each day of the week play a different type of music played on stringed instruments (classical, jazz, bluegrass, folk, country/western, rock and roll). As the music is playing have students draw what they see in their mind using colored chalk, crayons, tempera paints, or watercolors. Each day have students label their artwork with the type of music that was played and put their work into a portfolio. When all projects are completed, display the artwork and have students discuss the effect of different types of music on their art.

RELATED NONPRINT MATERIALS

Magic Flute. 16mm film. National Film Board of Canada, 1972.

Walt Disney's Fantasia. Video. The Walt Disney Company, 1991.

SENSES

Share the books *I See a Song* and *Color Dance* with small groups so they can see the illustrations. When all students have seen the books, discuss the following questions: How can you see a song? How can you dance a color? How can you see something you hear? How can you feel something you see? Discuss ways that our senses interact.

RELATED MATERIALS

Brown, Marcia. *Listen to a Shape*. Watts, 1979.

_____. *Touch Will Tell*. Watts, 1979.

_____. *Walk with Your Eyes*. Watts, 1979.

Jonas, Ann. *Color Dance*. Greenwillow, 1989.

RELATED NONPRINT MATERIALS

Listen, You'll See... 16mm film. National Film Board of Canada.

THEME UNIT

Students enjoy art, dance, and musical instruments, and many take lessons in one or more of these creative areas. Develop a unit on creativity and the arts, including nonfiction and fiction materials on art and artists, music and musicians, and dancing and dancers.

Encourage students to explore why people become artists, dancers, or musicians. Why do people create? Have students write about which of these areas they are interested in. Do they take lessons? How do they feel when they participate in the creation of an artwork, a musical piece, or a dance?

In the book *I See a Song*, the musician changes from the beginning to the end of the book as he creates music with his instrument. Have students verbally respond to this change. Invite community artists, musicians, and dancers to the classroom to talk about their art form and why creativity is important to them. Have them respond to the way the musician changes in this book.

RELATED MATERIALS

Agee, Jon. *The Incredible Painting of Felix Clousseau*. Farrar, Straus & Giroux, 1988.

dePaola, Tomie. *Art Lesson*. Putnam, 1989.

_____. *Oliver Button Is a Sissy*. Harcourt Brace Jovanovich, 1979.

Hurd, Thacher. *Mama Don't Allow*. Harper, 1984.

Isadora, Rachel. *Ben's Trumpet*. Greenwillow, 1979.

Lionni, Leo. *Matthew's Dream*. Knopf, 1991.

Martin, Bill, Jr., and John Archambault. *Barn Dance!* Illustrated by Ted Rand. Holt, 1986.

McKissack, Patricia. *Mirandy and Brother Wind*. Illustrated by Jerry Pinkney. Knopf, 1988.

Rylant, Cynthia. *All I See*. Illustrated by Peter Catalanotto. Orchard/Watts, 1988.

Thomas, Ianthe. *Willie Blows a Mean Horn*. Illustrated by Ann Toulmin-Rothe. Harper & Row, 1981.

RELATED NONFICTION MATERIALS

Ancona, George. *Dancing Is*. Dutton, 1981.

Bjork, Christina. *Linnea in Monet's Garden*. Illustrated by Lena Anderson. Farrar, Straus & Giroux, 1987.

Cole, Liliana. *Young Ballet Dancer*. McGraw-Hill, 1979.

Goffstein, M. B. *An Artist*. HarperCollins, 1980.

Krementz, Jill. *Very Young Dancer*. Knopf, 1976.

Zeck, Gerry. *I Love to Dance: A True Story About Tony Jones*. Carolrhoda, 1982.

RELATED NONPRINT MATERIALS

Why Man Creates. 16mm film. National Film Board of Canada, 1969.

LITERATURE STUDY

Share *I See a Song* and discuss how a song can be seen. Just as the musician is able to see a song, many listeners are able to hear word music when different types of poetry are read aloud. Poets are interested in both the meaning of a word and the sound that it makes when read aloud. In *Joyful Noise: Poems for Two Voices*, the sounds and movement of a variety of insects are re-created when read aloud. *Blackberry Ink* contains bouncy poems that are good for classroom chanting aloud. *Sea Songs* conjure up the musical sounds and sensations of the sea. Share a variety of poems aloud with students and have them discuss how the different poems have different rhythms and how they create different feelings in the listener.

Play selections from the recording *Musical Chairs*, which interweaves poetry of interest to children with the music of famous classical composers.

RELATED NONFICTION MATERIALS

Ciardi, John. *You Read to Me, I'll Read to You.* Illustrated by Edward Gorey. Lippincott, 1981.

cummings, e. e. *Hist Whist*. Illustrated by Deborah Kogan Ray. Crown, 1989.

Esbensen, Barbara Juster. *Words with Wrinkled Knees: Animal Poems*. Illustrated by John Stadler. Crowell, 1986.

Fleischman, Paul. *Joyful Noise: Poems for Two Voices*. Illustrated by Eric Beddows. Harper-Collins, 1988.

Greenfield, Eloise. *Under the Sunday Tree*. Illustrated by Amos Ferguson. HarperCollins, 1988.

Haseley, Dennis. *The Old Banjo*. Illustrated by Stephen Gammell. Macmillan, 1983.

Kennedy, X. J., and Dorothy Kennedy. *Knock at a Star: A Child's Introduction to Poetry*. Illustrated by Karen Weinhaus. Little, Brown, 1982.

Livingston, Myra Cohn. *Sea Songs*. Illustrated by Leonard Fisher. Holiday House, 1986.

Merriam, Eve. *Blackberry Ink*. Illustrated by Hans Wilhelm. Morrow, 1985.

Steele, Mary Q. *Anna's Summer Songs*. Illustrated by Lena Anderson. Greenwillow, 1988.

RELATED NONPRINT MATERIALS

Page, Linda. *Musical Chairs: A Classical Music Fantasy for Children*. Sound recording disc. Kids Records, 1982.

MUSIC, LIBRARY RESEARCH, AND BOOKMAKING

Share the four groups of musical instruments with students (brass, strings, percussion, woodwinds), and have each student choose a group that he or she wants to learn more about. Have students use library resources to gather information for a report on their group of instruments. Students can each select one instrument to concentrate on after starting the research.

Share the book *I See a Song* and have students use the format to make theor own accordian-folded book about their instrument. The title page should be followed by a one- to two-page carefully written report on the instrument. Make a set of copies of the musician from the beginning and end of *I See a Song* for each student. Following their report, students can glue the musician into their book and make a cutout of the instrument they have studied to place in the musician's hands. At the end of the book, they can glue into place the final picture of the musician holding the chosen instrument. On the pages between the two pictures of the musician, students can use crayons/markers/watercolors/tempera to draw the sounds they hear as they listen to music played by their instruments.

Carrier, Lark

The Snowy Path: A Christmas Journey
Picture Book Studio, 1989.
ISBN 0-88708-121-5; LC 89-8449

ABOUT THE AUTHOR AND HER BOOKS

Lark Carrier was born in Montana in 1947 and lived there until she was 11 years old. She credits those years with shaping her views of nature and the world. She graduated from the Parsons School of Design and has worked as a graphic designer and an advertising consultant. *The Snowy Path: A Christmas Journey* is her fifth picture book. Her first book, *There Was a Hill...* was an Ezra Jack Keats Award nominee.

Selected Books by the Author

A Christmas Promise. Picture Book Studio, 1986.

Do Not Touch. Picture Book Studio, 1988.

A Perfect Spring. Picture Book Studio, 1989.

Scout and Cody. Picture Book Studio, 1987.

There Was a Hill.... Picture Book Studio, 1985.

ABOUT THE SNOWY PATH

Snowy woods at twilight are the setting for this Christmas story. A brief introduction, which invites the reader to join a little girl who believes she is alone in the woods, suggests the sequence of the story: "Some footprints come first, some come next, some come last." A trail of boot prints leads to the child, who is following paw prints leading to a small dog. The little girl joins the dog in following tracks that lead to a rabbit, and the three of them then find a deer. Succeeding tracks lead to a skunk, a bear, and a turkey. The final tracks end on a snowy slope. Beyond the curve of the hill, in the starry night sky, the mystery is solved: The tracks were left by Santa's reindeer and sleigh as they raced up the hill to become airborne.

The little girl in this story is curious and observant, and the unusual format of the book invites the reader to participate with her as she makes her discoveries. Each set of tracks ends in a cutout flap which, when lifted, shows the character that made the tracks. When the flap is in place and the page is turned, the previously revealed character appears as part of the continuing search.

Each picture is seen at ground level, focusing on the tracks in the snow. The woods are indicated by the trunks of trees, dry weeds poking through the snow, and fallen leaves here and there. The soft, muted, winter colors seem to glow against the white background of snow. The form of each figure is softened and rounded, indistinct in outline or detail. A hint of habitat is given, such as the caves seen behind the bear. As each new animal joins the search, violet shadows increase. In the final picture, evening has arrived and the sky is full of stars glowing through a mist of fallen snow.

Although the pages are sturdy, the binding is weak, which makes the book poorly suited for much handling. The accurately depicted tracks giving a clue to each new animal are too small for the detail to be noted from any distance. This makes the book best shared with an adult one-on-one or with a few children at a time.

In the Library (or In the Classroom)

MAKING A DISPLAY

This story takes place in the woods in the winter. The book invites questions such as: Who made that track in the snow or mud? Where do animals go in the winter? What other discoveries can be made in the winter woods?

Use *The Snowy Path* as the center of a display. A background can be made simply with a white sheet. Collect some pine cones, a small log, and a few dried weeds to indicate the woods. Contact local naturalists from the state park or forestry service to borrow plaster casts of tracks. Identify the casts, or pose questions about each one: "This animal has a short tail and long ears. What is it?" Display related materials to help children answer the questions. Provide cut paper, rubber stamps of various animal paw prints, and ink pads with which children can make their own paw print bookmarks.

RELATED MATERIALS

Arnosky, Jim. *Crinkleroot's Book of Animal Tracking*. Bradbury, 1989.

Brimner, Larry Dane. *Animals That Hibernate*. Watts, 1991.

Docekal, Eileen M. *Nature Detective: How to Solve Outdoor Mysteries*. Sterling, 1989.

Markle, Sandra. *Exploring Winter*. Atheneum, 1984.

Nestor, William P. *Into Winter: Discovering a Season*. Illustrated by Susan Banta. Houghton Mifflin, 1982.

Riha, Susanne. *Animals in Winter*. Carolrhoda, 1989.

STORYHOUR

The little girl's search through the woods ends with a magical Christmas discovery. Use *The Snowy Path* with a small group to begin a program on Christmas searches. The group will be able to see that there are tracks in the snow even if they cannot see the details of the tracks, and their attention will be held by the device of folding back the flap to discover what made each set of tracks. Share *A Christmas Promise* by the same author. Do the children recognize the little girl and her dog? What is she searching for in this book? Tell a story in which Santa Claus is searching for a missing reindeer, such as *Where's Prancer?* by Syd Hoff. Follow with a booktalk of *What Did You Lose, Santa?* and then invite the children to make their own Christmas search for a good book to read.

RELATED MATERIALS ON SEARCHES

Amoss, Berthe. *What Did You Lose, Santa?* Harper, 1987.

Carrier, Lark. *A Christmas Promise*. Picture Book Studio, 1986.

Cunningham, Julia. *Onion Journey*. Illustrated by Lydia Cooley. Pantheon, 1957.

dePaola, Tomie. *Legend of Old Befana*. Harcourt Brace Jovanovich, 1980.

Drescher, Henrik. *Looking for Santa Claus*. Lothrop, Lee & Shepard, 1984.

Hoff, Syd. *Where's Prancer?* Harper, 1960.

Hyman, Trina Schart. *How Six Found Christmas*. Holiday House, 1991. (Reissue)

CRAFT PROGRAM

The maker of each set of snow prints is revealed in *The Snowy Path* when a flap is folded over. Have students use this book as a model to make their own flap books or snowy scenes with flaps. Discuss the things that might be hidden under the snow. Show Donnelly's *Dinosaur Day*, in which various city objects are hidden under the snow and appear to be dinosaur shapes. After discussing the way snow hides things, invite children to make an open-the-flap book or scene. Hint: Draw the object to be revealed before cutting out the flap. The object is drawn on the back of the paper, then partially cut out. A snowy scene is drawn on the front of the paper, with the hidden object covered with snow. When the flap is folded open, the hidden object is revealed.

RELATED MATERIALS

Donnelly, Liza. *Dinosaur Day*. Scholastic, 1987.

Assortment of lift-the-flap books.

STORY AND CRAFT PROGRAM

The snow on the ground made the various sets of tracks easy to follow in *The Snowy Path*. Use the book in a program centering on snow. Show either the film or the book *The Snowy Day* by Ezra Jack Keats to introduce the theme. Point out the tracks Peter made in the snow as a lead-in to *The Snowy Path*. Prior to sharing *The Snowy Path*, make enlarged drawings of each track on separate pieces of paper. As you turn each page, hold up the drawings of the tracks from that page, and ask children to guess what made the track. Then, fold the flap over to see if they are correct. The picture book version of *Stopping by Woods on a Snowy Evening* makes a good follow-up to this story. Continue with the snow theme with the book *Simon and the Snowflakes*. End the program by having children cut out snowflakes to count. Instructions for cutting out snowflakes can be found in *December Decorations*.

RELATED MATERIALS

Blades, Ann. *Winter*. Lothrop, Lee & Shepard, 1989.

Delaney, A. *Monster Tracks*. HarperCollins, 1981.

Frost, Robert. *Stopping by Woods on a Snowy Evening*. Illustrated by Susan Jeffers. Dutton, 1978.

Gundersheimer, Karen. *Happy Winter*. Harper & Row, 1982.

Keats, Ezra Jack. *The Snowy Day*. Viking, 1962.

Krahn, Fernando. *The Mystery of the Giant Footprints*. Dutton, 1977.

Parish, Peggy. *December Decorations*. Macmillan, 1975.

Tibo, Gilles. *Simon and the Snowflakes*. Tundra Books, 1988.

RELATED NONPRINT MATERIALS

Keats, Ezra Jack. *The Snowy Day*. 16mm film/video. Weston Woods, 1964.

Yolen, Jane. *Owl Moon*. 16mm film/video. Weston Woods, 1989.

CREATIVE DRAMATICS PROGRAM

In preparation you will need a number of white sheets, a sack of small treats such as small candy canes or bookmarks, and a hidden Santa Claus picture. Prepare the Santa Claus picture using two large sheets of white paper or poster board. Draw or paste a large picture of Santa on one sheet and cover with the other, making a flap that can be pulled to reveal the Santa Claus picture.

Invite program participants to bring a stuffed animal or animal puppet representing a creature that might be found in the woods (have extras for children who forget). Have children share the animal character they brought, then settle down to view what the adult has to share.

Share the book *The Snowy Path* with the children. You may want to share it several times to enable children to look under the flaps, look at the scenery, and pay attention to the accumulation of characters as they move from flap to flap.

Place children in small groups based on animals of like kind (all children with bears together, all with rabbits together, and so forth). Cover each group loosely with a white sheet. A child with a doll or unique animal could join the adult in "discovering" each group. As you walk around, "discover" a group by lifting up the sheet. That group joins the adult in finding the next group. Encourage children to imagine things they would see in the woods; follow a twisting path around the library or program room as you look for the hidden groups. When all of the "animals" have been located, have them wind around the room following the adult until they discover the poster board that hides the Santa Claus picture. Lift the cover to see Santa, then pull out the sack of treats from behind the picture to distribute as children leave. Display related winter woods and woodland Christmas books for checkout.

RELATED MATERIALS

Brown, Margaret Wise. *The Little Fir Tree*. Illustrated by Barbara Cooney. Crowell, 1954.

Gammell, Stephen. *Wake Up, Bear ... It's Christmas!* Lothrop, Lee & Shepard, 1981.

Holm, Mayling Mack. *A Forest Christmas*. Harper, 1977.

Holmes, Efner. *The Christmas Cat*. Illustrated by Tasha Tudor. Crowell, 1976.

Hutchins, Pat. *The Silver Christmas Tree*. Macmillan, 1974.

Mariana. *Miss Flora McFlimsey's Christmas Eve*. Illustrated by Caroline Howe and Mariana. Lothrop, Lee & Shepard, 1988. (Revised edition)

Miller, Edna. *Mousekin's Christmas Eve*. Prentice-Hall, 1965.

In the Classroom (or In the Library)

SCIENCE AND ART

Each animal in this book left a very distinct print in the snow. Compare the illustrated prints in the story with pictures of prints of the same animals in real life. Discuss how the feet of different animals make different prints.

Prepare for rubbings by either drawing or photocopying sets of various animal footprints (you may need to enlarge them). After backing the copy on cardboard, cover it with clear contact paper. Draw the outline of each print with white glue so that a thick, raised ridge is created. When the glue has dried, children can lay a sheet of paper over the print and rub it with the long side of a crayon. The resulting rubbings can be displayed with pictures of the animals.

RELATED MATERIALS

Branley, Franklyn. *Big Tracks, Little Tracks*. Illustrated by Leonard Kessler. Crowell, 1960.

Goor, Ron, and Nancy Goor. *All Kinds of Feet*. Crowell, 1984.

Kudlinski, Kathleen V. *Animal Tracks and Traces*. Illustrated by Mary Morgan. Watts, 1991.

Machotka, Hana. *What Neat Feet!* Morrow, 1991.

Pluckrose, Henry. *Paws and Claws*. Watts, 1989.

Selsam, Millicent E. *How to Be a Nature Detective*. Illustrated by Ezra Jack Keats. HarperCollins, 1966.

Webster, David. *Track Watching*. Watts, 1972.

BOOK REPORT

This book begins with a child's footprints in the snow that lead the reader into the story. Students can lead others to stories using their footprints. Have students trace around their own feet on white construction paper and cut out the tracing. This footprint can be used as a book report form to tell about a favorite book or a recently read book. Students need to include their own name, the author and title of the book, and enough information to interest another person in reading the book.

Create a snowy path of student footprints that lead to the school or classroom library, book corner, or table of books. Begin the snowy path with a sign that says, "The Snowy Path leads to good reading."

ACCUMULATION AND SEQUENCING GAME

As each flap is lifted in this story, a new character joins the other characters to follow the next set of prints in the snow. While sharing the book, point out how the characters accumulate as each flap is lifted (how many on each page?), and discuss the sequence of the characters (who came first? second? third?). You may want to share other books about accumulation or following before you have the class play the following game.

Have the class play the game of follow-the-leader using a technique similar to the one in the book. All students sit in their seats, and the first child "finds" the second child, who then follows the first child as they "find" the third child. The leader can be the one to always "find" the next student, or you can have the last student who was "found" be the one to "find" the next student. Each person must follow behind the last person found so there is a line of students who follow the leader. When all students are in line, have the leader lead the line around the school to discover Christmas displays.

RELATED MATERIALS

Brenner, Barbara. *The Snow Parade*. Illustrated by Mary Tara O'Keefe. Crown, 1984.

Brett, Jan. *The Mitten*. Putnam, 1989.

Burningham, John. *Mr. Gumpy's Outing*. Holt, Rinehart & Winston, 1970.

Crews, Donald. *Parade*. Greenwillow, 1983.

Ets, Marie Hall. *In the Forest*. Viking, 1944.

Galdone, Paul. *The Gingerbread Boy*. Clarion, 1975.

Sage, James. *The Little Band*. Illustrated by Keiko Narahashi. McElderry/Macmillan, 1991.

ART AND LANGUAGE ARTS

This story becomes a Christmas story when the characters see Santa Claus with his reindeer and sleigh as they begin to fly across the sky. Share a variety of winter holiday cards—Thanksgiving, Hanukkah, Christmas. For each card, have students look at the design of the card, the written message, and the way the two reinforce each other. Share the book and the way the flaps are integrated into the design. Students can design and make their own holiday cards that incorporate a flap.

RELATED MATERIALS

Purdy, Susan Gold. *Holiday Cards for You to Make*. Lippincott, 1967.

LANGUAGE ARTS

After sharing this story, have students discuss the time of year the story takes place, the animals in the story and their habitats, and the holiday that is occurring. Students can write their personal cumulative stories using different habitats and animals that live in that habitat. After selecting a habitat, students need to identify six or seven animals typical of that habitat. Examples:

City	—	Dogs, cats, birds, rats
Desert	—	Snakes, lizards, burrowing owls, roadrunners
Farm	—	Horses, cows, chickens, pigs
Ocean	—	Whales, sharks, octopuses, lobsters
Pond	—	Frogs, fish, tadpoles, insects

Other habitats might include a polar region or a rainforest. Students may select different times of the year and end their story with a symbol of any holiday during that season.

Collington, Peter

The Angel and the Soldier Boy
Knopf, 1987.
ISBN 0-394-88626-7; 0-394-98626-1 (lib)

ABOUT THE AUTHOR AND HIS BOOKS

Peter Collington was born on April 2, 1948, in Northcotes, England. He studied photography at the Bournemouth College of Art, then moved to New York City, where he started drawing in his spare time. He now lives in Dorset, England, with his wife and their daughter, Sasha. He got the idea for his first book, *Little Pickle*, from Sasha when she was a toddler. *Little Pickle* was a runner-up for England's prestigious Mother Goose Award. *The Angel and the Soldier Boy* was his second book, and it received the Smarties Prize in 1988.

Selected Books by the Author

Little Pickle. Dutton, 1986.

My Darling Kitten. Knopf, 1988.

On Christmas Eve. Knopf, 1990.

ABOUT THE ANGEL AND THE SOLDIER BOY

The angel and the soldier boy are two small dolls a little girl holds as she listens to a bedtime book about pirates, and then carefully places on her pillow as she falls asleep. A tiny purple-coated pirate, resembling the one on the book cover, comes up the lamp cord to rob the child's piggy bank, and the soldier boy attempts to stop him. In the ensuing adventure, the soldier boy is taken captive and the angel doll goes to the rescue. She undertakes a dangerous trip through the house, braving stairs, a cat, and a wasp, until she finds the ship model where the pirates live. The daring rescue and the restoration of the coin to the bank are completed before the child awakens and reaches for the two dolls beside her.

Pastel watercolors and colored pencil drawings appear in panels of varying sizes. The drawings are direct and representational, which makes the fantasy more believable. Perspective varies to emphasize the smallness of the figures in an environment sized to humans. The angel and the soldier boy are drawn as if they were real children in costume; as a result, it is easy for the reader to become involved in the adventure.

In the Library (or In the Classroom)

MAKING A DISPLAY

Soldier dolls and miniature toy soldiers have been popular with many children over the years and are sometimes collected by adults. Develop a display of fiction and nonfiction books about toy soldiers. Use wallpaper sample books to find a Victorian print similar to the wallpaper in the little girl's room in *The Angel and the Soldier Boy* and use it for a backdrop. Display soldier dolls with the books, including tin soldiers, plastic soldier models, G.I. Joe dolls, and others.

RELATED FICTION RESOURCES

Ambrus, Victor. *Brave Soldier Janosh*. Harcourt, Brace & World, 1967.

Clarke, Pauline. *The Return of the Twelve*. Gregg Press, 1981.

Delaney, M. C. *Not Your Average Joe*. Illustrated by Chris Burke. Dutton, 1990.

Emberley, Barbara. *Drummer Hoff*. Illustrated by Ed Emberley. Prentice-Hall, 1967.

Nicholson, William. *Clever Bill*. Farrar, Straus & Giroux, 1977.

Noll, Sally. *Off and Counting*. Greenwillow, 1984.

RELATED NONFICTION RESOURCES

Dilley, Roy. *Model Soldiers in Color*. Cathay Books, 1980.

Goodenough, Simon. *Military Miniatures*. Chilton, 1978.

Harris, Henry. *Model Soldiers*. Octopus, 1962.

Johnson, Peter. *Toy Armies*. B. T. Batsford, 1981.

Smeed, Vic, editor. *Encyclopedia of Military Modeling*. Octopus, 1981.

BOOKTALK

Begin by sharing the double-page spread of the pirate's ship on the piano in *The Angel and the Soldier Boy*. Invite participants to speculate on the ship: Who put it there? Why? What flag is it flying? Can anyone see the tiny figure approaching the ship? Is there anybody aboard the ship? Retell just the part of the plot in which the angel sneaks on board the ship and tiptoes past the sleeping pirates to discover the soldier boy tied hand and foot. To entice readers, hint at the rest of the adventure—both how the angel and the soldier boy get into the situation and what happens to them next.

If you are able to obtain a model ship, show it to the audience as you talk about the way in which looking at model ships seems to have stimulated the imagination of many authors. Select one or two other books to talk about as you share the model. Invite participants to create their own stories about the ship model you have, after they have read the Collington title or other books you mention. Leave the model on display in the library to stimulate writing or telling a story on audiotape.

RELATED MATERIALS

Faulkner, Matt. *The Amazing Voyage of Jackie Grace*. Scholastic, 1987.

Ginsburg, Mirra. *Four Brave Sailors*. Illustrated by Nancy Tafuri. Greenwillow, 1987.

Goffstein, M. B. *Me and My Captain*. Farrar, Straus & Giroux, 1974.

_____. *My Noah's Ark*. Harper & Row, 1978.

Paxton, Tom. *Jennifer's Rabbit*. Illustrated by Donna Ayers. Morrow, 1988.

Reavin, Sam. *Hurray for Captain Jane!* Illustrated by Emily Arnold McCully. Parents Magazine Press, 1971.

Zhitkov, Boris. *How I Hunted the Little Fellows*. Illustrated by Paul O. Zelinsky. Dodd, Mead, 1979.

RELATED NONFICTION MATERIALS

Gilbreath, Alice. *Making Toys That Swim and Float*. Follett, 1978.

COLLECTION DEVELOPMENT

Include *The Angel and the Soldier Boy* with other picture books depicting pirates in text sets, subject displays, and thematic units for comparison of artists' perceptions of pirate costumes and behavior.

RELATED MATERIALS

Burningham, John. *Come Away from the Water, Shirley*. HarperCollins, 1983.

Guillermo, Mordillo. *The Damp and Daffy Doings of a Daring Pirate Ship*. Harlin Quist, 1971.

Haseley, Dennis. *The Pirate Who Tried to Capture the Moon*. Illustrated by Susan Truesdell. HarperCollins, 1983.

Lofgren, Ulf. *Alvin the Pirate*. Carolrhoda, 1990.

Peppe, Rodney. *The Kettleship Pirates*. Lothrop, Lee & Shepard, 1983.

Ryan, John. *Pugwash Aloft: A Pirate Story*. Criterion, 1959.

_____. *Pugwash and the Buried Treasure: A Pirate Story*. Bodley Head, 1980.

Wilhelm, Hans. *Pirates Ahoy!* Parents Magazine Press, 1987.

BOOKSHARING PROGRAM

The perspective used in the illustration of *The Angel and the Soldier Boy* helps the reader imagine what it would be like to be tiny in a large world. Take children on an imaginary trip through the library pretending to be only 3 inches high. To help children's imaginations, use a flashlight with a strong, concentrated beam. The spot of light from the flashlight represents their imaginary small selves. Have the group describe what the tiny person is seeing and doing as you walk around. Include some challenging situations such as the ones the angel encounters, and have the children tell you how to proceed in each one. End the trip near a display of books about small beings in a large world.

RELATED MATERIALS

Banks, Lynne Reid. *The Indian in the Cupboard.* Illustrated by Brock Cole. Doubleday, 1980.

Blathwayt, Benedict. *Tangle and the Firesticks.* Knopf, 1987.

Heller, Linda. *Lily at the Table.* Macmillan, 1979.

Norton, Mary. *The Borrowers.* Illustrated by Beth Krush and Joe Krush. Harcourt Brace Jovanovich, 1953. (Several titles in series)

Peterson, John. *The Littles.* Illustrated by Roberta Clark. Scholastic, 1967. (Several titles in series)

Pratchett, Terry. *Truckers.* Delacorte, 1990.

Ross, Pat. *Hi Fly.* Illustrated by John Wallner. Crown, 1974.

Wallace, Barbara. *Barrel in the Basement.* Illustrated by Sharon Wooding. Atheneum, 1985.

CRAFT PROGRAM

The figures of the angel doll, the soldier boy, and the pirate captain can easily be turned into stick puppets. Make each figure 3 to 4 inches tall or "life size." If you project the figures with an opaque projector to draw them for reproduction, the images of the two dolls lying on the pillow on the first page and the image of the pirate captain on page 5 work well as puppet figures. Reproduce the figures in outline on heavy stock. Children can color the figures, cut them out, and attach them to either a popsicle stick or a plastic drinking straw to make a puppet.

The children can take turns telling part of the story with their stick puppets and can take the puppets home to tell continuing adventures of the characters.

In the Classroom (or In the Library)

LITERATURE SHARING

After students have had the opportunity to read *The Angel and the Soldier Boy*, read aloud the story *The Steadfast Tin Soldier* by Hans Christian Andersen. Invite students to compare and contrast the characters, settings, themes, and plots in the two books, charting their responses on the chalkboard.

RELATED MATERIALS

Andersen, Hans Christian. *The Steadfast Tin Soldier*. Illustrated by Marcia Brown. Scribner, 1953.

_____. *The Steadfast Tin Soldier*. Illustrated by Paul Galdone. Houghton Mifflin, 1979.

_____. *The Steadfast Tin Soldier*. Illustrated by Alain Vaes. Little, Brown, 1983.

ECONOMICS AND LANGUAGE ARTS

After the pirates stole the coin from the piggy bank, it was very important to the angel and the soldier boy to return it to the little girl's bank before she awoke. Discuss the importance of savings and ways that people budget their money so they can save. Invite students to share ways that they earn money and how and where they save it. Have students write a two-part paper in which they tell what they think the little girl was saving her money for, and what they would save money for.

RELATED MATERIALS

Cantwell, Lois. *Money and Banking*. Watts, 1984.

Kyte, Kathy. *The Kids' Complete Guide to Money*. Knopf, 1984.

Scott, Elaine. *The Banking Book*. Warne, 1981.

Zillions, a periodical for children. Consumers Union of the United States. (The publishers of *Consumer Reports* produce this guide on spending and saving for children.)

MUSIC

Ballads are songs that tell a story. The structure of a ballad is very repetitive, with a fixed stanza structure and a refrain repeated after each stanza. Introduce ballads by listening to several or by teaching children several to sing. Use *The Oxford Book of Ballads*, an anthology of the traditional ballads of Scotland and England as a resource for reading out loud. The ballads "The Ballad of Tam Lin" and "Waltzing Matilda" are available as picture books.

After students are familiar with ballad structure, create a ballad for *The Angel and the Soldier Boy*. Begin by determining the stanza structure and creating the refrain as a group activity. Small groups can then create stanzas based on the sequence of events in the story. These stanzas can be assembled into the final ballad and sung by the entire class.

RELATED MATERIALS

Kinsley, James, editor. *The Oxford Book of Ballads*. Oxford University Press, 1969.

Niles, John Jacob. *The Ballad Book*. Bramhall House, 1961.

Paterson, A. B. *Waltzing Matilda*. Illustrated by Desmond Digby. Holt, Rinehart & Winston, 1972.

Plotz, Helen. *As I Walked Out One Evening*. Greenwillow, 1976.

Yolen, Jane. *Tam Lin: An Old Ballad*. Illustrated by Charles Mikolaycak. Harcourt Brace Jovanovich, 1990.

RELATED NONPRINT MATERIALS

Seeger, Pete. *American Favorite Ballads*. Sound recording disc. Folkways, 1968.

_____. *Frontier Ballads*. Sound recording disc. Folkways.

LANGUAGE ARTS I

The angel and the soldier boy were favorite toys of the young girl in this book; she took them with her when she went to bed and put them near her as she fell asleep. The girl was unaware that her toys had an amazing adventure while she slept. Have students think about their favorite toy, either one they currently enjoy or one from the past. Have them write imaginary stories about an adventure that their favorite toy might have at their house when everyone else is sleeping.

RELATED MATERIALS

Freeman, Don. *Beady Bear*. Viking, 1954.

Goodall, John S. *The Midnight Adventures of Kelly, Dot, and Esmeralda*. Atheneum, 1972.

Gruelle, Johnny. *Original Adventures of Raggedy Ann*. Outlet, 1988.

Hissey, Jane. *Old Bear*. Philomel, 1986.

Wahl, Jan. *The Muffletump Storybook*. Illustrated by Cyndy Szekeres. Follett, 1975.

LANGUAGE ARTS II

As members of the class read this book, have them make a list of the different characters and the behaviors they exhibit. When all class members have read the book, compile a class list of the characters and their behaviors. List each of the behaviors on the chalkboard and write the characters underneath. As you discuss the behaviors, have students think of other characters from books or the media that exhibit similar behavior and tell why they think the character they mention should be added to the list.

In My Garden
Picture Book Studio, 1985.
ISBN 0-907234-05-4; LC 85-9402

In the Pond
Picture Book Studio, 1984.
ISBN 0-907234-43-7; LC 84-972

In the Woods
Picture Book Studio, 1983.
ISBN 0-907234-31-3; 0-88708-008-1; LC 83-8153

ABOUT THE AUTHORS AND THEIR BOOKS

Ermanno Cristini and Luigi Puricelli were both born in Italy. They attended the Milan Technical Academy, where each received a doctor of architecture degree. They have both also studied visual communication. The two have a design studio in Varese, Italy. They have been involved in communication with children for 20 years, and their picture books have been published in many countries around the world.

ABOUT IN MY GARDEN; IN THE POND; IN THE WOODS

Each of these titles is an ecological exploration of a specific environment. Each book shows a scene in panoramic fashion, with successive pages continuing the picture from the page before. As each book unfolds, it creates a mural of animals and plants typical of each habitat, as seen from the perspective of someone lying stomach-down on the ground. This close-up, ground-level view brings the environment into unusual focus. While the concept is the same, the treatment differs slightly from book to book.

In My Garden uses simple graphics with boldly painted colors to show the many life forms in a rural garden. Many of the animals shown are typical insects and small reptiles and amphibians; however, the hedgehog and the small songbird betray the European origin of the book. Domestic animals are part of the scene, but not a natural part. The rabbits looking through their wire enclosure, the horse stepping on the freshly turned earth, the cat and the hen hunting—all are shown as pure white animals, in contrast to the naturalistic colors of the wildlife.

In the Pond uses realistic paintings as the scene moves from one bank to another of a marshy wetland area. The water is shallow and full of plant and animal life, which is shown both below the surface of the water and just above it. Tadpoles, mayflies, and nesting birds indicate a spring setting for the panorama.

Richly colored paintings show the wealth of life on the forest floor in *In the Woods*. Animals and plants are seen in detail from the ground to about a foot high. The front legs of the deer are seen on one page, the browsing head on the next. The hawk is shown only as talons poised to strike above a hare. This use of partial clues to the animals challenges the reader to name the whole object after examining only a part.

In these nature studies, patience and careful observation yield rewards, just as they do in field study. Hints to the food chains and interactions between species are given. Just as one might identify a tree by examining a leaf or the bark, the portions of animals and plants shown serve as clues to the whole. The alert reader begins to notice the difference in similar things that enables identification and classification. The feeling of actual observation is strong, due to the attention to detail and the close-up, consistent point of view.

In the Library (or In the Classroom)

ACTIVITY AND DISPLAY

In springtime, visit a pond or creek and fill a bucket with water, mud, and plants. Establish a pond environment in a small aquarium.

Introduce the aquarium to the library or classroom by sharing *In the Pond* with a group. Invite the participants to observe the changes in the plants and animals for a few weeks. Place the aquarium at eye level for children. Put magnifying glasses, pencils, and paper close to it. Ask children to write out the names of the plants or animals they can identify, or observations they make, and put their writing on display next to the aquarium. You may want to have observations dated and put them in chronological order, or by Day 1, Day 2, and so forth. Place related materials nearby.

(Note: Once a week you will need to freshen the water with "aged" or pond water, pouring half the water out and replacing it. Watch for hatching and developing mosquitoes—you may want to place glass over the aquarium to prevent them from infesting the room.)

RELATED NONFICTION MATERIALS

Court, Judith. *Ponds and Streams*. Watts, 1985.

Dewey, Jennifer. *A Day at the Edge of the Pond*. Little, Brown, 1987.

Michels, Tilde. *At the Frog Pond*. Illustrated by Reinhard Michl. Lippincott, 1989.

Reid, George K. *Pond Life*. Illustrated by Sally Kaicher and Tom Dolan. Golden Press, 1967.

Schwartz, David M. *The Hidden Life of the Pond*. Photos by Dwight Kuhn. Crown, 1988.

Stone, Lynn M. *Pond Life*. Childrens Press, 1983.

RELATED NONPRINT MATERIALS

Sabin, Francene. *Wonders of the Pond*. Illustrated by Leigh Grant. Book/cassette. Troll Associates, 1983.

STORYHOUR

Invite children to come to your garden as you share the book *In My Garden*. Use a repeated phrase to encourage audience participation—something like, "In my garden, I see...." Take time to point out some of the more hidden animals in the book, such as the lizard and the mouse, and to guess what the partially seen animals are.

"In my garden," you might say, "there are plants, animals ... and stories. Some of the animals have their own stories." Use the pictures of the animals in this first book to introduce each story. For the hen, share Garth Williams's *The Chicken Book*, or Pat Hutchins's *Rosie's Walk*. For the turtle, Ron Maris's *I Wish I Could Fly* or Frank Asch's *Turtle Tale* can be told. The spider with its web goes with Eric Carle's *The Very Busy Spider*; be sure to let children touch the web and feel the strands. Ruth Brown's *Ladybug, Ladybug*, with its extended version of the traditional rhyme, also spotlights various animals in a rural area.

You may want to stretch this theme over several storyhours and use *In My Garden* as the central book for a whole series. Many stories can be found for other animals in the book—ladybugs, mice, hedgehogs, moles, and lizards are all featured as main characters in stories you can use. Be sure to include *The Tale of Peter Rabbit* for the rabbits in the garden.

RELATED MATERIALS

Asch, Frank. *Turtle Tale*. Dial, 1978.

Brown, Ruth. *Ladybug, Ladybug*. Dutton, 1988.

Carle, Eric. *The Very Busy Spider*. Philomel, 1984.

Hutchins, Pat. *Rosie's Walk*. Macmillan, 1968.

Maris, Ron. *I Wish I Could Fly*. Greenwillow, 1986.

Potter, Beatrix. *The Tale of Peter Rabbit*. Warne, 1902.

Williams, Garth. *The Chicken Book*. Delacorte, 1990.

LITERATURE SHARING

Compare these three titles with some books in which an artist has portrayed various aspects of an environment. As children look at the illustrations, encourage them to discover the ways in which the artist has selected details. How does the artist convey information? What is left out? Compare the work of various artists—how do they differ? Which is the most effective portrayal of a total environment? Compare these illustrations with photographs of the same environments. As a group, select the artist that children feel is most successful in portraying an environment.

RELATED MATERIALS

Arnosky, Jim. *In the Forest: A Portfolio of Paintings*. Lothrop, Lee & Shepard, 1989.

Baker, Alan. *Two Tiny Mice*. Dial, 1990.

Bash, Barbara. *Desert Giant: The World of the Saguaro Cactus*. Little, Brown, 1989.

Bellamy, David. *Our Changing World: The Forest*. Illustrated by Jill Dow. Potter, 1988.

Greeley, Valerie. *Field Animals*. Bedrick, 1984.

Parnall, Peter. *Woodpile*. Macmillan, 1990.

Tafuri, Nancy. *Rabbit's Morning*. Greenwillow, 1985.

RELATED PHOTOGRAPHIC WORKS

Hirschi, Ron. *Fall*. Photographs by Thomas D. Mangelsen. Cobblehill, 1991.

_____. *Spring*. Photographs by Thomas D. Mangelsen. Cobblehill, 1990.

_____. *Summer*. Photographs by Thomas D. Mangelsen. Cobblehill, 1991.

_____. *Winter*. Photographs by Thomas D. Mangelsen. Cobblehill, 1990.

Porter, Eliot. *Appalachian Wilderness: The Great Smoky Mountains*. Ballantine, 1973.

RELATED PERIODICALS

Chickadee. Buffalo, NY: The Young Naturalist Foundation.

Owl. Buffalo, NY: The Young Naturalist Foundation.

Ranger Rick. Vienna, VA: National Wildlife Federation.

BOOKTALK

Use the wordless diorama shown in the title *In the Woods* to begin a booktalk on woodland nonfiction. How were the artists able to see so much in the woods? Maybe they were like Crinklefoot in *I Was Born in a Tree and Raised by Bees*. Introduce this character and read the final page of the book, "Remember, there are pictures everywhere, puzzles hidden among the leaves and in the streams, and stories written on the snow...." The author who created Crinklefoot has also written a book, *Secrets of a Wildlife Watcher*, to help readers see things in the woods.

Before you go out to creep up on animals, it is helpful to know about *The Hidden Life of the Forest*. When you are out spying on creatures, you will see different things in the same place as the seasons change. Find out about some of these things in books by Carol Lerner, such as *A Forest Year* and *Flowers of a Woodland Spring*. Reading these books is almost like spending time in the woods. Before or after you go looking for secrets and hidden things in the woods, you will enjoy reading about Rebecca, a young explorer, who is searching for an elusive ovenbird in *One Day in the Woods*. Her Uncle Luke had said, "When you find an ovenbird, you will have found the wizard of the woods." Rebecca finds many enchantments in her day of exploration.

Listeners may want to write their own stories about a day in the woods after reading these books and exploring the woodlands themselves.

RELATED MATERIALS

Arnosky, Jim. *I Was Born in a Tree and Raised by Bees*. Bradbury, 1988. (Reprint of 1977 edition)

_____. *Secrets of a Wildlife Watcher*. Lothrop, Lee & Shepard, 1983.

George, Jean Craighead. *One Day in the Woods*. Illustrated by Gary Allen. Crowell, 1988.

Hirschi, Ron. *Forest*. Illustrated by Barbara Bash. Bantam, 1991. (Discover My World Series)

Lerner, Carol. *Flowers of a Woodland Spring*. Morrow, 1979.

_____. *A Forest Year*. Morrow, 1987.

Schwartz, David M., and Dwight Kuhn. *The Hidden Life of the Forest*. Crown, 1988.

BOOKSHARING AND ART PROGRAM

Share the Cristini/Puricelli books with children and invite them to create a mural based on their observations of a specific area nearby. Use drawing books by Jim Arnosky to discuss how to make nature drawings. After sketching ground-level plants and features such as rocks, puddles, or fence posts, the children take portions of the mural and add insects, birds, and other animals they have observed or know live in this area. Illustrator notes from each child about her or his portion might accompany the completed mural, along with copies of *In My Garden, In the Pond*, and *In the Woods*.

In the Classroom (or In the Library)

LANGUAGE ARTS

These three books offer a close-up view of nature as seen by artists. Have students explore the way in which the animals pictured may see the same scene. Introduce the idea of an animal's point of view through some of the titles by Joanne Ryder. Talk with the class about the concepts presented in *The View from the Oak*, and then read aloud from page 91, "Finding and understanding the keys."

Have students select one animal from one of the Cristini/Puricelli books and write about the environment from their animal's point of view, using a first-person narrative. Papers might be titled, "A _____'s View" (fill in the blank with the name of the animal). Show one book at a time and have students who have selected an animal from that book share their writing with the class. Compare the ways in which different animals might look at the same scene as you share each book.

RELATED MATERIALS

Ryder, Joanne. *Catching the Wind*. Illustrated by Michael Rothman. Morrow, 1989.

_____. *Chipmunk Song*. Illustrated by Lynn Cherry. Lodestar/Dutton, 1987.

_____. *Lizard in the Sun*. Illustrated by Michael Rothman. Morrow, 1990.

_____. *White Bear, Ice Bear*. Illustrated by Michael Rothman. Morrow, 1989.

RELATED NONFICTION MATERIALS

Kohl, Judith, and Herbert Kohl. *The View from the Oak*. Illustrated by Roger Bayless. Little, Brown, 1988.

SCIENCE AND VISUAL DISCRIMINATION

Use the three Cristini/Puricelli titles to practice observational skills before taking a class field trip. Students can look at one of the books and make notes on what they see in several double-page spreads. Have students work in groups of three or four to compare their notes on the same book. Work with each small group to point out the things they might not have listed. Discuss things that might move if startled and how to watch for them. Discuss things in the illustration that are fragile and might be damaged if they are stepped on or touched.

As a class, discuss the observation techniques to be used on the field trip. Students need to be prepared for the field trip by having their own notepads and pencils and access to a measuring stick and magnifying glass. After the trip, create a class record of the observations. What do students know about observation that they might not have known before? Why is observation an important scientific tool?

RELATED NONFICTION MATERIALS

Leslie, Clare Walker. *Nature All Year Long*. Greenwillow, 1991.

SCIENCE AND LIBRARY RESEARCH I

As a class, discuss ecology and what constitutes an ecosystem. Use these three books to enable students to discover some of the ways in which scientists look at living systems. Divide the class into three groups. Each group will work with one of the titles. As students study their book, they should record their observations and make inferences about the ecosystems portrayed. Most of the direct observation will deal with the biotic factors; students can make inferences about abiotic factors. Introduce the concepts of habitat and niche, food chains and food webs, trophic levels, and the flow of energy and matter through the system as students discover indications of each in the books' illustrations. Student groups might use library resources to gather additional information. A final report from each group should indicate the things students learned about environmental science.

SCIENCE

Scientists classify living things into two main groups—the plant kingdom and the animal kingdom. Use these three books to begin a unit on classification. As you share the books, have students decide which things on each page belong to each kingdom. Then, introduce the idea that animals are classified by separating them by their differences and grouping them by their likenesses. Select one of the books and discuss observable characteristics, such as the number of legs on an animal or the type of body covering. Students can then work together in pairs or small groups to decide which animals in each book go together, giving reasons for their groupings and showing differences or likenesses. Make a chart for each group the students have chosen, listing the characteristics they have used for each group determination. Compare student classification with the way scientists place animals into kingdom, phylum, class, order, family, group, and species.

RELATED NONFICTION MATERIALS

Burnie, David. *How Nature Works*. Reader's Digest, 1991.

SCIENCE AND LIBRARY RESEARCH II

Have each student select one animal found in either *In the Pond* or *In the Woods*. Challenge students to find as many facts as possible about their animals using basic research tools such as encyclopedias and identification guides. Research may take several days. Students may start by trying to locate only very specific information; you can point out ways in which they can use general information about a type of animal to discover facts about their specific animal. Encourage students to borrow ideas and share resources as their lists grow longer. Students can illustrate their lists with a picture of their animal before putting the lists in a class display.

Drescher, Henrik

The Yellow Umbrella
Bradbury, 1987.
ISBN 0-02-733240-3

ABOUT THE AUTHOR AND HIS BOOKS

Henrik Drescher was born in Denmark in 1955. During his childhood Drescher read many books by European graphic artists, and his own unique style of illustration is attributed to the influence of the books he read and the richness of the graphic arts in northern Europe, where he grew up. He has been primarily self-taught and started drawing political illustrations for his own enjoyment. A friend encouraged him to do a children's book, and the result was his first book, *The Strange Appearance of Howard Cranebill, Jr.* Drescher believes that children's books should be pleasurable. He has written and illustrated fiction and nonfiction picture books. Henrik Drescher currently lives in New York and travels quite a lot.

Selected Books by the Author

Look-Alikes. Lothrop, Lee & Shepard, 1985.

Looking for Santa Claus. Lothrop, Lee & Shepard, 1984.

Simon's Book. Lothrop, Lee & Shepard, 1983.

The Strange Appearance of Howard Cranebill, Jr. Lothrop, Lee & Shepard, 1982.

Whose Furry Nose? Australian Animals You'd Like to Meet. Lippincott, 1987.

Whose Scaly Tail? African Animals You'd Like to Meet. Lippincott, 1987.

Selected Books Illustrated by the Author

All Clean! by Harriet Ziefert. Harper & Row, 1986.

Brer Rabbit and the Wonderful Tar Baby. Edited by Joel C. Harris and Eric Metaxas. Picture Book Studio, 1990.

No Plain Pets by Marc Barasch. HarperCollins, 1991.

Poems of A. Nonny Mouse by Jack Prelutsky. Knopf, 1989.

Selected Media from the Author's Books

Simon's Book. Video. Great Plains National Instructional Television Library, 1984. (Reading Rainbow Series)

ABOUT THE YELLOW UMBRELLA

This small yellow book uses scratchy pen-and-ink drawings with a pale yellow wash to tell a story that can be read on many levels. The sketches use childlike shapes to reflect a child's view of the world, in which geography and natural science elements are simplified and jumbled together to tell a story rather than to reflect reality.

The tale begins with a crowded city of skyscrapers, all concrete with black streets and no trees. High stone walls surround an old-fashioned zoo in the center of the city, where animals are confined in tiny enclosures. A father and daughter come in just as the zoo opens and go directly to see the sad mother monkey and her child. As the humans laugh at the monkeys, the father's umbrella falls into the enclosure. The monkeys are curious and cheered by finding it in their enclosure, and, as they hold it, the umbrella blows open and carries them out of the zoo, above the heads of astonished people. The monkeys fly high above mountains and over the sea, where a storm forces them down—but the open upside-down umbrella serves as a boat and floats up a river to a jungle home. There the mother and child are reunited with the father monkey, and they find their own place. The umbrella becomes a roof over the family as they sleep happily in a tree.

The illustration is reminiscent of Dr. Seuss in the double curves in the giraffe's neck and the elongated snakelike curves of the elephant's trunk. Animals from different parts of the world are mixed together in various environments; for instance, lions, tigers, and leopards play together in the jungle.

The story can be read as a fable of any journey from confinement to freedom, with the yellow umbrella serving as a symbol for whatever makes the journey possible. However, younger children can read it as a story with a simple-to-follow plot and an emotionally satisfying ending. Older readers and adults can find this title to be a good discussion starter for issues such as animals' rights. The small size of the book and the use of the yellow wash behind the sketches, crowded with tiny lines and forms, make this a book for individual reading or one-on-one sharing.

In the Library (or In the Classroom)

MAKING A DISPLAY

Open a colorful umbrella as a backdrop to a display of books that feature unusual, magical, or extraordinary umbrellas. Open *The Yellow Umbrella* to the illustration in which the monkeys are being carried away from the city above the mountains while holding onto the umbrella. Make a bookmark that features a drawing of an umbrella and includes a list of books about umbrellas, and have bookmarks available for distribution near the display.

RELATED MATERIALS

Bright, Robert. *My Red Umbrella*. Morrow, 1959.

Goodall, John S. *The Surprise Picnic*. Atheneum, 1977.

Meyers, Odette. *The Enchanted Umbrella: With a Short History of the Umbrella*. Illustrated by Margot Zemach. Harcourt Brace Jovanovich, 1988.

Pinkwater, Daniel. *Roger's Umbrella*. Illustrated by James Marshall. Dutton, 1982.

Platt, Kin. *Big Max*. Illustrated by Robert Lopshire. HarperCollins, 1965.

_____. *Big Max in the Mystery of the Missing Moose*. Illustrated by Robert Lopshire. HarperCollins, 1977.

Travers, P. L. *Mary Poppins*. Harcourt Brace Jovanovich, 1962; 1981.

LITERATURE SHARING

Use a monkey puppet to welcome children and to begin a discussion about monkeys. Participants can volunteer what they know about monkeys and where they have seen them.

Invite children to take on the role of the monkeys in the story *Caps for Sale*. "You monkeys you" is a refrain the peddler uses in the story, which can be used to make a transition to booktalking other books: "You monkeys you—you like books!"

Introduce *The Yellow Umbrella*, a story about a mother and baby monkey who find an extraordinary umbrella. Show the two-page spread in which the umbrella is carrying the monkeys above mountains, through a flock of birds. In *The Yellow Umbrella*, the monkeys escape from a zoo. In the book *Where's Wallace?* the reader has to find the small orange orangutan in busy two-page spreads each time he escapes. George escapes from the zoo in *Curious George Takes a Job*. Share the illustration in which everyone is looking for George, noticing all of the places they search. George ends up with his friend, the Man with the Yellow Hat. The mother monkey and her child found a yellow umbrella. What else might a monkey like that is yellow? Bananas! That is what the monkey in *The Monkey and the Crocodile* wants, and it gets him into trouble. Invite the audience to see what kind of trouble by doing the finger play from the book *Five Little Monkeys Sitting in a Tree*.

RELATED MATERIALS

Christelow, Eileen. *Five Little Monkeys Sitting in a Tree*. Clarion, 1991.

Galdone, Paul. *The Monkey and the Crocodile: A Jataka Tale from India*. Seabury Press, 1969.

Knight, Hilary. *Where's Wallace?* HarperCollins, 1964.

Rey, H. A. *Curious George Takes a Job*. Houghton Mifflin, 1947.

Slobodkina, Esphyr. *Caps for Sale*. HarperCollins, 1947.

COLLECTION DEVELOPMENT

The journey of the monkeys in *The Yellow Umbrella* is a return to their original home, where they are welcomed back and reunited as a family. Include this book in displays, booklists, text sets, thematic units, and programs on homecomings.

RELATED MATERIALS

Burnford, Sheila. *Incredible Journey*. Illustrated by Carl Burger. Atlantic/Little, Brown, 1961.

Chorao, Kay. *Cathedral Mouse*. Dutton, 1988.

Flack, Marjorie. *Angus Lost*. Doubleday, 1932; 1989.

Johnson, Crockett. *Harold and the Purple Crayon*. Harper & Row, 1955.

Kent, Jack. *Joey Runs Away*. Prentice-Hall, 1985.

Lyon, David. *The Runaway Duck*. Lothrop, Lee & Shepard, 1985.

CRAFT AND CREATIVE DRAMATICS PROGRAM

The mother monkey and her child in *The Yellow Umbrella* go through a sequence of situations together. Introduce the sequences to participants using the filmstrip of the book. Outline the scenes of the story on a large piece of paper. Divide the group of children into pairs and give each pair a part of the story. The length of each part can be adjusted so that the entire story is covered.

Have each child, working in pairs, create a paper bag monkey puppet; one child can make a mother monkey using a larger paper bag and the other child can use a smaller paper bag to make the monkey child.

After the puppets are made, have the children enact the story, creating dialogue between the mother and baby for each scene. For example, what do the mother monkey and her child say while they are in the zoo? What do they say when the umbrella falls into their enclosure? What are they saying as they fly away?

Use the frames of the filmstrip as the background for each skit by projecting them onto a wall and having the children stand in front with their puppets.

RELATED NONFICTION MATERIALS

Mehrens, Gloria, and Karen Wick. *Bagging It with Puppets*. Fearon, 1988.

Oldfield, Margaret. *Tell and Draw Paper Bag Puppet Book*. Creative Storytime, 1981.

RELATED NONPRINT MATERIALS

The Yellow Umbrella. Sound filmstrip. American School Publishers.

WRITING INTEREST CENTER

Several copies of *The Yellow Umbrella* can be placed in a writing area. Invite children to read the book and create a sequel. Invite them to pick one of the other animals in the zoo and to tell that animal's story. Does this animal escape? How did this animal feel when the monkeys blew into the sky holding onto the umbrella?

You may want to make a master to reproduce as a starter for this independent writing project. Copy the page on which the child runs to the monkey's cage and the other four animals are looking into the page. Cut out each animal and paste it to the top of a blank page giving each page a title such as "The Lion's Story."

As children finish writing their stories, each new story can be put into a loose-leaf binder kept in the writing area or in another part of the library where they can be read. Index dividers can be used to separate sections so all lion stories are kept together, and so forth.

In the Classroom (and In the Library)

NATURAL SCIENCE AND LANGUAGE ARTS

When the mother monkey and her child finally return to the jungle, the other monkeys are very happy to see them and they are reunited with the father monkey. Use this as a springboard to discuss how animals are taken from the wild to be put into zoos. Look at the traffic in wild animals and discuss problems that arise in the animal trade. Have students form teams to research and debate the advantages and disadvantages of keeping exotic animals in zoos throughout the world.

RELATED NONFICTION MATERIALS

Cajacob, Thomas, and Teresa Burton. *Close to the Wild: Siberian Tigers in a Zoo*. Carolrhoda, 1986.

Curtis, Patricia. *Animals and the New Zoos*. Lodestar/Dutton, 1991.

Guernsey, JoAnn Bren. *Animal Rights*. Crestwood House, 1990.

Johnston, Ginny, and Judy Cutchins. *Windows on Wildlife*. Morrow, 1990.

Schick, Alice, and Sara Ann Friedman. *Zoo Year*. Lippincott, 1978.

Scott, Jack Denton. *City of Birds and Beasts*. Putnam, 1978.

Thomson, Peggy. *Keepers and Creatures at the National Zoo*. Photographs by Paul Conklin. Crowell, 1988.

NATURAL SCIENCE AND LIBRARY RESEARCH

Have students, working individually or in pairs, look through *The Yellow Umbrella* and make a list of the different habitats that are shown (city, mountains, ocean, shore, jungle). For each habitat have them include environmental characteristics the author noted, including the plant and animal life. Students can use the library to determine why the monkeys were better suited to the jungle environment than to any of the other habitats.

LANGUAGE ARTS

The yellow umbrella in this book may be used as a symbol for any agent that liberates. This small book can serve as a springboard for the exploration of symbol and metaphor. How might a person, or a group of people, be imprisoned? For each imprisonment, the umbrella would represent a different liberating agent. As an example, consider those who are illiterate and the ways in which their lives are confined by the inability to read. Discuss the umbrella as a symbol for learning to read, and the way in which the story could be interpreted as a metaphor for the journey of the new reader to becoming a part of the literate society. Encourage students to create different interpretations of the story based on such potentially restrictive situations such as poverty, race, age, disability, or imprisonment.

ART

After sharing this book, have students notice that all of the illustrations are done in black and yellow on white paper. The yellow wash varies in intensity and the umbrella is always the deepest hue. Discuss possible reasons why the author/illustrator chose yellow instead of another color. Have students design an art project using only black, white, and yellow. They might use tempera paints, crayons, markers, chalk, torn tissue paper, or construction paper. Have each student work on an individual project with limited direction, and then have students share the results of their creativity with the class.

RELATED MATERIALS

Alexander, Martha. *Maggie's Moon*. Dial, 1982.

Isadora, Rachel. *Ben's Trumpet*. Greenwillow, 1979.

Jonas, Ann. *Round Trip*. Greenwillow, 1983.

Neumeier, Marty, and Byron Glaser. *Action Alphabet*. Greenwillow, 1985.

Rice, Eve. *Goodnight, Goodnight*. Greenwillow, 1980.

Sara. *Across Town*. Orchard, 1991.

MUSIC

Have students look through the book to determine what different emotions the monkeys might be feeling. What is the mood at the beginning of the book when the two monkeys huddle at the top of the mound in their cage? When the humans laugh and point at them? When they find and explore the umbrella? When the umbrella carries them out of the cage to fly above the zoo? When they fly high in the air amidst a flock of birds? When they encounter a storm? When the umbrella lands and becomes a boat? When they float through the desert? When they see an alligator? When they escape down the waterfall? When they see the other monkeys in the jungle? When they fall asleep as a family in their jungle home?

Discuss ways that music is used to set a mood. Play a variety of musical selections and invite students to discuss the different moods that are elicited. Have students go through the list of emotions the monkeys have felt and find music that might be used to set the mood for each emotion.

Dubois, Claude K.

He's MY Jumbo!
Viking Kestrel, 1989.
ISBN 0-670-83029-1

Looking for Ginny
Viking Kestrel, 1989.
ISBN 0-670-83030-5

ABOUT THE AUTHOR AND HER BOOKS

Claude Dubois was born in Liège, Belgium. She studied illustration at l'Institut Saint Luc de Liège, and later taught there. She has drawn the illustrations for stories and games in children's magazines for several years. Claude Dubois lives in Belgium with her husband, who is a cartoonist, and their two daughters.

Selected Book Illustrated by the Author

Jeanette and Josie by Claude Lager. Viking, 1989.

ABOUT HE'S MY JUMBO! AND LOOKING FOR GINNY

These companion books feature a young brother and sister bear in two stories of typical sibling behavior. Rounded soft forms of the bear children and light pastel colors combine with an expressive drawing style to create an atmosphere of warmth and humor.

In *Looking for Ginny*, brother and sister are arguing over a guinea pig in a small wire cage. When brother grabs sister, the cage is knocked over and opens, and as sister bites brother, the little long-haired guinea pig scurries away. The argument is forgotten as the two search throughout the house for their missing pet. The personable guinea pig seems to be playing hide-and-seek as it follows them from room to room, and the reader can discover it hiding in each illustration. The guinea pig returns to its cage for a nap and is found there by the relieved bear children.

Sister has a large elephant doll in *He's MY Jumbo!* Her older brother watches her dress the doll, read it a book, and put it in a doll bed. As he watches, brother becomes increasingly glum, and he finally takes the doll away from his little sister. When she bawls, he has to give it back, but he goes on watching and wanting the doll through dinner and bedtime. After sister is asleep, brother takes Jumbo from her bed and happily cuddles the doll as he falls asleep. In the morning, Jumbo is gone. Brother discovers his sister has Jumbo in the kitchen, and the story ends with both sharing the coveted doll.

Themes of competition and sharing, and fighting and cooperation lift the simple plots and engage readers. The illustration is framed on each page, and the background detail does not intrude on the central action. These books can be shared with small groups provided a little description is added, especially of facial expression, and certain details are pointed out.

In the Library (or In the Classroom)

LIBRARY ACTIVITY

Make a cutout figure of a long-haired guinea pig like Ginny. Cover it with clear contact paper or laminate it. Place the figure in a different spot in the library each day and challenge children to find it. Have a booklist prepared of books that contain hidden objects.

RELATED MATERIALS

Cartwright, Steven. *Find the Duck*. Illustrated by C. Zeff. Usborne, 1983.

Handford, Martin. *Where's Waldo?* Little, Brown, 1987.

Knight, Hilary. *Where's Wallace?* HarperCollins, 1964.

Nims, Bonnie Larkin. *Where Is the Bear?* Illustrated by John Wallner and Alex Wallner. Whitman, 1988.

Tafuri, Nancy. *Have You Seen My Duckling?* Greenwillow, 1984.

Zacharias, Thomas. *But Where Is the Green Parrot?* Delacorte, 1968.

COLLECTION DEVELOPMENT

Use these two books with others in which brothers and sisters have conflicts. Include them in text sets, thematic units, booklists, and displays to begin discussions about siblings and emotions.

RELATED MATERIALS

Alexander, Martha. *Marty McGee's Space Lab, No Girls Allowed*. Dial, 1981.

Blume, Judy. *The Pain and the Great One*. Illustrated by Irene Trivas. Bradbury, 1984.

Brandenberg, Franz. *I Wish I Was Sick, Too!* Illustrated by Aliki. Greenwillow, 1976.

Hoban, Lillian. *Arthur's Honey Bear*. Harper, 1974.

Hoban, Russell. *Best Friends for Frances*. Illustrated by Lillian Hoban. Harper, 1969.

Van Leeuwen, Jean. *Amanda Pig and Her Big Brother Oliver*. Illustrated by Ann Schweninger. Dial, 1982.

Viorst, Judith. *I'll Fix Anthony*. Illustrated by Arnold Lobel. Harper, 1969.

Wells, Rosemary. *Max's Dragon Shirt*. Dial, 1991.

STORY PROGRAM

Looking for Ginny has a plot that encourages children's participation in storytelling. After the argument and the guinea pig's escape, use repetitive language to enable children to help you tell the story. "Brother looked...(where?); Sister looked...(where?); But they didn't see Ginny! Where was Ginny? Ginny was...(where?)."

After children help you tell the story with the book, use flannel board pieces to retell the story. Make large pieces for the brother, the sister, the cage, Ginny, a basket, a vase, a chair, an armoire, a laundry basket, a robe, and a bed. Cut a slit in each of the objects in which the guinea pig figure can be inserted. Retell the story with the audience participating, and let the children place the guinea pig figure in each object as it is put on the flannel board.

Have available other books in which pets are lost and found again.

RELATED MATERIALS

Barton, Byron. *Where's Al?* Houghton Mifflin, 1972.

Blegvad, Leonore. *The Great Hamster Hunt*. Harcourt, 1969.

Carle, Eric. *Have You Seen My Cat?* Picture Book Studio, 1987.

Carroll, Ruth. *The Chimp and the Clown*. Walck, 1968.

Hill, Eric. *Where's Spot?* Putnam, 1980.

Keats, Ezra Jack. *My Dog Is Lost!* Crowell, 1960.

MAKING A DISPLAY

An empty cage with the door open and the book *Looking for Ginny* beside it can be the center of a display inviting children to "find guinea pigs in stories." A stuffed toy guinea pig, or a cutout, can be tucked behind a book, and other books can be incorporated into the display.

RELATED MATERIALS

Bond, Michael. *The Tales of Olga da Polga*. Macmillan, 1989.

Brooks, Andrea. *The Guinea Pigs' Adventure*. Little, Brown, 1980.

Duke, Kate. *Guinea Pig ABC*. Dutton, 1983.

_____. *Guinea Pigs Far and Near*. Dutton, 1984.

_____. *What Would a Guinea Pig Do?* Dutton, 1988.

Hess, Lilo. *Making Friends with Guinea Pigs*. Scribner, 1983.

Potter, Beatrix. *The Tale of Tuppenny*. Illustrated by Marie Angel. Warne, 1971.

STORYTELLING AND GAME

Introduce the book *He's MY Jumbo!* by showing a stuffed toy elephant or elephant puppet. As you share the book, create a story and voices for the characters. Discuss the bear children and their feelings about Jumbo, and then play a memory game. Begin the game by saying "He's MY Jumbo, and I love him because _____." Hand the toy to a child and let that child give a reason, then have the whole group repeat the reason—"He's MY Jumbo and I love him because he's soft!" The first child then gives the toy to another child to give a different reason, which the whole group repeats. Continue until all children have had a chance to hold the elephant and give reasons why they love him. Older children might give their reasons in alphabetical order (...because he's adorable, brave, cuddly, and so forth), with either the individual or the whole group repeating the entire list of qualities that make Jumbo lovable.

In the Classroom (or In the Library)

LANGUAGE ARTS I

After sharing the story *Looking for Ginny* with a small group of students, have them recall where the characters looked for Ginny and make a list of those places. When students think they have listed all the places, go back through the book and find each spot, then cross it off the list. Were there any places that were not on the list? Were there any places on the list that weren't in the book?

LANGUAGE ARTS II

After sharing the book *Looking for Ginny* with small groups until the entire class has seen it, develop a class story about Ginny. Pretend that Ginny came for a visit to your classroom and got loose. You can begin the story and then go from student to student to ask where Ginny was hiding. With younger students you may want to continue part of the story by saying, "We looked in _____," and the students responding, "But Ginny was hiding in _____." With older students you may want to let half of them take the first part and the other half take the second part.

SCIENCE

After sharing the book *Looking for Ginny*, discuss fictional and real guinea pigs. Many children have guinea pigs for pets. Study guinea pigs and how to take care of them. If possible, bring a guinea pig into the classroom to share.

RELATED MATERIALS

Bare, Colleen. *Guinea Pigs Don't Read Books*. Dodd, Mead, 1985.

Bielfeld, Horst. *Guinea Pigs: A Complete Pet Owner's Manual*. Barron's, 1983.

Broekel, Ray. *Gerbil Pets and Other Small Rodents*. Childrens, 1983.

Burton, Jane. *Gipper the Guinea Pig*. Random House, 1988. (How Your Pet Grows! Series)

Henrie, Fiona. *Guinea Pigs*. Watts, 1980. (Junior Petkeeper's Library)

Hess, Lilo. *Making Friends with Guinea Pigs*. Scribner, 1983.

ART AND LANGUAGE ARTS

Have students make flat poster board masks that they can hold in front of them while they pretend to be the characters in these books. Make a pattern of the head and face of the brother and the sister bear, which students can trace onto poster board. Masks can be colored or painted, then cut out and attached to a clean tongue depressor or paint stirring stick.

As students look through either of these books, they will notice that the brother and sister characters are doing a lot of talking to one another. Pair students and have them develop one scene or sequence with each student taking one part. After students have practiced their parts, have a dramatic presentation with students following the sequences in each book.

LANGUAGE ARTS III

Sharing is not always easy for children, especially when it concerns their favorite toy. Most children have had an experience where another child wanted to play with something of theirs, or where they wanted to play with something that belonged to someone else. In small groups, share the book *He's MY Jumbo!* and then have students write about an experience they have had, giving their paper the title "It's MY _____." Have them tell about the object, who wanted it, and how the conflict was resolved.

<u>**Dupasquier, Philippe**</u>

The Great Escape
Houghton Mifflin, 1988.
ISBN 0-395-46806-X; LC 87-21500

ABOUT THE AUTHOR AND HIS BOOKS

Born in Switzerland, Philippe Dupasquier studied art in France. He currently lives in England with his wife and two children.

Selected Books by the Author

The Airport. Putnam, 1984.

The Building Site. Putnam, 1984.

Dear Daddy... Bradbury, 1985.

The Factory. Putnam, 1984.

The Harbor. Putnam, 1984.

I Can't Sleep. Orchard, 1990.

Our House on the Hill. Viking Kestrel, 1987.

A Robot Named Chip. Viking, 1991.

The Service Station. Putnam, 1984.

Selected Books Illustrated by the Author

Going West by Martin Waddell. HarperCollins, 1984.

The Sandal by Tony Bradman. Viking, 1990.

ABOUT THE GREAT ESCAPE

The cover of this humorous book reveals the slapstick nature of the action inside. The title is being painted on a stone wall, with a long smear at the end as the painter and his ladder are falling. Paint is spilling onto three policemen who run underneath chasing after an escaping prisoner.

Throughout the book the action is fast and funny, the pictures are crowded with detail, and the madcap nature of the chase is reminiscent of the Keystone Cops films. Vigorous line drawing and bright color enhance the comic nature of the story, presented in comic book-style panels. The chase follows the prisoner through city scenes such as a department store, a museum, a movie theater, and a burning building, then continues to rural scenes, from a circus and a fox hunt to a small church wedding. The comic possibilities are thoroughly explored, with a subplot involving a motorcyclist with his wife in a sidecar. The prisoner is inventive and kind to animals; the police chasing him are inept and clumsy. The prisoner is caught by accident when he crawls up a drain right into the middle of the prison yard. Back in his cell, the prisoner hears a bird singing, climbs up to his barred window, inadvertently breaks a bar, and the book ends with the prisoner escaping and the chase beginning again.

Style and content combine harmoniously to appeal to a wide range of readers. Little details and jokes will be picked up each time the book is reread. The first time through, it's easy for readers, focusing on the fast-paced action, to miss some of the hidden clues that contribute to the plot development. The story is both complex and entertaining, making this book a good choice for the older child or the adult who is a poor reader. It is an especially good choice for writing with upper grade or gifted students.

In the Library (or In the Classroom)

MAKING A DISPLAY

Use this book as the center of a display of books about escapes. Create the backdrop by painting a picture of the wall of the prison with its barred windows. Tie scraps of material together to form a rope as the prisoner does in the second escape at the end of the book. Attach one end of the rope to a window toward the top of the display and dangle it down to the book.

RELATED MATERIALS

Alter, Robert Edmond. *Who Goes Next?* Putnam, 1966.

Bunting, Eve. *Someone Is Hiding on Alcatraz Island.* Clarion, 1984.

Hergé. *Cigars of the Pharaoh.* Little, Brown, 1971.

Holm, Anne. *North to Freedom.* Harcourt, Brace & World, 1965.

Household, Geoffrey. *Escape into Daylight.* Bodley Head, 1976.

Macken, Walter. *The Flight of the Doves.* Macmillan, 1968.

Williams, Gurney. *True Escape and Survival Stories.* Watts, 1977.

GAME

Working with a small group of older children, create a board game for younger children to play in the library. Use a poster board for the game board, and position the prison at both the beginning and the ending of the game. With the children, determine what the middle event is and what the path will look like. Fill in the events in pencil, determining the "safe" spots where the prisoner can hide. Once the path and events are penciled in, have the group draw and color the scenes in the sequence in which they occur in the story, as indicated by the sequence of events you have penciled in along the path. The children may model small figures from a modeling compound to represent the prisoner and police. The game rules can be written up by the group, based on traditional Parcheesi rules, using a regular die to determine the moves. After the game has been completed, place it in the library with the book for younger children to enjoy.

WORKSHOP

Introduce children to three artists who create humor through their art styles and visual storytelling: Philippe Dupasquier, Mercer Mayer, and Stephen Kellogg. Divide the group into smaller groups of three and give each member a book by one of the three authors. The participants are to look only at illustration and the way it creates comic effect, and to discuss the techniques and devices used, comparing and contrasting the three artists. Participants may end by sharing with the entire group the scene they consider to be the funniest in their three books.

RELATED MATERIALS

Kellogg, Steven. *A Rose for Pinkerton!* Dial, 1981.

_____. *Tallyho, Pinkerton!* Dial, 1982.

Mayer, Mercer. *Frog Goes to Dinner*. Dial, 1974.

_____. *The Great Cat Chase*. Four Winds, 1974.

_____. *OOPS*. Dial, 1977.

WRITING INTEREST CENTER

Display *The Great Escape* in a writing interest center set up as a desk with an in box and an out box. Place stationery in the in box and pencils nearby. Use a large envelope as the center of a display inviting children to write a letter to the prisoner in this book. They can write to him signing their own names, or that of any one of the characters in the book. Completed letters can be placed in the out box for other children to read.

MEDIA PROGRAM

Request that participants read *The Great Escape* prior to the program. Briefly review the book before showing a film or video of a humorous silent film that includes a chase scene. Buster Keaton, Harold Lloyd, and the Keystone Cops all used slapstick chase scenes in various films, and many of those early films are available in video format. Compare the humor in the film to the humor in the book. What are the elements that make slapstick humor funny? Why does this type of humor work well in both silent films and wordless picture books? Share other humorous wordless picture books.

RELATED MATERIALS

Amoss, Berthe. *What Did You Lose, Santa?* Harper, 1987.

Henstra, Friso. *Mighty Mizzling Mouse*. Lippincott, 1983.

Mayer, Mercer. *Frog on His Own*. Dial, 1973.

RELATED NONPRINT MATERIALS

The following black-and-white films are available as videos.

The Desperate Scoundrel. (1916)

Golden Age of Comedy. (1957)

The Kid. (1920)

Tillie's Punctured Romance. (1914)

In the Classroom (or In the Library)

LITERATURE STUDY

Have students preview the story and make notes on sequences/scenes. Then develop a class list of sequences on the chalkboard, leaving room to write beside it. After identifying the scenes, have the students identify the following:

Where does the scene take place?
How does the main character get there?
What other characters are in the scene?
What humor takes place in the scene? What chaos?
How does the main character escape from that scene to the next? (movement of action)
How do the details in each scene add to the story?

This is a circular story. Begin with the second chase and have students develop the framework for a class story. Record on the board student ideas for new scenes, being sure that they don't use the same ideas as the author.

Where does the character go?
What is the action (humor/chaos)?
What other characters are in the scene?
How does the main character escape from that scene to the next?

Students can then work alone, or in pairs, to develop one detailed sequence, either in writing or through illustration. When completed, the sequences can be put together into a class book or mural.

VISUAL DISCRIMINATION AND LANGUAGE ARTS

As students reread *The Great Escape*, have them locate the subplots and minor characters in the book, such as the couple on the motorcycle. Why did the author include them?

Have students locate examples of foreshadowing, such as the flat scenery elephant on the movie set and the circus elephant.

Discuss the character of the prisoner and how it is revealed. Note his many kindnesses to animals.

JOURNALISM

Have each student choose a scene and look carefully at the many characters in that scene. Students then choose one character from their scene and write a description of what happened. One student, selected to be the newscaster broadcasting news of this Great Escape, can ask different people to describe what they saw.

OBSERVATION

Stage a disturbance in the classroom and then ask students what they saw or heard. Record their responses on the chalkboard. Discuss how different people notice different things and can come up with very different views of what went on.

Then, take one scene from the book and have students choose different characters from that scene and write descriptions of what happened from those characters' points of view. Have students read their descriptions aloud. What are the similarities and differences in what each character observed?

LANGUAGE ARTS

Discuss how we define people by what they are wearing. As a class, or in small groups, have students list the characters in each scene of *The Great Escape*, noting what the characters are wearing and what the clothing tells the reader about them. (The men in uniforms are policemen chasing a prisoner in a striped suit; the man in the loincloth is an actor playing Tarzan, and so forth.) Are there other details that help you define people? (The man at the museum in the loose green coat and hat is shown to be a janitor by the mop and pail he carries.)

Graham, Alastair

Full Moon Soup, or the Fall of the Hotel Splendide
Dial Books for Young Readers, 1991.
ISBN 0-8037-1045-3; LC 91-10276

ABOUT THE AUTHOR AND HIS BOOKS

Alastair Graham lives in Warwickshire, England, with his wife and two children. He has worked as an advertising writer/designer, and as a designer/producer with an animation studio. Graham currently illustrates children's books full-time. He enjoys reading and listening to music, and he plays conga drums in a modern jazz group.

Selected Book Illustrated by the Author

Down on the Funny Farm by P. E. King. Random House, 1986.

ABOUT FULL MOON SOUP

Pay attention to every detail in this book, from the endpapers to the pictures on the hotel wall, because every bit contributes to the cumulative madness of this hilarious account of catastrophe. The title alerts you to locate the soup in the first busy double-page spread, picturing the hotel in cutaway with each room furnished with elements that will transmute as the pages are turned. After noting the clutter in the attic, the lovers on the balcony, and the activity in the bedrooms, halls, stairs, lobby, and dining room, you will spot the sickly green soup in the basement kitchen. When a sip of the soup turns the chef into a werewolf, the zany events of the night accelerate to the final disaster.

Exaggeration and caricature fill each crowded page. Not one, but over a dozen stories unfold in a series of mishaps, each more preposterous than the last. The cast of characters includes maids, policemen, lovers, a decorator, a vampire, a grandmother with her spoiled granddaughter, a family with a bawling baby, a curmudgeon, a Scotsman, and a cat. Many of the characters are transformed into something else, and the ghosts, aliens, assorted animals, and monsters that join the cast add to the confusion. The book can be read by following the tale through one room of the hotel, by following one character, or by examining each page for all the plot lines and activity; but, however the book is approached, it takes more than one reading to fully explore its possibilities. Frequently, the setup for a joke is subtle, and the reader has to look back to see what led to it. The vigorous black line drawing, bright hues, and oversize pages contribute to the humorous effect. The reader is amused and dazed, with the feeling of having inadvertently stumbled into a weird world where none of the usual rules apply, and where sly references are made to things one feels one ought to recognize, and where things that were funny enough in themselves simply get wilder and funnier as they become more and more elaborate.

In the Library (or In the Classroom)

MAKING A DISPLAY

Commercially produced "Slime" comes in a sick green color similar to the color of the soup in this story. You can also produce your own gross-looking concoction using laundry starch, white glue, and food coloring, using the recipe for "Gloopy Glop" in *The Spook Book*. Fill a bowl with "soup" and situate it with the book against a dark night sky backdrop. Suspend a moon above it—either a cutout full moon or a painted styrofoam ball. Letter a legend such as "Do you dare to try Full Moon Soup?" and place it nearby.

RELATED MATERIALS

Marks, Burton, and Rita Marks. *The Spook Book*. Illustrated by Lisa Campbell Ernst. Lothrop, Lee & Shepard, 1981.

WORKSHOP

There are so many visual jokes in *Full Moon Soup* that it is a good start for a joke writing workshop. Introduce the program by telling some monster jokes and inviting participants to tell ones they know or to share jokes from related joke books on display. Talk about joke writing. Showing the book will require quite a bit of explanation, and you may want to show only the endpapers, title page, and one of the full-page spreads. Have multiple copies of the book available for small groups to refer to as they develop jokes. Supply each person with paper and pencil to record jokes as they are created. Individual jokes can be shared with the group at the completion of the workshop. You may want to have the jokes copied into a Full Moon Soup Joke Book, which can be placed near the original book for library browsing. Or, choose jokes to write on large cards and display in the library to attract attention to the book.

RELATED MATERIALS

Adler, David. *The Twisted Witch and Other Spooky Riddles*. Illustrated by Victoria Chess. Holiday House, 1987.

Bernstein, Joanne, and Paul Cohen. *Unidentified Flying Riddles*. Illustrated by Meyer Seltzer. Whitman, 1983.

Brown, Marc. *Spooky Riddles*. Random House, 1983.

Corbett, Scott. *Jokes to Read in the Dark*. Illustrated by Annie Gusman. Dutton, 1980.

Keller, Charles. *Count Draculations! Monster Riddles*. Illustrated by Edward Frascino. Prentice-Hall, 1986.

Phillips, Louis. *Haunted House Jokes*. Illustrated by James Marshall. Viking, 1987.

Rosenbloom, Joseph. *Monster Madness: Riddles, Jokes, Fun*. Illustrated by Joyce Behr. Sterling, 1980.

Seltzer, Meyer. *Hide-and-Go-Shriek Monster Riddles*. Whitman, 1990.

WRITING INTEREST CENTER

Place several copies of *Full Moon Soup* in a writing interest center. You might also include copies of *Stringbean's Trip to the Shining Sea*, which shows postcards a small boy sends to his family. Place a bulletin board in or near the interest center. Supply the center with 5-by-7-inch index cards, pens, pencils, and fine-tip colored markers or colored pencils. Each reader can pretend to be a character from the book and create a postcard to send home from the Hotel Splendide signed by that character. One side of the postcard can be used for a picture and/or message; the other side is for the address. When the postcard is completed, it can be stamped with the U.S. Ghostage Stamp rubber stamp and pinned to the bulletin board.

RELATED MATERIALS

Williams, Vera. *Stringbean's Trip to the Shining Sea*. Illustrated by Jennifer Williams and Vera Williams. Greenwillow, 1988.

RELATED NONPRINT MATERIALS

"Ghostage" rubber stamp. Kidstamps.

PRODUCTION PROGRAM

Work with a small group to create a soundtrack for this book as if it were a movie. Script the major events and then select sounds related to each. Provide sound effects on records and cassette tapes and have a variety of instruments and sound props available. (A synthesizer will be useful for this program.) Provide for ways to get the sound effects on tape. Rehearse the sounds before taping them. This project will take several meetings in both the planning and production stages. The final production can be dubbed onto several cassette tapes to be circulated with the book, and for library listening.

WORKSHOP

Nearly every character in *Full Moon Soup* suffers some form of transformation before the story is completed. Invite children to transform themselves with makeup or masks to become full moon monsters.

Local theatrical groups may have a makeup technician who can demonstrate some techniques for applying theatrical makeup. For practical reasons, you may want to limit the children to two or three choices of faces, such as the werewolf, the vampire, and an alien. Makeup and application devices may be donated, and mirrors may be loaned to you by a local theater group. Clear instructions for preparing skin for makeup, for applying the makeup, and for later removing it can be found in several books.

An alternate program would involve making monster masks or providing several masks for children to put on to transform themselves.

This program is a natural for the full moon in October and for taking before-and-after photographs of each child—just like the endpaper photographs in the book!

RELATED MATERIALS

Cox, Marcia Lynn. *Make-Up Monsters*. Grossett & Dunlap, 1976.

Haldane, Suzanne. *Painting Faces*. Dutton, 1988.

Smith, Dick. *Dick Smith's Do-It-Yourself Monster Make-Up*. Harmony/Crown, 1985.

In the Classroom (or In the Library)

LANGUAGE ARTS AND LIBRARY RESEARCH

To begin a unit on monsters, have students brainstorm famous monsters from books, stories, and films. Develop a set of monster materials that includes folktales and fairy tales, classic monster stories, monsters in picture books, movie monsters, and monsters in poems and rhymes. Students can choose a monster to read and learn about. Using the set of monster materials and other library materials, have each student choose a monster to learn and write about. After reading stories about the monster, students can use library reference materials to see if they can locate additional information. Students can do reports on their monster that include a detailed description of the monster, its country of origin, how it became a monster (if that is known), what the monster is like, and what stories the monster appears in.

SOCIAL STUDIES

As a class, discuss what stereotyping means. List the following characters from *Full Moon Soup* on the chalkboard and have a class discussion about stereotypical views that people have about each. Write comments on the board beside each of the characters.

Chef	Cat	Maid
Scotsman	Preacher	Waiter
Bellboy	Gypsy Fiddler	Decorator
Vampire	Policeman	Newlyweds
Baby	Aliens	Eskimo

Have students work individually or in pairs to choose one of these characters and follow it through the story. Does the character reinforce the stereotype? Write about how the character is alike or different from the stereotype that has been established for that character. Follow with a class discussion about student observations of each character.

JOURNALISM

Have students write radio commercials for the Hotel Splendide, working in pairs or small groups. Each group can put its commercial on audiotape, using sound effects or background music as appropriate. When the commercials are completed, play them back to the class. Or, have students work in small groups to produce video commercials.

VISUAL PERCEPTION

Divide the class into two teams. Working in separate rooms, each team looks through the book carefully to develop 25-30 questions (and answers) about *Full Moon Soup* for the other team to attempt to answer. After both teams have their questions prepared, have a game with the team captain from one team asking a member of the other team a question. If the answer is correct, that team receives a point and the opportunity for a different member of their team to answer a question. If the answer is incorrect, that team captain asks a member of the other team a question. The first team to reach 20 points wins the game.

COOKING AND ART

As a class, discuss the title of the book and the sequence of events in the book. What part does the pot of soup play? What might happen at your school if the cook in the school cafeteria made some Full Moon Soup? What would the principal do? The teachers? Students? Others? Are there pictures that might come to life? Create a school version of *Full Moon Soup* in mural form.

When the mural is completed, share other books about unusual foods. Have a meal consisting of puree of pea soup and runny lime jello.

RELATED MATERIALS

Lyon, George Ella. *The Outside Inn*. Illustrated by Vera Rosenberry. Orchard, 1991.

Pelham, David. *Sam's Sandwich*. Dutton, 1991.

Rockwell, Thomas. *How to Eat Fried Worms*. Illustrated by Emily McCully. Watts, 1973.

Seuss, Dr. *Green Eggs and Ham*. Beginner, 1960.

Hutchins, Pat

Changes, Changes
Macmillan, 1971.
ISBN 0-02-745870-9; LC 70-123133

ABOUT THE AUTHOR AND HER BOOKS

Pat Hutchins was born June 18, 1942, in Yorkshire, England. She grew up in a large family, and the children spent much of their time watching the wildlife in the surrounding woods and fields. Pat attended Darlington School of Art near her home for two years and then went to Leeds College of Art, where she received a National Diploma in Design. Upon graduation, she worked in an advertising agency in London. She and her husband spent a year and a half in the United States and currently live in London, England.

Selected Books by the Author

Clocks and More Clocks. Macmillan, 1970.

Don't Forget the Bacon! Greenwillow, 1987.

The Doorbell Rang. Greenwillow, 1986.

Good-Night, Owl! Macmillan, 1972.

Happy Birthday, Sam. Greenwillow, 1978.

One Hunter. Greenwillow, 1982.

Rosie's Walk. Macmillan, 1968.

The Surprise Party. Macmillan, 1969.

The Tale of Thomas Mead. Greenwillow, 1980.

The Very Worst Monster. Greenwillow, 1985.

The Wind Blew. Macmillan, 1974.

You'll Soon Grow into Them, Titch. Greenwillow, 1983.

ABOUT CHANGES, CHANGES

This story of transformation brings two wooden dolls and their world to life. Simple geometric forms in colors typical of a child's set of wooden blocks are used in stiffly composed pictures that convey the woodenness of both characters and setting. The two dolls have the look of European folk toys, with their painted features and pegged arms. The outlined forms of the illustrations are completed with elaborate lines within each form, and such elements as fire, smoke, and water are stylized and patterned.

In the beginning of the book, the dolls are building a house using wooden blocks. When the house begins to burn, they start a series of transformations by first using the blocks to make a fire engine. They use the fire engine to put out the fire, but there is too much water, so they change the fire engine into a boat and float away. When the dolls reach land, they change the boat into a truck, and then into a train on a block track. Finally, they use the blocks to once again begin building a house.

The transformations remind one of a child's play sequence. The bright colors, the large size of the pictures, and the identifiable toys make this book especially appealing to younger audiences and children who have special needs.

In the Library (or In the Classroom)

PROGRAM I

Changes, Changes can easily be shared in a picture book presentation, with children participating in the storytelling by first guessing, then identifying each new object that the dolls build. Follow the book presentation with the film *Tchou Tchou*, in which blocks are animated and two characters solve a problem by transforming a block dragon into a train. In both titles, the characters change their environment to deal with a problem. Complete the program with a final book, *Just One More Block*, in which an older brother responds to the problem of his little sister knocking over his tower of blocks by teaching her how to build a tower of her own.

When the program is completed, participants could be invited to build their own block structures.

RELATED MATERIALS

Mayers, Pat. *Just One More Block*. Illustrated by Lucy Hawkinson. Whitman, 1970.

Stevenson, Robert L. *Block City*. Illustrated by Ashley Wolff. Dutton, 1988.

RELATED NONPRINT MATERIALS

Tchou Tchou. 16mm film/video. National Film Board of Canada, distributed by Encyclopaedia Britannica Educational Corporation.

Matrioska. 16mm film/video. National Film Board of Canada.

MAKING A DISPLAY

The two characters in this story are animated wooden dolls. Use the double-page spread of the dolls and blocks as the center of a display on old-fashioned wooden folk toys. You can build a block structure as a background for the display and use wooden alphabet blocks to spell out "READ." Small wooden wagons can be filled with picture books, and wooden toys can be incorporated into the display. Collect stories about wooden toys and nonfiction books about folk toys to accompany the display.

RELATED FICTION MATERIALS

Bailey, Carolyn. *Miss Hickory*. Illustrated by Ruth Gannett. Viking, 1946.

Dalgliesh, Alice. *The Little Wooden Farmer*. Illustrated by Anita Lobel. Macmillan, 1968.

Field, Rachel. *Hitty: Her First Hundred Years*. Illustrated by Dorothy Lathrop. Macmillan, 1957.

Goffstein, M. B. *Me and My Captain*. Farrar, Straus & Giroux, 1974.

_____. *My Noah's Ark*. Harper, 1978.

Jacques, Faith. *Tilly's House*. Atheneum, 1979.

RELATED NONFICTION MATERIALS

Esterman, M. M. *A Fish That's a Box: Folk Art from the National Museum of American Art, Smithsonian Institution*. Great Ocean, 1990.

Fowler, Virginie. *Folk Toys Around the World and How to Make Them*. Prentice-Hall, 1984.

Kalman, Bobbie. *Early Pleasures and Pastimes*. Crabtree, 1983.

Loeper, John J. *The Shop on High Street: The Toys and Games of Early America*. Atheneum, 1978.

Schnacke, Dick. *American Folk Toys*. Putnam, 1973.

CRAFT PROGRAM

As children arrive, have small, brightly colored table blocks for them to manipulate. Discuss the block shapes and colors as you collect them to begin the program. After sharing the book or showing the video or film-strip of *Changes, Changes*, invite the participants to discuss the objects they might have made with the blocks.

Have brightly colored paper cut into geometric shapes available, as well as white paper and glue. Children can select and position shapes on the white paper to construct a variety of objects. When they have one they are pleased with, they can be shown how to glue the shapes into place.

RELATED NONFICTION MATERIALS

Emberley, Ed. *Drawing Book: Make a World*. Little, Brown, 1972.

_____. *Picture Pie*. Little, Brown, 1984.

RELATED NONPRINT MATERIALS

Changes, Changes. 16mm film/sound filmstrip/video. Weston Woods, 1973.

PROGRAM II

Pat Hutchins has written and illustrated numerous picture books. Many of these books have successfully been made into nonprint formats. Prepare a background display of books by this author along with the filmstrips and videocassettes that go along with them. After sharing information about the author, read one of her books and then show the film of the same title. Invite participants to discuss the similarities and differences in the formats.

Provide cut paper, a stamp pad, and a stamp of either Rosie or Rosie's fox and allow children to make their own Pat Hutchins bookmark before they leave.

RELATED NONPRINT MATERIALS

Changes, Changes. 16mm film/sound filmstrip/video. Weston Woods, 1973.

Goodnight Owl. Sound filmstrip. Weston Woods, 1982.

"Rosie" or "Rosie's Fox" rubber stamps. Kidstamps.

Rosie's Walk. 16mm film/sound cassette in English or Spanish/video. Weston Woods, 1972.

Tale of Thomas Mead. Sound filmstrip. Random House, 1982.

Titch. Book cassette. Weston Woods, 1989.

The Very Worst Monster. Sound filmstrip. Weston Woods, 1985.

COLLECTION DEVELOPMENT

The only characters in *Changes, Changes* are two wooden dolls that busily manipulate the blocks as the environment changes. Include this title in displays, booklists, text sets, thematic units, and programs in which toys are the main characters.

RELATED MATERIALS

Conrad, Pam. *The Tub People*. Illustrated by Richard Egielski. Harper & Row, 1989.

Goffstein, M. B. *Me and My Captain*. Farrar, Straus & Giroux, 1974.

Goodall, John S. *The Midnight Adventures of Kelly, Dot, and Esmeralda*. Atheneum, 1972.

Gruelle, Johnny. *The Raggedy Ann and Andy Storybook*. Putnam, 1980.

Hissey, Jane. *Old Bear*. Philomel, 1986.

Mariana. *Miss Flora McFlimsey's Valentine*. Lothrop, Lee & Shepard, 1987.

Maris, Ron. *Are You There, Bear?* Greenwillow, 1985.

Milne, A. A. *House at Pooh Corner*. Dutton, 1956.

Waddell, Martin. *Park in the Dark*. Illustrated by Barbara Firth. Lothrop, Lee & Shepard, 1989.

Williams, Margery. *Velveteen Rabbit: Or, How Toys Become Real*. Illustrated by William Nicholson. Doubleday, n.d.

Wright, Dare. *The Lonely Doll*. Doubleday, 1957.

In the Classroom (or In the Library)

STORYTELLING

The two characters and the blocks in *Changes, Changes* can be easily copied and cut out for a flannel board presentation. Use felt pieces or draw patterns on Pellon purchased at the fabric store. Pellon is lightweight, and you can use marking pens or crayons to color the pieces. A large flannel board can be used for group presentations. Clean pizza boxes can be used for individual flannel board stories: Glue flannel or felt on the inside cover of the box and store pieces in the box.

Share the book *Changes, Changes*, having students note the way that blocks are used and reused to construct different objects. Use the flannel board and retell the story or create a new story. Students can be paired to tell stories to one another, or older students can work with younger students in developing new stories and constructions.

RELATED MATERIALS

Sierra, Judy. *Flannel Board Storytelling Book*. H. W. Wilson, 1987.

LANGUAGE ARTS AND SOCIAL SKILLS

The two characters in *Changes, Changes* work cooperatively to build each new construction. After sharing the book with small groups of students, have them work in pairs. Set up a work center with table blocks, paper, and pencils. The first pair of students makes a construction with the blocks and records what they have made with a sketch of their construction. They return to their desks, and the second pair sits at the work center to change the construction, recording in a sketch what they have done. Continue until the entire class has had an opportunity to work with the blocks. Have each pair number their paper in the order that they have worked.

Place the sketches in numerical order on a bulletin board or on the chalkboard and create a class narrative about the changes that took place as each pair of students worked together on a new construction.

ART

The two wooden characters in this book look very similar to Jumping Jack toys that move when a string is pulled. A simple movable toy can be made by making a pattern of the characters and transferring the pattern to a heavy poster board or cardboard. Make one pattern for the body, two for the arms, and two for the legs. Students can cut out and color the pieces. Use an eyelet punch to make holes and brass brads to attach the arms and legs to the body.

RELATED MATERIALS

Newsome, Arden. *Crafts and Toys from Around the World*. Messner, 1972.

VISUAL DISCRIMINATION

After sharing *Changes, Changes* with students the first time, share it a second time and have them notice the different sizes and shapes of the blocks. Share other books on shapes. Have students look around the classroom and locate different shapes in common objects.

RELATED MATERIALS

Fisher, Leonard E. *Look Around! A Book About Shapes*. Viking Kestrel, 1987.

Hoban, Tana. *Circles, Triangles and Squares*. Macmillan, 1974.

_____. *Shapes, Shapes, Shapes*. Greenwillow, 1986.

Pluckrose, Henry. *Shape*. Photographs by Chris Fairclough. Watts, 1986. (Think About Series)

Reiss, John. *Shapes*. Bradbury, 1974.

Turner, Gwenda. *Shapes*. Viking, 1991.

LANGUAGE ARTS

Use the book *Fortunately* to introduce the concept of predicting what will happen next in a story. Before opening the book, discuss what the words *fortunately* and *unfortunately* mean. Before you turn each page, invite students to guess what might happen next, and encourage the group to help with the story by saying *fortunately* or *unfortunately* as appropriate.

Share the book *Changes, Changes*, using the same format. Students can predict what is going to happen next as the characters have a misfortune and then reconstruct their blocks to provide a fortunate scene. (Example: Unfortunately the house started burning; fortunately they built a fire truck.)

RELATED MATERIALS

Charlip, Remy. *Fortunately*. Parents Magazine Press, 1964.

Clementina's Cactus
Viking, 1982.
ISBN 9-670-22517-7; LC 82-2630

ABOUT THE AUTHOR AND HIS BOOKS

Ezra Jack Keats was born March 11, 1916, in Brooklyn, New York, where he grew up and attended public schools. His parents were Polish immigrants and never had much money. Keats began drawing when he was four years old and, as a child, taught himself to paint using any materials he could find. Although he won three scholarships, he was unable to attend art school due to the Great Depression in the late 1930s. During World War II, he was a camouflage expert in the U.S. Army. Keats illustrated more than 20 of his own writings and almost 50 of other writers' books. His works have received many awards and honors, including the 1963 Randolph Caldecott Medal for *The Snowy Day*. *Goggles* was a Caldecott Honor Book in 1970. Many of Keats' books have been adapted into films, filmstrips with cassettes, and videocassettes. Ezra Jack Keats died of a heart attack in New York City on May 6, 1983.

Selected Books by the Author

Apt. 3. Macmillan, 1971.

Hi, Cat! Macmillan, 1970.

A Letter to Amy. Harper, 1968.

Louie. Greenwillow, 1975.

Maggie and the Pirate. Four Winds, 1979.

Pet Show! Macmillan, 1972.

Psst! Doggie. Watts, 1973.

Skates. Watts, 1973.

The Snowy Day. Viking, 1962; 1972.

Whistle for Willie. Viking, 1964.

Selected Books Illustrated by the Author

In a Spring Garden. Edited by Richard Lewis. Dial, 1989. Reprint of 1965 edition.

The King's Fountain by Lloyd Alexander. Dutton, 1971.

Over in the Meadow by Olive A. Wadsworth. Scholastic, 1985.

Selected Media from the Author's Books

Apt. 3. 16mm film/video. Weston Woods.

Goggles. 16mm film/video. Learning Corporation of America, 1988.

Hi, Cat! 16mm film/video. Learning Corporation of America, 1989.

Peter's Chair. 16mm film/video. Weston Woods.

The Snowy Day. 16mm film/video. Weston Woods, 1964.

ABOUT CLEMENTINA'S CACTUS

A dry, sun-washed setting with a vista of cacti and buttes sets this book in the U.S. Southwest. An elongated, long-haired, bearded man is walking with a tiny girl in a sunbonnet holding onto his finger. They examine a short, fat cactus that has dry clumps of buds on its top. The man watches while the girl explores and discovers the sharp point to the thorns on the cactus. She settles to watch the cactus, but he picks her up and hurries her away just before a violent thunderstorm hits. The end of the storm brings a brilliant rainbow over their desert shack. Inside, the tiny girl listens to a bedtime book by lamplight. Outside, the cactus is shown under the starry sky, its buds swelling. The child wakens and runs out into the pink sunrise to find large orange-yellow flowers blooming on the cactus.

The dramatic colors of the southwestern landscape are used in the paintings. All of the colors are textured and shaded. The sky, a plain white backdrop in the beginning, gradually assumes importance as the clouds gather and the storm breaks. The rainbow, the night sky full of stars, and the early morning sky awash with color all emphasize the prominence of the western sky in the landscape. Several scenes are shown in silhouette against the colors of the sky.

The child, barely more than a toddler, is appealing in reds and blues. The blue of her eyes is picked up in the blues of the bonnet, the red of her hair in the red of her dress. The very thin man with his long legs and long arms may represent a child's-eye view of a tall, slender adult. He is shown as a loving caretaker. The simplicity of their lifestyle is reflected in the sparse landscape around them. The watercolor painting is effective in moving from a dry to a wet scene. The colors of the rainbow on the wet tin roof of the shack and the splotchy, wet paper technique of the storm cloud painting are just right for this. The perspectives may be somewhat confusing to younger children, as the extended distances of the desert are shown with smaller hills and outcroppings in the background, while the very tall man seems to loom over them in the foreground. The uncluttered pages and the bright, contrasting colors make it possible to share this book with a group, even though the book is small in size.

In the Library (or In the Classroom)

LITERATURE SHARING

Use this book to introduce a storyhour on the U.S. Southwest. The book is easily shared as a question-and-answer presentation, and the slight plot benefits from the embellishment of the audience. Due to the small size of the pages, the group needs to be fairly close to the presenter.

In *Desert Voices*, inhabitants of the desert speak of their home. The spadefoot toad that waits down in the earth until rain falls and the final "desert person" would be appropriate parts of that book to share along with *Clementina's Cactus*. Clementina and her father live simply, yet there is much to celebrate in the desert. In *I'm in Charge of Celebrations,* a desert dweller finds cause for celebration in such things as rainbows and coyotes.

Desert views in books by Kirk and Siebert can be compared with those of Keats. In *Mojave*, poetic text accompanies full-page paintings by Wendell Minor to explore the animals and landscapes of the Mojave Desert. Compare the summer storm here with the one in *Clementina's Cactus*. In *Desert Life,* simple text accompanies photographic views of the plants and animals of the desert. The section on rain shows a real rainbow to compare with the illustration by Keats. Invite participants to explore this special region through books.

RELATED MATERIALS

Baylor, Byrd. *Desert Voices*. Illustrated by Peter Parnall. Scribner, 1981.

_____. *I'm in Charge of Celebrations*. Illustrated by Peter Parnall. Scribner, 1986.

Kirk, Ruth. *Desert Life*. Natural History Press, 1970.

Siebert, Diane. *Mojave*. Illustrated by Wendell Minor. Crowell, 1988.

MAKING A DISPLAY

Clementina's interest in the cactus and its flowering is central to this story. Many cacti are grown as house plants and can be found in any part of the country. Borrow a variety of live cacti to set up in a display to accompany this book. A simple background for the display can be made of sandy-colored burlap. A more elaborate backdrop can be created by children using either torn tissue for a collage, or sponge printing to imitate the landscape in *Clementina's Cactus*. Children may also collect simple facts about cacti to print on small cards, which can be placed in the display. Signs near the display might pose questions to motivate viewers to find the answers in nonfiction and reference sources: How is a cactus like a rose? Who uses cacti for a home? What parts of a cactus might you eat?

RELATED MATERIALS

Bash, Barbara. *Desert Giant: The World of the Saguaro Cactus*. Little, Brown, 1989.

Guiberson, Brenda Z. *Cactus Hotel*. Illustrated by Megan Lloyd. Holt, 1991.

PROGRAM

Use *Clementina's Cactus* to introduce an exploration of the people and animals living in the desert. Clementina holds a Hopi kachina doll while she listens to a story and later hangs the kachina on the wall of her bedroom. The kachina can be used to introduce the Native American tribes that live in the Southwest. Where could Clementina have gotten her kachina doll? What other tribes might live near Clementina? What animals would Clementina become familiar with? *Along Sandy Trails* is a first-person narrative of a young Papago Indian girl who goes walking in the Arizona desert the day after a rain. The photographs include flowering cacti. Have children compare this book with the book by Keats.

RELATED MATERIALS

Blood, Charles L., and Martin Link. *The Goat in the Rug*. Illustrated by Nancy W. Parker. Parents Magazine Press, 1976.

Brenner, Barbara. *Lizard Tails and Cactus Spines*. Harper & Row, 1975.

Bronin, Andrew. *The Desert: What Lives There*. Illustrated by Nathalie Van Buren. Coward, McCann & Geoghegan, 1972.

Clark, Ann Nolan. *Along Sandy Trails*. Viking, 1969.

Cobb, Vicki. *This Place Is Dry!* Illustrated by Barbara Lavallee. Walker, 1989.

dePaola, Tomie. *The Legend of the Bluebonnet*. Putnam, 1983.

Nunes, Susan. *Coyote Dreams*. Illustrated by Ronald Himler. Atheneum, 1988.

Spencer, Guy. *A Living Desert*. Illustrated by Tim Fuller. Troll, 1988.

COLLECTION DEVELOPMENT

Clementina and her father share a very nurturing relationship. As you develop programs, text sets, and displays on families, include *Clementina's Cactus* as an example of the single father/single child family. Include this book with Father's Day lists and displays. Develop a collection of materials about nurturing father/child relationships.

RELATED MATERIALS

Ormerod, Jan. *Sunshine*. Lothrop, Lee & Shepard, 1981.

Stecher, Miriam. *Daddy and Ben Together*. Lothrop, Lee & Shepard, 1981.

Steptoe, John. *Daddy Is a Monster ... Sometimes*. Lippincott, 1980.

Thompson, Susan. *One More Thing, Dad*. Whitman, 1980.

Zolotow, Charlotte. *A Father Like That*. Illustrated by Ben Shecter. Harper, 1971.

_____. *The Summer Night*. Illustrated by Ben Shecter. Harper, 1974.

STORY AND CRAFT PROGRAM

The rare event of the rain in the desert is important in both *Clementina's Cactus* and *Bringing the Rain to Kapiti Plain: A Nandi Tale*. Share the two books along with more familiar rain and rainy day stories for contrast and comparison. *Mushroom in the Rain* shows another plant that responds to the rain; compare it to the cactus Clementina examines. Another small girl waits anxiously for rain in *Umbrella*. By contrast, share *Peter Spier's Rain*, which shows the response of children familiar with rainy days and their preparation with boots, raincoats, and umbrellas. Discuss with children how the environment varies in each of these books. End the program with an art activity in which children can make a rainy day picture.

RELATED MATERIALS

Aardema, Verna. *Bringing the Rain to Kapiti Plain: A Nandi Tale*. Illustrated by Beatriz Vidal. Dial, 1981.

Cole, Sheila. *When the Rain Stops*. Illustrated by Henri Sorensen. Lothrop, Lee & Shepard, 1991.

Ginsberg, Mirra. *Mushroom in the Rain*. Illustrated by José Arvego and Ariane Dewey. Macmillan, 1974.

Spier, Peter. *Peter Spier's Rain*. Doubleday, 1982.

Yashima, Tara. *Umbrella*. Viking, 1958.

In the Classroom (or In the Library)

LANGUAGE ARTS I

As students look through the book, they can compare Clementina's life with their own. Have students divide a sheet of paper and write their name on the top of one side, and "Clementina" on the other side. Leaving space between each item, they should write down information on topics such as their family members, house, bedroom, outdoor environment, flora and fauna, and things to do. Using this form, students can make notes that can then be developed into paragraph form comparing their life with Clementina's.

Or, have students use their outline form to develop a wordless picture book about a day in their own life that parallels the day in Clementina's life. For an example of a comparison of two children who live in different parts of the world, use the book *A Country Far Away*.

RELATED MATERIALS

Gray, Nigel. *A Country Far Away*. Illustrated by Philippe Dupasquier. Orchard, 1988.

LIBRARY RESEARCH

Clementina and her father live in the desert in the U.S. Southwest. Have students study how people live in the desert areas of the southwestern part of the United States. What is the environment like? Include geography, climate, and types of flora and fauna. Who lives in the desert? What types of dwellings are best in the desert? What foods do people eat and why? What type of transportation is used? How is this part of the country different from other areas of the United States?

RELATED NONFICTION MATERIALS

Bronin, Andrew. *The Desert: What Lives There*. Illustrated by Nathalie Van Buren. Coward, McCann & Geoghegan, 1972.

Cobb, Vicki. *This Place Is Dry!* Illustrated by Barbara Lavallee. Walker, 1989.

Larson, Peggy P. *A Sierra Club Naturalist's Guide to the Deserts of the Southwest*. Sierra Club Books, 1977.

Posell, Elsa Z. *Deserts*. Childrens Press, 1982.

Wiewandt, Thomas. *Hidden Life of the Desert*. Crown, 1990.

Zwinger, Ann. *The Mysterious Lands: A Naturalist Explores the Four Great Deserts of the Southwest*. Dutton, 1989.

LANGUAGE ARTS II

It takes special skills and precautions to stay alive in the desert. Have students, working in pairs, create desert survival guides. Have each pair decide the contents of their guide, the format, and the style they will use. Some may be serious; some may be humorous, with cartoonlike characters. Students may want to include such things as the importance of water, what to do if you run out of water, how to deal with rattlesnakes, how to tell directions in the desert, or why you should avoid cactus plants. When all guides are completed, have each pair present their guide to the class.

Either preceding or following this assignment you might want to read aloud the book *Lost in the Devil's Desert*, which is about an 11-year-old boy who finds himself alone and lost in the Utah desert with only his wits to help him survive.

RELATED MATERIALS

Skurzynski, Gloria. *Lost in the Devil's Desert*. Lothrop, Lee & Shepard, 1982.

RELATED NONFICTION MATERIALS

Catchpole, Clive. *Deserts*. Illustrated by Brian McIntyre. Dial, 1984. (The Living World Series)

Pitt, Valerie. *A Closer Look at Deserts*. Illustrated by Roy Coombs. Watts, 1975.

Sabin, Louis. *Wonders of the Desert*. Illustrated by Pamela B. Ford. Troll, 1982.

Smith, Howard E., Jr. *You Can Survive*. McGraw-Hill, 1982.

DRAMATICS

Have students pay particular attention to Clementina's father as they read this book. What do they learn about him? Discuss monologues and have students write monologues from the father's point of view. These might include why he lives in the desert, how he supports himself and Clementina, what it's like to be a single parent, what he likes and dislikes about desert life, and so forth. Review the monologues and allow time for rewriting. Students can present their monologues to the rest of the class.

ART

Clementina's Cactus shows beautiful desert sky scenes. Students can use wet paper painting to create their own desert skies. Use watercolor paper or finger paint paper. Wet the paper thoroughly before beginning, blotting any puddles with a sponge. Use limited colors—pink and orange were used for the sunrise page, blue and purple for the storm scene. Drop paint on the paper, or apply it directly with a brush, allowing the colors to run together.

Variations: (1) By crumpling the paper before wetting, the colors will be emphasized in the lines formed by the wrinkles; (2) use watercolors instead of tempera paint; (3) sprinkle powdered tempera from salt shakers on very wet paper.

After papers have dried, students can cut out silhouettes of cacti and landscapes from dark construction paper to paste on their paintings.

Koontz, Robin Michal

Dinosaur Dream
Putnam, 1988.
ISBN 0-399-21669-3; LC 88-18171

ABOUT THE AUTHOR AND HER BOOKS

Robin Michal Koontz was born in Wheaton, Maryland. Her mother was an artist, so Robin grew up around art. She attended the Maryland Institute of Art before moving to the Pacific Northwest. Koontz owns and operates a design company and has illustrated greeting cards, gift tags, and preschool books as well as children's picture books. Robin Koontz and her husband live in a house they built in Noti, Oregon.

Selected Books by the Author

I See Something You Don't See: A Riddle-Me Picture Book. Cobblehill/Dutton, 1992.

Pussycat Ate the Dumplings: Cat Rhymes from Mother Goose. Dodd, Mead, 1987.

This Old Man: The Counting Song. Dodd, Mead, 1988.

Selected Books Illustrated by the Author

In a Cabin in a Wood by Darcie McNally. Cobblehill/Dutton, 1991.

Victoria Flies High by Becky Ayres. Cobblehill/Dutton, 1990.

ABOUT DINOSAUR DREAM

A boy who loves dinosaurs is the main character in this colorful story. He has pictures of dinosaurs hanging on his wall and decorating his pajamas, bedspread, and curtains. The boy is reluctant to leave his large dinosaur toys to go to bed, but as he sleeps, a long neck stretches through his window, and a yellow and brown striped Apatosaurus carries him off to a prehistoric world.

Bright two-page watercolors depict large and small dinosaurs and other prehistoric creatures. The boy's pleasant exploration is interrupted by the arrival of the Tyrannosaurus. The friendly dinosaurs scatter, and the boy is placed safely up in a tall plant. A Triceratops rescues the child and takes him home, trundling off over the horizon as the sun rises. Alert readers will notice that the boy falls asleep hugging his Apatosaurus doll and will relate this to the Apatosaurus that carries him away. The boy is returned to his window by a Triceratops, and in the final scene, he is hugging his Triceratops doll. A plump cat appears in the opening and closing illustrations, reacting to the supposedly imaginary dinosaurs. A final guide page tells the names and pronunciations for the dinosaurs and challenges readers to locate over 30 dinosaurs in the story.

The large size of the illustrations, the use of color, and the composition of the scenes make the book accessible for a group presentation; however, the boy is somewhat hard to distinguish in some scenes unless the presenter points him out.

In the Library (or In the Classroom)

LITERATURE SHARING

The boy in *Dinosaur Dream* has filled his room with dinosaurs. After sharing this book with children, discuss the fascination people have with prehistoric times. Children may volunteer information about toys, clothes, models, games, or other things they have collected with the theme of dinosaurs or prehistoric animals.

Follow with the book or video of *Will's Mammoth*. Are the two boys in these stories alike or different? What is the same about the two stories? What is different? Invite children to look at other books on the same theme.

RELATED MATERIALS

Donnelly, Liza. *Dinosaur Day*. Scholastic, 1987.

Martin, Rafe. *Will's Mammoth*. Illustrated by Stephen Gammell. Putnam, 1989.

Nolan, Dennis. *Dinosaur Dream*. Macmillan, 1990.

RELATED NONPRINT MATERIALS

Martin, Rafe. *Will's Mammoth*. Video or sound filmstrip. American School Publishers, 1991.

MAKING A DISPLAY

Display dinosaur models or toys with this book as the center of a display. Use light green or yellow for a backdrop to bring out the light, pleasant colors in the book. Notice the use of simple leaf forms in the foreground of many of the illustrations. Cut similar forms from dark green paper and mount them in the front of the display to give it depth. Place dinosaur books nearby for circulation.

RELATED MATERIALS

Aliki. *Digging Up Dinosaurs*. Crowell, 1981.

_____. *Dinosaur Bones*. Crowell, 1988.

_____. *My Visit to the Dinosaurs*. Crowell, 1969.

Barton, Byron. *Bones, Bones, Dinosaur Bones*. Crowell, 1990.

_____. *Dinosaurs, Dinosaurs*. Crowell, 1989.

Gibbons, Gail. *Dinosaurs*. Holiday House, 1987.

Most, Bernard. *Littlest Dinosaurs*. Harcourt Brace Jovanovich, 1989.

BOOKTALK

In Robin Koontz's *Dinosaur Dream*, the boy is taken back to prehistoric times. Use this book to introduce the idea of time travel as a genre of fantasy literature. Follow it with *Dinosaur Dream* by Dennis Nolan, in which the little boy goes to the time of the Apatosaurus. Display and briefly introduce either a variety of other time travel fiction or fiction that features dinosaurs.

RELATED MATERIALS

Bunting, Eve. *The Day of the Dinosaurs*. Illustrated by Judith Leo. E.M.C., 1975.

Butterworth, Oliver. *The Enormous Egg*. Illustrated by Louis Darling. Little, Brown, 1956.

Carrick, Carol. *Patrick's Dinosaurs*. Illustrated by Donald Carrick. Clarion, 1983.

Fleischman, Paul. *Time Train*. Illustrated by Claire Ewart. HarperCollins, 1991.

Harrison, Sarah, and Mike Wilks. *In Granny's Garden*. Holt, Rinehart & Winston, 1980.

Nolan, Dennis. *Dinosaur Dream*. Macmillan, 1990.

Richler, Mordecai. *Jacob Two-Two and the Dinosaur*. Illustrated by Norman Eyolfson. Knopf, 1987.

STORYTELLING AND PARTICIPATION PROGRAM

The boy in *Dinosaur Dream* collects everything that has to do with dinosaurs. Use the book to begin a discussion on theme collections. After sharing the story, or introducing the first three pages, have the group identify all the things in the boy's room that have to do with dinosaurs.

Invite participants to list other things that someone could collect. Suggest other favorite animals, current popular media creations, and things such as rocks or postcards. Read the list back to the group, then introduce the books you have gathered on collecting for them to enjoy. Finish the program with the book *Josephina the Great Collector*, in which Josephina's passion for collecting creates problems with her sister who shares her room.

Provide cutout paper strips and a dinosaur stamp and ink pad or stickers so that children can make a bookmark to take home with them.

RELATED MATERIALS

Allen, Judy. *Usborne Guide to Stamps and Stamp Collecting*. Usborne, 1981.

Daeschler, Ted. *Start Collecting Fossils*. Running Press, 1988.

Engel, Diana. *Josephina the Great Collector*. Morrow, 1988.

Lewis, Shari. *Things Kids Collect!* Holt, Rinehart & Winston, 1980.

McComas, Tom. *Collecting Toy Trains*. Childrens Press, 1979.

Russell, Margo. *Start Collecting Coins*. Running Press, 1989.

Srogi, LeeAnn. *Start Collecting Rocks and Minerals*. Running Press, 1989.

Villiard, Paul. *Collecting Things*. Doubleday, 1975.

RELATED NONPRINT MATERIALS

"Dinosaur" rubber stamps by Palmer Cox. Kidstamps.

"Dinosaur" stamps by Bernard Most. Kidstamps.

"Reading Dino" stamp by Aliki. Kidstamps.

BOOKSHARING AND WRITING PROGRAM

After sharing *Dinosaur Dream*, talk about when the boy wakes up—will he think the dream was real? Does he wish dinosaurs were still alive? A character who does is Danny in the story *Danny and the Dinosaur*. After sharing this book about Danny, discuss what would happen if dinosaurs did return. One author has ideas for you in the book *If the Dinosaurs Came Back*.

Invite children to write and illustrate a page showing the dinosaur they would like to have and what might happen if their wish came true. Compile these pages into a book for library browsers to read.

RELATED MATERIALS

Hoff, Syd. *Danny and the Dinosaur*. Harper & Row, 1958.

Most, Bernard. *If the Dinosaurs Came Back*. Harcourt Brace Jovanovich, 1978.

In the Classroom (or In the Library)

VISUAL DISCRIMINATION AND SOUNDS

After sharing *Dinosaur Dream* with a small group, share it a second time and ask students to pay careful attention to what is going on in the background. During the first viewing of a picture book, readers usually observe the main character and what happens to that character. However, there is other activity going on in *Dinosaur Dream*. As the book is shared a second time, have students discuss the background activities that are going on as the boy goes through his dream.

Although we cannot hear them, we can imagine that there are many background sounds that the character in this book might hear. Share the book a third time and invite viewers to tell about the sounds that might be heard and to make those sounds.

ART AND MURAL MAKING

The boy in this story has a dinosaur poster on his bedroom wall, a dinosaur quilt on his bed, and a border of different dinosaurs on the wall going around the room. Have students make a large class mural that includes all of the dinosaurs from the back of the book in a prehistoric habitat.

RELATED MATERIALS

Ames, Lee J. *Draw 50 Dinosaurs and Other Prehistoric Animals*. Doubleday, 1977.

Emberley, Michael. *Dinosaurs! A Drawing Book*. Little, Brown, 1980.

_____. *More Dinosaurs! and Other Prehistoric Beasts; A Drawing Book*. Little, Brown, 1983.

NATURAL SCIENCE AND LIBRARY RESEARCH

As the young boy in this story travels through prehistoric times in his dream, he sees more than 31 different types of dinosaurs. At the back of the book is a list of the dinosaurs that appear in the story. Copy this list and have each student choose one of the dinosaurs as his or her favorite.

Students can use library resources to learn everything they can about their dinosaur, including the time period the dinosaur lived, its size, what it ate, and so forth. Students can make individual books in the shape of their dinosaurs. Books can include factual information from the students' research and student illustrations.

RELATED NONFICTION MATERIALS

Davidson, Rosalie. *Dinosaurs from A to Z*. Childrens Press, 1983.

Elting, Mary. *The Macmillan Book of Dinosaurs and Other Prehistoric Creatures*. Illustrated by John Hamberger. Macmillan, 1984.

Sattler, Helen Roney. *Dinosaurs of North America*. Illustrated by Anthony Rao. Lothrop, Lee & Shepard, 1981.

_____. *New Illustrated Dinosaur Dictionary*. Illustrated by Joyce Powzyk. Lothrop, Lee & Shepard, 1990.

Selsam, Millicent E., and Joyce Hunt. *A First Look at Dinosaurs*. Illustrated by Harriett Springer. Walker, 1982.

RELATED NONPRINT MATERIALS

The Age of Dinosaurs. Sound filmstrip. National Geographic Society, 1990.

Cohen, Daniel. *Dinosaurs*. Sound filmstrip. Listening Library, 1986.

LANGUAGE ARTS AND WRITING

The boy in *Dinosaur Dream* dreams that he has traveled to prehistoric times. There are many books in which dreams seem like real adventures. Share several wordless picture books that depict dream adventures. Students can pretend that they are the main character in one of the stories. Upon awakening, they write a first-person journal entry that tells about their dream journey and the adventures they had.

RELATED MATERIALS

Barton, Byron. *Elephant*. Seabury Press, 1971.

Tafuri, Nancy. *Junglewalk*. Greenwillow, 1988.

Wiesner, David. *Free Fall*. Lothrop, Lee & Shepard, 1988.

Wright, Cliff. *When the World Sleeps*. Ideal Children's Books, 1989.

ART

The boy in this story has his room filled with different types of stuffed animal toys. Fill the classroom with different types of student-made dinosaurs.

Students can make their own stuffed dinosaurs by folding brown paper in half and drawing a pattern on one side, then carefully cutting out the two shapes. Features can be added with paint or marking pens, and the dinosaur can be colored or painted. Using a large blunt needle and yarn, stitch the two pieces together, leaving an opening that can be stitched shut after the creature is stuffed. Stuff the dinosaur with wadded paper. Other types of dinosaurs can be made from papier-mâché or other materials.

RELATED NONFICTION MATERIALS

Caket, Colin. *Model a Monster: Making Dinosaurs from Everyday Materials*. Sterling, 1986.

Hawcock, David. *Paper Dinosaurs: How to Make 20 Original Paper Models*. Sterling, 1988.

West, Robin. *Dinosaur Discoveries: How to Create Your Own Prehistoric World*. Illustrated by Bob Wolfe and Diane Wolfe. Carolrhoda, 1989.

Moonlight
Lothrop, Lee & Shepard, 1982.
ISBN 0-688-00846-1; 0-688-00847-X (lib); LC 81-8290

Sunshine
Lothrop, Lee & Shepard, 1981.
ISBN 0-688-00552-7; 0-688-00553-5 (lib); LC 80-84971

ABOUT THE AUTHOR AND HER BOOKS

Jan Ormerod was born on September 23, 1946, in Bunbury, Western Australia. She received a degree in graphic design from the Western Australian Institute of Technology and a teacher's certificate from Claremont Teachers College in Perth, Western Australia. She has worked as an art teacher; a lecturer in art education, drawing, and basic design; and an author and illustrator of children's books. Jan Ormerod lives in Cambridge, England, with her husband and two daughters. Her book *Sunshine* has won numerous awards and honors, including the Mother Goose Award and the Australian Picture Book of the Year Award.

Selected Books by the Author

Be Brave, Billy. Dent, 1983.

Bend and Stretch. Lothrop, Lee & Shepard, 1987.

Just Like Me. Lothrop, Lee & Shepard, 1986.

Mom's Home. Lothrop, Lee & Shepard, 1987.

101 Things to Do with a Baby. Lothrop, Lee & Shepard, 1984.

Saucepan Game. Lothrop, Lee & Shepard, 1989.

The Story of Chicken Licken. Lothrop, Lee & Shepard, 1986.

This Little Nose. Lothrop, Lee & Shepard, 1987.

Selected Books Illustrated by the Author

Chewing-Gum Rescue and Other Stories by Margaret Mahy. Overlook Press, 1991.

Hairs in the Palm of the Hand by Jan Mark. Viking Kestrel, 1981.

Happy Christmas, Gemma by Sarah Hayes. Lothrop, Lee & Shepard, 1986.

One Ballerina Two by Vivian French. Lothrop, Lee & Shepard, 1991.

Peter Pan by James M. Barrie. Viking, 1987.

Rhymes Around the Day. Compiled by Pat Thompson. Lothrop, Lee & Shepard, 1983.

Stamp Your Feet by Sarah Hayes. Lothrop, Lee & Shepard, 1988.

ABOUT MOONLIGHT *AND* SUNSHINE

These companion volumes show a young child in two sequences very recognizable to children. *Sunshine* shows the early morning hours as a family wakens and prepares for the day, while *Moonlight* shows a typical bedtime routine. Warm relationships between the family members make these everyday experiences a pleasure to share. The family—a mother, father, and young daughter—share chores, with the father and the daughter shown in the kitchen cooking and cleaning up.

In *Sunshine*, the little girl wakens early and reads in bed before going to wake her bearded father with a kiss. Together they make breakfast and take it to the mother in bed. As the relaxed morning proceeds, the father enjoys the newspaper and the mother falls back asleep. The little girl gets up and dresses herself before showing them the time. The morning becomes hectic as the adults hurry to dress and be off. The little girl leaves with her mother, with the implication that both parents are going off to work.

Moonlight follows the evening from the end of dinner to sleep, with several detours on the way. As the father cleans up, the little girl makes herself a boat from a melon rind and prepares and takes a bath. When she is ready for bed, a typical series of requests prolongs the final goodnight. Her father falls asleep on her bed, so the little girl joins her mother on the couch. When the father awakens, he finds both the mother and daughter asleep over their reading.

The illustration in both books uses line drawing with watercolor. Many humorous touches are emphasized by the use of color—for example, the father, rushing to get ready for work, has one bright red sock on. Multiple images show action broken into small stages. The sequences of the child changing clothes are very detailed and easy to follow. Although the incidents are ordinary, the illustration is illuminating. For example, the anticipation of disaster is shown as the smoke from the toaster gradually thickens and blackens, while the father is absorbed in the morning newspaper.

Although the plot is extremely simple in these books, the careful presentation attracts and rewards readers. Each book is filled with homey details and subtle humor. The independence and personality of the little girl make her an attractive character. The sharing of chores and the contemporary feel of the family's life are appealing. The true charm of these sequences lies in the affection between family members and in the good-natured respect they exhibit for one another. As a plus, reading is shown as an integral part of the family's morning and evening, with each person incorporating reading and books into their individual activities; reading is clearly also a family activity.

In the Library (or In the Classroom)

STORYHOUR

Use the theme of trouble sleeping for an evening storytime with parents and children together, or as a theme for a regular daytime storyhour. The song "Stay Awake" from Walt Disney's *Mary Poppins* can be used to open the program. *Moonlight* shows a little girl who can't sleep in a familiar family setting. However, some situations in which characters can't sleep are not so typical. Use the fingerplay of "Five Little Monkeys Jumping on the Bed" as an example of fooling around instead of going to sleep. Russell Hoban's character, Frances, had trouble at bedtime and can be used as one of the stories. The little mouse in *Mother, Mother, I Want Another* has a different kind of problem. End the program with a song that is meant to be sung to a crying baby who won't sleep—"Hush, Little Baby," which can be found as a sing-along filmstrip.

RELATED MATERIALS

Chevalier, Christa. *Spence and the Sleepytime Monster*. Whitman, 1984.

Hoban, Russell. *Bedtime for Frances*. Illustrated by Garth Williams. Harper, 1960.

Keller, Holly. *Ten Sleepy Sheep*. Greenwillow, 1983.

Polushkin, Maria. *Mother, Mother, I Want Another*. Illustrated by Diane Dawson. Crown, 1978.

Rodgers, Frank. *I Can't Get to Sleep*. Simon & Schuster, 1991.

Stevenson, James. *We Can't Sleep*. Greenwillow, 1982.

Wells, Rosemary. *Good Night, Fred*. Dial, 1981.

Zolotow, Charlotte. *The Summer Night*. Illustrated by Ben Shecter. HarperCollins, 1991. (Reissue)

RELATED NONPRINT MATERIALS

Hush Little Baby. Illustrated by Aliki. 16mm film/video. Weston Woods.

WORKSHOP

Because these two books show very familiar situations, they are excellent tools for teaching a beginning sign language vocabulary. Introduce words that will be used in the story. Have children practice the words while they retell the story as a group. Children will enjoy searching in similar books for illustrations to match words they have learned. The sections "In the Morning" and "Nighttime" in *Sesame Street Sign Language Fun* show many words you might use.

RELATED MATERIALS

Brown, Margaret Wise. *A Child's Good Night Book*. Illustrated by Jean Charlot. Harper & Row, 1950.

Himler, Ronald. *Wake Up, Jeremiah*. Harper & Row, 1979.

Rockwell, Anne. *Bear Child's Book of Hours*. Crowell, 1987.

Ziefert, Harriet. *Say Good-Night!* Illustrated by Catherine Siracusa. Viking Kestrel, 1987.

Zinnemann-Hope, Pam. *Time for Bed, Ned*. Illustrated by Kady MacDonald Denton. Atheneum, 1986.

Zolotow, Charlotte. *Wake Up and Good Night*. Illustrated by Leonard Weisgard. HarperCollins, 1971.

RELATED NONFICTION MATERIALS

Sesame Street Sign Language Fun. With Linda Bove. Illustrated by Tom Cooke. Random House, 1980.

GAME PROGRAM

After sharing these books, go back to the sequences in which the family is getting dressed. In *Moonlight*, look at how fast the parents must get dressed. Play a game in which participants must practice dressing and undressing quickly. Divide the group into two or more teams. Have a box of oversize clothing for each team—a coat, hat, boots, tie, and so forth. Each person races to the box, puts on the clothes, races back, and takes off the clothes; the next person puts them on, races to the box, takes them off, and so forth. The fun of the game is not so much winning as it is seeing the funny things that people do when they try to dress quickly.

RELATED MATERIALS

Kuskin, Karla. *The Dallas Titans Get Ready for Bed*. Illustrated by Marc Simont. Harper, 1986.

_____. *The Philharmonic Gets Dressed*. Illustrated by Marc Simont. Harper, 1982.

Maestro, Betsy, and Giulio Maestro. *On the Town: A Book of Clothing Words*. Crown, 1983.

Watanabe, Shigeo. *How Do I Put It On?* Illustrated by Yasuo Ohtomo. Philomel, 1984.

Wells, Rosemary. *Max's New Suit*. Dial, 1979.

Zinnemann-Hope, Pam. *Find Your Coat, Ned*. Illustrated by Kady MacDonald Denton. Macmillan, 1988.

LITERATURE SHARING

Look at the works of two illustrators/authors: Jan Ormerod and Helen Oxenbury. Notice how often and in what circumstances their characters are reading. Can participants find other books in which characters read? How many ways do characters in books use reading? Where do book characters read? What might the characters be reading? Have participants find a book to share with their family and help them to check the book out.

RELATED MATERIALS

Ormerod, Jan. *Reading*. Lothrop, Lee & Shepard, 1985.

Oxenbury, Helen. *Tom and Pippo Read a Story*. Macmillan, 1988.

MAKING A DISPLAY

Open *Moonlight* to the page on which the child is in the bathtub. Drape a large red bath towel for a backdrop. Place various homemade tub toys around the book. A sign can point out that the child in this story made her own toy boat. Invite children to make their own toys that float, similar to the samples you have set out. You might also invite them to imagine what story the little girl is telling herself as she plays with the boat, and to put their story ideas on cards to be displayed.

RELATED MATERIALS

Anderson, Lena. *Bunny Bath*. R & S Books, 1990.

Burningham, John. *Time to Get Out of the Bath, Shirley*. Crowell, 1978.

Faulkner, Matt. *The Amazing Voyage of Jackie Grace*. Scholastic, 1987.

Lindgren, Barbro. *Sam's Bath*. Illustrated by Eva Eriksson. Morrow, 1983.

Watanabe, Shigeo. *I Can Take a Bath!* Illustrated by Yasuo Ohtomo. Philomel, 1987.

Wood, Audrey. *King Bidgood's in the Bathtub*. Illustrated by Don Wood. Harcourt Brace Jovanovich, 1985.

Ziefert, Harriet. *Harry Takes a Bath*. Illustrated by Mavis Smith. Viking Kestrel, 1987.

RELATED NONFICTION MATERIALS

Blocksma, Mary. *Easy-to-Make Water Toys That Really Work*. Illustrated by Art Seiden. Prentice-Hall, 1985.

Gilbreath, Alice. *Making Toys That Swim and Float*. Illustrated by Joe Rodgers. Follett, 1978.

In the Classroom (or In the Library)

LANGUAGE ARTS I

Share the book *Sunshine* with the class, paying particular attention to the pages where the young girl eats breakfast and prepares breakfast in bed for her mother. As a group, discuss why breakfast is important and which breakfast foods provide good nutrition. Plan a well-balanced nutritional menu that children could prepare and serve to their parent(s) in bed.

RELATED MATERIALS

Krementz, Jill. *The Fun of Cooking*. Knopf, 1985.

Sanders, Sandra. *Easy Cooking for Kids*. Illustrated by Mike Quon. Scholastic, 1979.

Toth, Robin. *Naturally It's Good ... I Cooked It Myself*. Betterway, 1982.

RELATED NONPRINT MATERIALS

Nutrition for Children. "Break the Fast." Sound filmstrip. Polished Apple, 1976.

Nutrition: Who Cares? You Should. "Choosing Foods"; "Choices from Breakfast to Dinner." Sound filmstrips. Guidance Associates, 1982.

LANGUAGE ARTS II

Share the book *Moonlight* with the group and invite them to discuss the different things that the little girl and her parents do in the evening. Write the activities on a chart labeled "Evening." The next day, share the book *Sunshine* and invite students to discuss the activities of the little girl and her parents in the morning; write them on a chart labeled "Morning." As a class, brainstorm what the little girl and her parents might do during the day. You may want to make separate "Daytime" charts for the little girl, the mother, and the father. Each student can select one of the characters and make a book about that character's daytime activities. Books could include text, text with illustration, or illustrations only.

SOCIAL STUDIES AND LANGUAGE ARTS I

Discuss family dynamics and the roles each family member takes. As you share these two books, have students discuss the roles of the different members of *this* family. How might the roles of the family change if there were additional members (grandparents, a baby, adopted siblings, cousins, and so forth)?

SOCIAL STUDIES AND LANGUAGE ARTS II

Discuss what it means to learn to be independent and to do things for oneself. Why is it important to learn to do things independently? As you share each book, have students look for the things the little girl is able to do for herself and the ways her parents are helping her learn to be independent. Make a list of the things the little girl is able to do in each book. Have students discuss the things *they* are able to do for themselves and make a class list (dress themselves, tie shoes, walk to school, feed pets, and so forth).

MATHEMATICS

As you share each book, discuss how the passage of time is shown in the illustrations. *Sunshine* shows a clock in several of the pictures. Discuss how time is measured in hours and minutes. How do we know when it is time for bed? Time to get up? Time to do different activities? Why is it important to be able to tell time using a clock or watch? Share the book *Bear Child's Book of Hours*, which shows the hands of a large clock moving hour by hour on one page and Bear Child engaged in appropriate activities on the opposite page. Have students make a book of hours for themselves. Begin with a clock showing 6:00 a.m. and go to 10:00 p.m. Students can draw pictures for each hour showing what activities they might be engaged in on a typical school day. A brief text might be included for each time period.

RELATED MATERIALS

McMillan, Bruce. *Time to....* Lothrop, Lee & Shepard, 1989.

Pluckrose, Henry. *Time*. Photographs by Chris Fairclough. Watts, 1988.

Rockwell, Anne. *Bear Child's Book of Hours*. Crowell, 1987.

Schwerin, Doris. *The Tomorrow Book*. Illustrated by Karen Gundersheimer. Pantheon, 1984.

Time. Photographs by Steven Oliver. Random House, 1991. (My First Look At Series)

RELATED NONPRINT MATERIALS

It's About Time. "A Day Goes By." Sound filmstrip. National Geographic Society, 1988.

Learning About Telling Time. Sound filmstrip. SVE, 1984.

Sara

Across Town
Orchard, 1991.
ISBN 0-531-05932-4; 0-531-08532-5 (lib); LC 90-7982

ABOUT THE AUTHOR AND HER BOOKS

Sara was born on March 17, 1950, in Nantes, France, near the mouth of the Loire River in the chateau country. A painter since she was quite young, Sara first studied in a studio when she was only nine years old. She moved to Paris when she was 20 and continued her studies and her painting in the art workshops (*ateliers*) of Montparnasse. Sara did editorial work for magazines and newspapers for 10 years before changing her profession to work in graphics and magazine layouts. Sara lives in the Montparnasse area of Paris with her three children and their three mice. *Across Town* is based on an incident Sara saw on the Boulevard Sébastopol in Paris.

Selected Book by the Author

The Rabbit, the Fox, and the Wolf. Orchard, 1991.

ABOUT ACROSS TOWN

An elegant, understated style creates a richly atmospheric story. The dark side of a lonely city night is first apparent as a man in a slouch hat makes his way on foot through deserted streets. The cinematic style of the torn paper collage illustration provides a mood reminiscent of a 1940s black-and-white mystery movie. Suspense builds as two eyes peer through the darkness under a bridge, creating an anxious mood; then the plot turns to the other side of the city night, as the man first caresses, then carries off a white cat.

The dramatic use of space and shape sets the illustration in this book apart from others. The artwork is sophisticated in the use of only three colors—black, white, and beige. A contrast is created between the slick, smooth black, which has been cut with precise, straight lines, and the textured, rough, natural-colored paper with its torn, irregular edges. Perhaps because of the minimal detail, the book evokes from students imaginative writing and emotional response. Older readers may appreciate the artistry and respond to the atmosphere set by the book more than younger readers.

In the Library (or In the Classroom)

BOOKTALK

Use *Across Town* as the beginning of a booktalk on novels that are set in cities and reveal surprising encounters. The illustrations in this title are easily shared with a group. The city of Paris is the background for *Across Town*, in which a man finds unexpected companionship. San Francisco is the setting for another story in which a lonely person finds unexpected companionship: Nina in *The Court of the Stone Children* discovers a strange girl in an unusual museum. Another museum (the Metropolitan Museum of Art) and another city (New York City) are the setting for a third unusual encounter in *From the Mixed-Up Files of Mrs. Basil E. Frankweiler*.

In *Across Town*, finding the cat provides the happy ending, but in *Tails of the Bronx*, a missing cat is the beginning of an investigation by neighborhood children who uncover some surprising things about the city block that they thought they knew so well. In *The Scariest Night*, everything about the neighborhood and the city of Milwaukee is unfamiliar to Erin and her family. When Rufus, the cat, slips out of their borrowed apartment in a building that doesn't allow pets, Erin begins a summer of unusual meetings. These stories all reveal city surprises, just as *Across Town* does.

RELATED MATERIALS

Cameron, Eleanor. *The Court of the Stone Children*. Dutton, 1973.

Konigsburg, E. L. *From the Mixed-Up Files of Mrs. Basil E. Frankweiler*. Atheneum, 1980.

Pinkwater, Jill. *Tails of the Bronx*. Macmillan, 1991.

Wright, Betty Ren. *The Scariest Night*. Holiday House, 1991.

LITERATURE SHARING

The white cat hiding under the bridge in *Across Town* is a city animal. Many other books feature cats that live in cities. Share *Across Town* and *Hi, Cat!* with a group. Invite the participants to compare the two stories. After thinking about the similar idea of a person meeting a city cat, talk about the many differences in the experiences. Then encourage the group members to think about the ways in which the two artists used many of the same elements to create very different moods and very different illustrations. Have a display of stories about city cats that children may check out.

RELATED MATERIALS

Baker, Leslie. *The Third-Story Cat*. Little, Brown, 1987.

Brown, Marcia. *Felice*. Scribner, 1958.

Coats, Laura Jane. *Goodyear the City Cat*. Macmillan, 1987.

Foreman, Michael. *Cat & Canary*. Dial, 1985.

Keats, Ezra Jack. *Hi, Cat!* Macmillan, 1970.

Miles, Miska. *Nobody's Cat*. Illustrated by Jon Schoenherr. Little, Brown, 1969.

Poulin, Stéphane. *Have You Seen Josephine?* Tundra Books, 1986.

RELATED NONPRINT MATERIALS

Foreman, Michael. *Cat & Canary*. Sound filmstrip. Weston Woods, 1986.

Keats, Ezra Jack. *Hi, Cat!* 16mm film. Learning Corporation of America, 1989.

BOOKSHARING AND ART PROGRAM

Share the expressive illustrations in this book with a group and discuss the art technique of torn and cut paper that Sara has used. Invite participants to create their own pictures using only black, gray, or beige paper on a white background. Suggest combining torn and cut forms as Sara has done. Children can write a short caption for their picture. Captioned pictures can be displayed in the library near copies of *Across Town*.

MEDIA PROGRAM

There are several picture books that feature Paris or France. Use these books in a multimedia program. Begin the program with the film *Rendezvous*; just as a car in this film goes through the city of Paris, so does the man in *Across Town*. After sharing *Across Town*, have participants suggest some of the words they would use in telling the story, such as *man, hat, night*, and *cat*. Teach students how to say several of these words in French, then have them participate in telling the story using the French words as you share the book. You may want to share other picture books with the group, or teach them a simple French song. Sample French bread before selecting books to check out and take home.

RELATED MATERIALS

Bemelmans, Ludwig. *Madeline*. Viking, 1963.

Bingham, Mindy. *Minou*. Illustrated by Itoko Maeno. Advocacy Press, 1987.

dePaola, Tomie. *Bonjour, Mr. Satie*. Putnam, 1991.

Fender, Kay. *Odette: A Bird in Paris*. Illustrated by Philipe Dumas. Prentice-Hall, 1978.

Goode, Diane. *Where's Our Mama?* Dutton, 1991.

Kalman, Maira. *Max Makes a Million*. Viking, 1990.

Titus, Eve. *Anatole over Paris*. Illustrated by Paul Galdone. Bantam, 1991. (Reprint)

RELATED NONFICTION MATERIALS

A Child's Picture English-French Dictionary. Illustrated by Dennis Sheheen. Adama, 1984.

RELATED NONPRINT MATERIALS

Cronan, Mary, and Judy Mahoney. *Teach Me French*. Coloring book and sound cassette. Teach Me Tapes, 1985.

Lamorisse, Albert. *The Red Balloon*. 16mm film. Nelson Entertainment, 1988.

Lelouch, Claude. *Rendezvous*. 16mm film. Pyramid, 1977.

COLLECTION DEVELOPMENT

Include *Across Town* in displays, booklists, text sets, thematic units, and programs that offer a look at the different moods of night.

RELATED MATERIALS

Grifalconi, Ann. *Darkness and the Butterfly*. Little, Brown, 1987.

Martin, Bill, Jr., and John Archambault. *The Ghost-Eye Tree*. Illustrated by Ted Rand. Holt, 1985.

Pizer, Abigail. *Harry's Night Out*. Dial, 1987.

Ressner, Philip. *At Night*. Photographs by Charles Pratt. Dutton, 1967.

Rice, Eve. *Goodnight, Goodnight*. Greenwillow, 1980.

Ryder, Joanne. *Step into the Night*. Illustrated by Dennis Nolan. Four Winds, 1988.

In the Classroom (or In the Library)

LANGUAGE ARTS I

Using an opaque projector, share *Across Town* with a small group or the whole class up to the page where the man sees the two eyes. Stop the story, close the book, and have students complete the story in writing. Reopen the book to the same page and have students read aloud their ending to the story before sharing the rest of the illustrated story by Sara. Discuss the following: Was the author's ending predictable or was it a surprise? Did any of the students end their story in the same way as Sara? How many variations of the ending of the story did the students have? How did Sara's illustrations affect the mood and setting of the stories that students wrote?

LANGUAGE ARTS II

Provide multiple copies of *Across Town* to enable students to work individually or in pairs; or set up a writing center with this book where students can work one at a time. As students read the book, have them do a stream of consciousness writing from the main character's point of view. When all students have had the opportunity to write, allow them to share their work orally with the class and discuss the variations.

VISUAL LITERACY

Discuss the atmosphere of *Across Town* with the class and talk about how the author developed a mood or feeling through setting and artistic techniques. How does the moon change through the story? Illustration can create an emotional climate that establishes a viewer's attitudes and expectations toward what they are viewing.

Visual communication is a very powerful tool that is used by the advertising industry to promote all types of products and messages. As a class, brainstorm moods and feelings and list them on the chalkboard. Then, have students look through a variety of magazines for illustrated advertisements. What type of atmosphere is created by different ads? What mood is created? What type of emotional reaction is the ad designed to elicit in the reader?

Have students each select a feeling or mood to work with and have them make a collage of magazine pictures that depict that mood. Create a bulletin board of student collages.

LANGUAGE ARTS III

The man in *Across Town* encounters a large white cat, picks it up, and takes the cat with him as the book ends. Many people have cats as pets. Survey the class to see how many students have a pet cat in their immediate or extended family. What types of cats do they have? Make a list of the types of cats and of the names that people give their cats. Discuss why each cat was given the name it was given. Have students tell about the different personalities their cats have and whether their cats are indoor or outdoor animals.

Many poems have been written about cats and their different personalities and characteristics. Share a variety of cat poems with the class before having students write their own poems about their own cats, or the one in this book. Poems can be illustrated using a torn paper technique such as the one used in *Across Town*.

RELATED MATERIALS

Cat Poems. Selected by Myra Cohn Livingston. Illustrated by Trina Schart Hyman. Holiday House, 1987.

Cats Are Cats. Compiled by Nancy Larrick. Illustrated by Ed Young. Philomel, 1988.

deRegniers, Beatrice Schenk. *This Big Cat and Other Cats I've Known*. Illustrated by Alan Daniel. Crown, 1985.

Eliot, T. S. *Growltiger's Last Stand: And Other Poems*. Illustrated by Errol LeCain. Farrar, Straus & Giroux, 1939.

_____. *Old Possum's Book of Practical Cats*. Illustrated by Edward Gorey. Harcourt Brace Jovanovich, 1982.

SOCIAL STUDIES

Across Town can be used to introduce a discussion on stray animals and their treatment. Although the cat in this book is picked up and taken away by the man, many animals are not so fortunate. *A Cat's Nine Lives* is a photo-essay of a purebred Persian cat as she goes from owner to owner, is put in an animal shelter, becomes injured while homeless, and, finally, finds a good home with a caring youngster. *Pets Without Homes* is a photo-essay that looks at pet neglect and pet adoption as it follows a lost dog that is picked up by an animal control officer and taken to an animal shelter. *The Animal Shelter* explores the issues of irresponsible pet ownership and the difficulties of operating an animal shelter. An animal control officer from a local animal shelter can be invited to speak to the class about responsible pet care.

RELATED NONFICTION MATERIALS

Arnold, Caroline. *Pets Without Homes*. Clarion, 1983.

Curtis, Patricia. *The Animal Shelter*. Lodestar/Dutton, 1984.

Hess, Lilo. *A Cat's Nine Lives*. Scribner, 1984.

Poynter, Margaret. *Too Few Happy Endings: The Dilemma of the Humane Societies*. Atheneum, 1981.

Mouse Around
Farrar, Straus & Giroux, 1991.
ISBN 0-374-35080-9; LC 90-56156

ABOUT THE AUTHOR AND HER BOOKS

Pat Schories was born in Ohio on July 30, 1952. As a child, she loved looking at the pictures in books while her mother read to her. She graduated from Kent State University in Ohio in 1974 with a B.F.A. in graphic design and illustration. After college she moved to New York and worked as a freelance graphic designer. Her first book assignment was illustrating a cloth baby book with simple objects in bright colors. Pat enjoys visiting schools and talking about making books. She also enjoys outdoor activities, including gardening and canoeing. *Mouse Around* is Pat Schories first book; she is currently working on another book for the same publisher. She lives in Cold Springs, New York.

Selected Books Illustrated by the Author

Baby's Games. Edited by Debby Slier. Checkerboard Press, 1990.

Quiet as a Mouse by Carol Roth. Checkerboard Press, 1991.

Young Abraham Lincoln, Log-Cabin President by Andrew Woods. Troll, 1991.

ABOUT MOUSE AROUND

The cover of *Mouse Around* shows a curious little mouse poking his head out of a snug basement nest to look at drops of water going by. Warm browns and tans convey the security of the dark basement, but the little mouse soon leaves this safe environment for bright daylight and adventure. He overbalances as he peeks out, falls into a plumber's pocket, and is carried upstairs. The mouse creeps out of the pocket and into a box of doughnuts. He is carried out of the house while tucked inside a doughnut he's nibbling. Curiosity and a desire to nibble on various tasty treats lead the tiny character from one hiding place to another as he is carried on a lengthy journey through the city. The small mouse finally rides on a lady's hat back to the original kitchen, where he slips down to his own nest and his mother's welcome.

An interesting technique is used to show the sequence in this book, in which larger pictures set the overall scene, middle-size pictures show intermediate activity, and small close-up pictures show the mouse in his current hiding place. These pictures are overlapped in various arrangements on cream pages, with the overlapping indicating the order in which to read the pictures. The pleasant watercolors are clear. Although the mouse is not always visible, clues allow the reader to guess where he might be. Readers enjoy following the mouse's journey and predicting where he will turn up next. People in the bustling town are oblivious to the mouse, creating humor as the reader knows how upset the humans would be if they knew a mouse was there. Other animals in the book sense the mouse, but humans pay them no attention. The chance journey includes drama as well as humor — for example, the scene in which the mouse is in a cup on the street as a car drives directly toward him.

In the Library (or In the Classroom)

COLLECTION DEVELOPMENT

Mice are timid creatures, but many authors and illustrators have made them the central characters in adventure stories. Include *Mouse Around* with other titles in displays, booklists, text sets, thematic units, and programs in which mice have unusual adventures.

RELATED MATERIALS

Barbaresi, Nina. *Firemouse*. Crown, 1987.

Emberley, Michael. *Ruby*. Little, Brown, 1990.

Jacques, Brian. *Redwall*. Philomel, 1986.

King-Smith, Dick. *Magnus Powermouse*. Illustrated by Mary Rayner. Harper & Row, 1982.

McCully, Emily Arnold. *Picnic*. Harper, 1984.

Miller, Edna. *Mousekin's Frosty Friend*. Simon & Schuster, 1990.

Selden, George. *Harry Kitten and Tucker Mouse*. Illustrated by Garth Williams. Farrar, Straus & Giroux, 1986.

Sharp, Margery. *The Rescuers*. Illustrated by Garth Williams. Little, Brown, 1959.

Titus, Eve. *Basil of Baker Street*. Illustrated by Paul Galdone. Simon & Schuster, 1958.

MEDIA PROGRAM AND BOOKTALK

Use the film or video of *The Mouse and the Motorcycle* to introduce books in which mice characters travel and have adventures. Follow the film with a booktalk that includes *Mouse Around*.

RELATED MATERIALS

Buchanan, Heather. *Emily Mouse's First Adventure*. Dial, 1985.

Cleary, Beverly. *The Mouse and the Motorcycle*. Illustrated by Louise Darling. Morrow, 1965.

———. *Runaway Ralph*. Illustrated by Louise Darling. Morrow, 1970.

Geraghty, Paul. *Look Out, Patrick!* Macmillan, 1990.

Noll, Sally. *Watch Where You Go*. Greenwillow, 1990.

Peppe, Rodney. *The Mice and the Clockwork Bus*. Lothrop, Lee & Shepard, 1986.

Steptoe, John. *The Story of Jumping Mouse*. Lothrop, Lee & Shepard, 1984.

RELATED NONPRINT MATERIALS

The Mouse and the Motorcycle. 16mm film/video. Churchill Films, 1986.

GAME

Create a bulletin board game for younger children based on *Mouse Around*. Place a picture of the little mouse in the center of the board. Make a pocket on one side of the board to hold game cards, and two pockets on the other side for sorting the cards. One sorting pocket should be labeled "Yes" and the other "No." Make 22 game cards with a picture of an object on each. Eleven of the cards should be pictures of the places where little mouse is shown hiding in the book, and 11 should be unrelated places, such as a telephone or a clock. Challenge children to sort the cards while they check in the book to be sure the mouse actually hides in each place.

STORY AND CRAFT PROGRAM

Settle children down with a fingerplay rhyme such as "There's such a tiny little mouse" or "Little mice." Introduce *Mouse Around* with the cover picture of the tiny mouse leaning out of his nest. The story can be told with help from the children. After helping you tell the story, children may make a little mouse finger puppet. Cut two pieces of felt for the mouse body and two small circles of felt for the ears. Children make the puppet by gluing the seams together, gluing the ears on, and drawing the face with a permanent marker. While the glue dries, the children can select a mouse story to read. To conclude the program, you may want to invite children to wear their puppets and recite the same fingerplay that you began the session with.

RELATED MATERIALS

Arnosky, Jim. *Mouse Writing*. Harcourt Brace Jovanovich, 1983.

Freeman, Don. *Norman the Doorman*. Viking, 1959.

Lionni, Leo. *Mouse Days*. Pantheon, 1981.

Miller, Edna. *Mousekin's Mystery*. Prentice-Hall, 1983.

Potter, Beatrix. *The Tale of Two Bad Mice*. Warne, 1904.

Titus, Eve. *Anatole*. Bantam, 1990. (Reprint)

Turk, Hanne. *Rainy Day Max*. Neugebauer Press, 1983.

Vincent, Gabrielle. *Ernest and Celestine*. Greenwillow, 1982.

Wells, Rosemary. *Noisy Nora*. Dial, 1973.

RELATED NONFICTION MATERIALS

Ring a Ring O' Roses: Stories, Games and Fingerplays for Pre-School Children. Flint Board of Education, 1981.

BOOKTALK

Mice live in many of the same places as people. Authors and illustrators can imagine mice in many different kinds of houses. The illustration on the cover of *Mouse Around* shows a mouse house built in the basement of a human house. Oscar Mouse in *Oscar Mouse Finds a Home* lives in a similar nest with many brothers and sisters, but he wants a new home.

Not every mouse lives in a human house. *The Supermarket Mice* are happy living in a store until a cat moves in. Churches are another place where mice might live. In *Cathedral Mouse*, another little mouse is looking for a home. Graham Oakley's *Church Mouse* is happy living in a British church. These mice are all city mice, but some mice live in the country. In fact, there is even a traditional story about mice in the city and in the country that has also been told by Beatrix Potter as *The Tale of Johnny Town-Mouse*.

Mice in the country might live in a wall, as Frederick does. They might find a nest to live in, as Mousekin does. They might have an unusual home, like the mouse in *Two in a Pocket*. An imaginary home in the country shows mice living in a tree in *The Secret Staircase*. The mouse in *The House* uses his teeth and his wits to create his own home out of the pages of the book that he is in. Perhaps the strangest house of all is the one in *The Maid and the Mouse and the Odd-Shaped House*. Like the little mouse in *Mouse Around*, all these mice are glad to be home by the end of the book.

RELATED MATERIALS

Aesop. *The Town Mouse and the Country Mouse*. Illustrated by Lorinda Bryan Cauley. Putnam, 1984.

Barklem, Jill. *The Secret Staircase*. Philomel, 1983.

Chorao, Kay. *Cathedral Mouse*. Dutton, 1988.

Felix, Monique. *The House*. Creative Education, 1991.

Gordon, Margaret. *The Supermarket Mice*. Dutton, 1984.

Lionni, Leo. *Frederick*. Pantheon, 1967.

Miller, Edna. *Mousekin's Golden House*. Simon & Schuster, 1964.

Miller, Moira, and Maria Majewska. *Oscar Mouse Finds a Home*. Dial, 1985.

Oakley, Graham. *The Church Mouse*. Atheneum, 1972.

Potter, Beatrix. *The Tale of Johnny Town-Mouse*. Warne, 1918.

Ravilious, Robin. *Two in a Pocket*. Little, Brown, 1991.

Zelinsky, Paul O. *The Maid and the Mouse and the Odd-Shaped House*. Dodd, Mead, 1981.

In the Classroom (or In the Library)

LANGUAGE ARTS AND ART

As you share this book, notice all the places the little mouse hides while traveling from place to place. Make a list on the chalkboard of all the places the students remember, then organize the list by sequences.

Discuss ways that the little mouse might travel around your school. Where would he hide? Have students develop a class story with one student starting the story and the next student continuing it. Record student ideas on the board. When the story is finished, students can make individual books by writing the class story in their book and then illustrating each sequence. Or, have students make a class mural with the story written along the bottom.

DRAMATICS

As the little mouse travels around, he overhears many different conversations: the plumber and the mother; the mother and the brother and sister; the man with the wrecked car and the tow truck driver; the man with the wrecked car and the auto repairman; the mother and her small child at the store; the two women having coffee.

Have students each select one scene and imagine that they are the little mouse overhearing the conversation in that scene. Conversations should be written down using dialogue format. Students can choose a partner and rehearse their dialogue to be presented in a short skit in front of the class (or, for another class). Arrange the skits in sequential order according to the book, and have a little mouse character that can go from scene to scene to tie the skits together.

LANGUAGE ARTS I

In the last illustration of *Mouse Around* the little mouse is returning to his home after an adventure-filled day. There are many different ways for the little mouse to tell his mother about where he has been. He might relate his adventures by understating them, as the child did in *The Day Jimmy's Boa Ate the Wash*. Or he could use the format of unfortunately/fortunately found in the book *Fortunately*. The little mouse could also relate his adventures in a narrative form. Students can pretend they are the little mouse and write what they would tell their mouse mother about their day. When finished, students can read their accounts aloud and then display them on a bulletin board.

RELATED MATERIALS

Charlip, Remy. *Fortunately*. Four Winds/Macmillan, 1984. (Reprint)

Noble, Trinka Hakes. *The Day Jimmy's Boa Ate the Wash*. Illustrated by Steven Kellogg. Dial, 1980.

LANGUAGE ARTS II

Read aloud the book *Two Terrible Frights*, in which a young girl and a small mouse meet and frighten one another when they go to get a bedtime snack. When they run to their own mothers for comfort, they are told that the other was probably more frightened than they were. You may also want to share *Mouse and Tim*, in which the two characters alternate in telling their experiences by way of their inner thoughts.

As the young mouse in *Mouse Around* travels through his day, he comes in contact with numerous other characters. Working individually or in pairs, students can write the inner thoughts of both the mouse and the character in a particular scene. What is the plumber thinking as he works on the basement pipes? What does the little mouse think as he sees the plumber and falls into his pocket? What does the young boy think as he rides his bicycle off to deliver newspapers? What does the little mouse think as he rides along in the paper bag? And so forth.

RELATED MATERIALS

Aylesworth, Jim. *Two Terrible Frights*. Illustrated by Eileen Christelow. Atheneum, 1987.

McNulty, Faith. *Mouse and Tim*. Illustrated by Marc Simont. Harper & Row, 1978.

SCIENCE AND LIBRARY RESEARCH

Use *Mouse Around* to begin a discussion and research on real mice. As children ask questions about mice, record the questions on the chalkboard for later research. Typical questions might include: Where do mice live? What do they eat? Are mice good pets? Do mice carry disease? Students can select a question and work individually or in small groups to gather information to answer that question.

RELATED NONFICTION MATERIALS

Broekel, Ray. *Gerbil Pets and Other Small Rodents*. Childrens Press, 1983.

Burton, Robert. *The Mouse in the Barn*. Photographs by Oxford Scientific Films. Gareth Stevens, 1988.

Lavine, Sigmund. *Wonders of Mice*. Dodd, Mead, 1980.

Oxford Scientific Films. *House Mouse*. Photographs by David Thompson. Putnam, 1978.

Pope, Joyce. *Taking Care of Your Mice and Rats*. Watts, 1987.

Silverstein, Alvin, and Virginia Silverstein. *Mice: All About Them*. Lippincott, 1980.

Steinberg, Phillip Orso. *Rodents and Rabbits*. Illustrated by Christine Cummings. Lerner, 1979.

Wexler, Jerome. *Pet Mice*. Whitman, 1989.

How Anansi Obtained the Sky God's Stories:
An African Folktale from the Ashanti Tribe
Childrens, 1991.
ISBN 0-516-45134-0; LC 91-7581

ABOUT THE AUTHOR AND HER BOOKS

Janice Skivington was born in Colorado. When she was a baby, her family moved and she grew up in the Philippine Islands, where her parents were missionaries. She returned to the United States for college and studied art, enjoying it so much that it took her six years of courses to finish a four-year B.F.A. degree. She wanted to illustrate children's books and learned about publishing by working for magazines and advertising agencies before she began illustrating children's books. She and her husband have four children and live in Wheaton, Illinois.

Selected Books Illustrated by the Author

The Free Pigs by Monard Sanford. Mill Creek Enterprises, 1987.

Girl from the Sky: An Inca Folktale. Childrens Press, 1992. (Adventures in Storytelling Series)

A Tale of Foreverland. Intervarsity Press, 1992.

A Tangled Web by Kristi Holl. Standard, 1991.

Trusting in the Dark by Kristi Holl. Standard, 1990.

Two of a Kind by Kristi Holl. Standard, 1990.

ABOUT HOW ANANSI OBTAINED THE SKY GOD'S STORIES

In the introduction of this book, the idea of storytelling as a cultural activity is emphasized. The wordless content is not intended here to supply the entire plot of the story, but to provide the context for the oral interpretation of the story in the reader's own language. Afterward, one version of the tale is printed as a guide for those who are unfamiliar with the story. The book is a bridge between the nonreader and books, since the story is not completely comprehensible from the illustrations, yet the illustration is sufficient to recall the story from a prior knowledge of it.

The human storyteller sits in an African village, holding up a story bag, and begins the tale. The bag becomes the bag in the hands of the sky god, as Anansi the spider goes to ask for stories. The sky god sets three tasks as the price of the stories, and Anansi's cleverness enables him to trap three creatures—a hornet, a snake, and a leopard—and pay the required price. As the trickster climbs down a thorn tree, the bag catches on a thorn, and the stories are spread throughout the world. The final illustration returns to the human storyteller.

Large size and bright color make the illustrations easy to share with a group. Unlike some other representations of Anansi, here he is not made to appear human, but is a large black spider. Only his eyes show a minimum of expression. Careful touches of African culture convey the background of the story—the sky god wears a mask, the stories are represented by stylized animal figures, and Anansi's web is made of geometrical forms similar to Ashanti fabric designs.

In the Library (or In the Classroom)

CRAFT AND CREATIVE DRAMATICS PROGRAM

Share this story with a group, pointing out the mask that the sky god wears. Show illustrations from two other African folktales, *Who's in Rabbit's House?* and *Why the Sun and the Moon Live in the Sky*, which have characters wearing masks. Demonstrate a method of making masks—either paper masks from grocery bags as shown in *Make-Up, Costumes and Masks for the Stage*, or original masks as shown in *Papercrafts*. Participants can select a character from the story and create a mask of their character. After the masks are made, have the group enact the story while it is being told.

RELATED MATERIALS

Aardema, Verna. *Who's in Rabbit's House? A Masai Tale*. Illustrated by Leo Dillon and Diane Dillon. Dial, 1977.

Dayrell, Elphinstone. *Why the Sun and the Moon Live in the Sky: An African Folktale*. Illustrated by Blair Lent. Houghton Mifflin, 1968.

RELATED NONFICTION MATERIALS

Bruun-Rasmussen, Ole, and Grete Petersen. *Make-Up, Costumes and Masks for the Stage*. Sterling, 1972. ("Paper Masks")

Corwin, Judith Hoffman. *Papercrafts: Origami, Papier-Mâché, and Collage*. Watts, 1988.

Cosner, Sharon. *Masks Around the World, and How to Make Them*. Illustrated by Ann George. McKay, 1979.

Glubok, Shirley. *The Art of Africa*. Harper & Row, 1965.

Monti, Franco. *African Masks*. Hamlyn, 1969.

Price, Christine. *Dancing Masks of Africa*. Scribner, 1975.

COLLECTION DEVELOPMENT

Include *How Anansi Obtained the Sky God's Stories* in displays, booklists, text sets, thematic units, and programs on African folktales in picture books.

RELATED MATERIALS

Aardema, Verna. *Bringing the Rain to Kapiti Plain: A Nandi Tale*. Illustrated by Beatriz Vidal. Dial, 1981.

_____. *Why Mosquitoes Buzz in People's Ears: A West African Tale*. Illustrated by Leo Dillon and Diane Dillon. Dial, 1975.

Bowden, Joan Chase. *Why the Tides Ebb and Flow*. Illustrated by Marc Brown. Houghton Mifflin, 1979.

Grifalconi, Ann. *The Village of Round and Square Houses*. Little, Brown, 1986.

Knutson, Barbara. *How the Guinea Fowl Got Her Spots: A Swahili Tale of Friendship*. Carolrhoda, 1990.

_____. *Why the Crab Has No Head: An African Tale*. Carolrhoda, 1987.

Lexau, Joan M. *Crocodile and Hen*. Illustrated by Joan Sandin. Harper, 1969.

MAKING A DISPLAY

Use the fake spider webs sold at Halloween time to create the image of webs around this book. Position several large plastic spiders on the webs or dangling from them. Surround the display with other books that have spiders as main characters, and invite children to read them.

RELATED MATERIALS

Baker, Jeannie. *One Hungry Spider*. André Deutsch, 1982.

Carle, Eric. *The Very Busy Spider*. Philomel, 1989.

Climo, Shirley. *The Cobweb Christmas*. Illustrated by Joe Lasker. Crowell, 1982.

Kraus, Robert. *How Spider Saved Easter*. Hastings House, 1988.

McNulty, Faith. *The Lady and the Spider*. Illustrated by Bob Marstall. HarperCollins, 1986.

White, E. B. *Charlotte's Web*. Illustrated by Garth Williams. Harper, 1952.

Yolen, Jane. *Spider Jane*. Illustrated by Stefen Bernath. Coward, 1978.

RELATED NONFICTION MATERIALS

Climo, Shirley. *Someone Saw a Spider: Spider Facts and Folktales*. Illustrated by Dirk Zimmer. Crowell, 1985.

BOOKSHARING AND WRITING PROGRAM

Storytelling has had an important role in most cultures. Share several tales about the origin of stories before inviting participants to create their own written myth about the origin of stories.

RELATED MATERIALS

Bruchac, Joseph. *Turkey Brother and Other Tales: Iroquois Folk Stories*. Crossing Press, 1975. (pp. 15-16)

DeWitt, Dorothy. *The Talking Stones: An Anthology of Native American Tales and Legends*. Greenwillow, 1979. (pp. 5-9)

Guirma, Frederic. *Tales of Mogho: African Stories from Upper Volta*. Macmillan, 1971.

Haley, Gail E. *A Story, A Story: An African Tale*. Atheneum, 1970.

Parker, Arthur Caswell. *Skunny Wundy: Seneca Indian Tales*. Illustrated by George Armstrong. Whitman, 1926; 1970.

Rockwell, Anne. *The Story Snail*. Macmillan, 1974.

Troughton, Joanna. *How Stories Came into the World: A Folk Tale from West Africa*. Bedrick/Blackie, 1989.

BOOKTALK

In the folklore of many cultures, characters have been challenged to travel to the sky, and many different methods have been imagined. Share the illustrations and story of *How Anansi Obtained the Sky God's Stories* with a group. As you retell the story, note that Spider is shown spinning a web to a cloud to get up in the sky. When Spider has to carry the bag down, he climbs down a thorn tree. In many other stories, characters get to the sky in other unusual ways. The most familiar is probably *Jack and the Beanstalk*, which you can introduce by describing Jack's method of getting to the sky, and letting the participants guess the story. Other methods are not as familiar: taping ladders together as the characters do in *Painting the Moon*, or shooting arrows into each other as the boy does in *The Angry Moon*. The boy in *Arrow to the Sun* is actually shot as an arrow to the sky. The most unusual method of getting to the sky is in a Japanese folktale. Badger's magic fan causes his nose to lengthen until it reaches the sky, taking him with it.

RELATED MATERIALS

Johnston, Tony. *The Badger and the Magic Fan: A Japanese Folktale*. Illustrated by Tomie dePaola. Putnam, 1990.

Kellogg, Steven. *Jack and the Beanstalk*. Morrow, 1991.

McDermott, Gerald. *Arrow to the Sun: A Pueblo Indian Tale*. Viking, 1974.

Sleator, William. *The Angry Moon*. Illustrated by Blair Lent. Little, Brown, 1970.

Withers, Carl. *Painting the Moon: A Folktale from Estonia*. Illustrated by Adrienne Adams. Dutton, 1970.

In the Classroom (or In the Library)

SOCIAL STUDIES AND LIBRARY RESEARCH

The Ashanti (also spelled Asante) are the largest and most powerful ethnic group in the West African country of Ghana. There are approximately one and a half million Ashanti living in the Ashanti region of south central Ghana. Introduce the Ashanti with this book. As you share the story, have students notice the environment, including plant and animal life. What type of houses are shown? What type of clothing do the people wear? Have students use library resources to learn about the Ashanti. Include the following:

- Political history, including British colonial period

- Language(s)

- Environment, types of shelter, foods, clothing, education

- Family life

- Music, arts, and crafts

RELATED NONFICTION MATERIALS

Barnett, Jeanie. *Ghana*. Chelsea House, 1989.

Bleeker, Sonia. *The Ashanti of Ghana*. Morrow, 1966.

Ghana in Pictures. Lerner, 1988.

Hintz, Martin. *Ghana*. Childrens Press, 1987.

Musgrove, Margaret. *Ashanti to Zulu: African Traditions*. Illustrated by Diane Dillon and Leo Dillon. Dial, 1976.

Sale, J. Kirkpatrick. *The Land and People of Ghana*. Lippincott, 1972.

LITERATURE SHARING

Anansi the Spider is a favorite West African story character, and there are many stories about him. (His name is spelled Ananse in some versions.) Share Skivington's version with students and then the Caldecott Award version, *A Story, A Story* by Gail E. Haley. Have students compare the two versions. How are they alike? How do they differ? Each day share another Anansi story aloud with the class and have students react to it.

Students can design bulletin board displays of Anansi and his various adventures.

RELATED MATERIALS

Aardema, Verna. *Anansi Finds a Fool: An Ashanti Tale*. Illustrated by Bryna Waldman. Dial, 1992.

Anansi Goes Fishing. Retold by Eric A. Kimmel. Illustrated by Janet Stevens. Holiday House, 1991.

Appiah, Peggy. *Ananse the Spider: Tales from an Ashanti Village*. Illustrated by Peggy Wilson. Pantheon, 1966.

Arkhurst, Joyce Cooper. *The Adventures of Spider: West African Folk Tales*. Illustrated by Jerry Pinkney. Little, Brown, 1964.

Bryan, Ashley, reteller. *The Dancing Granny*. Atheneum, 1977.

Cole, Joanna, selector. *Best-Loved Folktales of the World*. Illustrated by Jill Karla Schwarz. Doubleday, 1983. ("Anansi and His Visitor, Turtle," pp. 618-19; "Anansi Play with Fire, Anansi Get Burned," pp. 741-814; "Anansi's Hat Shaking Dance," pp. 615-17; "How Spider Obtained the Sky-God's Stories," pp. 620-23).

Haley, Gail E. *A Story, A Story: An African Tale*. Atheneum, 1970.

McDermott, Gerald. *Anansi the Spider: A Tale from the Ashanti*. Holt, Rinehart & Winston, 1972.

Sherlock, Philip M. *Anansi, the Spider Man: Jamaican Folk Tales*. Illustrated by Marcia Brown. Crowell, 1954.

RELATED NONPRINT MATERIALS

Ananse's Farm. 16mm film/video. National Film Board of Canada.

ART AND LANGUAGE ARTS

As you share this story, have students notice the fabric that the people's clothing is made of. Ashanti weavers are famous for producing the colorful kente cloth, from which the national dress of Ghana is made. Have students notice the beautiful story bag that the sky god keeps his stories in. Students can make individual story bags and write a story to put in it, or the class can work on a large, colorful class story bag, with each student contributing an original story to the bag to be shared with the class.

Simple individual story bags can be made by decorating white paper lunch bags. Fabric bags can be made using a simple pattern and fabric crayons.

RELATED MATERIALS

Trowell, Kathleen. *African Designs*. Praeger, 1971.

TEXT SET AND THEME UNIT

Anansi is a trickster. There are stories of tricksters in many cultures. Use *How Anansi Obtained the Sky God's Stories* to introduce trickster tales. Read aloud a variety of trickster tales and invite class discussion on their similarities and differences. Is it possible by listening to the story to tell what culture the story is from?

RELATED MATERIALS

Edmonds, I. G. *Trickster Tales*. Illustrated by Sean Morrison. Lippincott, 1966.

Galdone, Paul. *The Turtle and the Monkey: A Philippine Tale*. Clarion, 1983.

Goble, Paul. *Iktomi and the Buffalo Skull*. Orchard, 1990.

Harris, Joel Chandler. *The Complete Tales of Uncle Remus*. Compiled by Richard Chase. Houghton Mifflin, 1955.

Hodges, Margaret. *The Fire Bringer: A Paiute Indian Legend*. Illustrated by Peter Parnall. Little, Brown, 1972.

Robinson, Gail, and Douglas Hill. *Coyote, the Trickster: Legends of the North American Indians*. Illustrated by Graham McCallum. Crane Rusak, 1976.

_____. *Raven, the Trickster: Legends of the North American Indians*. Illustrated by Joanna Troughton. Atheneum, 1982.

NATURAL SCIENCE AND LIBRARY RESEARCH

This story mentions four different animals—Anansi the spider, Momboro the hornet, Onini the python, and Osebo the leopard. Have each student choose one of the animals to research using library resources. The students will want to find out all they can about their animal, including its habitat, food, shelter, life cycle, and so forth. Have students form four animal groups—spider, hornet, python, and leopard. Invite the groups to share their information with one another and decide how they will tell the rest of the class about their animals. They might develop a skit, a booklet, a multimedia presentation, or other.

Turkle, Brinton

Deep in the Forest
Dutton, 1976; 1987.
ISBN 0-525-28617-9; 0-525-44322-3 (pbk); LC 76-21691

ABOUT THE AUTHOR AND HIS BOOKS

Brinton Turkle was born on August 15, 1915, in Alliance, Ohio. He went to school at the Carnegie Institute of Technology (now called Carnegie-Mellon University) and the School of Boston Museum of Art. He works as an illustrator and is interested in music and in the theater. Brinton Turkle lives in New York City.

Selected Books by the Author

Do Not Open. Dutton, 1981.

The Fiddler of High Lonesome. Viking, 1968.

The Magic of Millicent Musgrave. Viking, 1967.

Mooncoin Castle. Viking, 1970.

Obadiah the Bold. Viking, 1965.

The Sky Dog. Viking, 1969.

Thy Friend, Obadiah. Viking, 1969.

Selected Books Illustrated by the Author

The Boy Who Didn't Believe in Spring by Lucille Clifton. Dutton, 1973.

The Elves and the Shoemaker by Freya Littledale. Four Winds, 1984.

Granny and the Indians by Peggy Parish. Macmillan, 1969.

If You Grew Up with Abraham Lincoln by Ann McGovern. Scholastic, 1980.

Over the River and Through the Woods by Lydia M. Child. Coward, McCann & Geoghegan, 1974.

Selected Media from the Author's Books

Rachel and Obadiah. Sound filmstrip. Live Oak Media, 1978.

Thy Friend, Obadiah. Sound filmstrip. Live Oak Media, 1971.

ABOUT DEEP IN THE FOREST

In this reversal of the traditional story of the three bears, a curious bear cub wanders away from his family and explores a cabin belonging to a frontier family. His destruction of the baby's bowl and chair and his crawling under the baby's quilt parallel the adventures of Goldilocks.

The little bear finds a rough-hewn table and crawls up on it to poke a curious nose into each successive bowl, tasting from papa's bowl, mama's bowl, and finally eating everything in the baby's bowl. He sits in each chair and breaks the baby's chair. The little bear then falls asleep in the baby's trundle bed.

The family returns: a bearded father, a comfortable mother, and a plump barefooted toddler with thick twisted curly locks. The family discovers the disarray of their home and chases the cub out. The bear then creeps away to rejoin his family in the woods.

Charcoal sketches create the deep woods setting in realistic detail. Gray and tan washes, and the orange of the cover, establish the time as autumn. The narrative quality of the pictures is enhanced by the occasional uses of frames, various size panels, backgrounds that vary from highly detailed to plain wash, and even a panel that wraps over pages.

In the Library (or In the Classroom)

STORYTELLING

Without suggesting the role reversal in *Deep in the Forest*, share the book with a small group. After the group realizes that the story is a reversed folktale, share the book a second time. Notice how their awareness affects the words the children suggest as they participate in telling the story the second time. Ask the group to suggest other stories that are very well known and ways the stories might be reversed. Another way a story might be changed is through changing the main character. Tell *The True Story of the 3 Little Pigs by A. Wolf* to demonstrate this. Invite the group to explore other altered tales.

RELATED MATERIALS

Emberley, Michael. *Ruby*. Little, Brown, 1990.

French, Fiona. *Snow White in New York*. Oxford University Press, 1987.

Gwynne, Fred. *Pondlarker*. Simon & Schuster, 1990.

Hewitt, Kathryn. *The Three Sillies*. Harcourt Brace Jovanovich, 1986.

Scieszka, Jon. *The Frog Prince, Continued*. Illustrated by Steve Johnson. Viking, 1991.

_____. *The True Story of the 3 Little Pigs by A. Wolf: As Told to Jon Scieszka*. Illustrated by Lane Smith. Viking Kestrel, 1989.

Williams, Jay. *The Practical Princess*. Illustrated by Frisco Henstra. Parents Magazine Press, 1969.

Yolen, Jane. *Sleeping Ugly*. Illustrated by Diane Stanley. Coward, 1981.

PROGRAM

The interior of the frontier cabin in *Deep in the Forest* is drawn in detail. Use the two-page illustration of the cabin as the bear goes in the door of the cabin to begin a program on pioneer life. Invite the participation of local historical societies, historical museums, or craftspeople to show children artifacts connected with frontier life.

RELATED MATERIALS

Edmonds, Walter D. *The Matchlock Gun*. Illustrated by Paul Lantz. Dodd, Mead, 1941.

Gorsline, Marie, and Douglas Gorsline. *The Pioneers*. Random House, 1978.

Henry, Joanne Landers. *Log Cabin in the Woods*. Illustrated by Joyce Andy Zarins. Four Winds, 1988.

Kalman, Bobbie. *The Early Family Home*. Crabtree, 1982.

Parish, Peggy. *Let's Be Early Settlers with Daniel Boone*. Illustrated by Arnold Lobel. Harper & Row, 1967.

Tunis, Edwin. *Frontier Living*. Crowell, 1961.

LITERATURE SHARING

In this book, the bear cub enters the human home and causes some destruction; however, the humans have also entered the bear's habitat and caused some destruction. The relationship between the woods and woodland creatures and the people who move into their environment can be explored by small groups of participants who compare and discuss related books set out in a display. In *A Clearing in the Forest*, a human family builds a cabin in the woods, and the animals attempt to drive them out of the woods; the humans are finally accepted. In the book *Miss Maggie*, the main character lives in a cabin in the woods and has a pet raven who has been tamed to live in the cabin with her.

RELATED MATERIALS

Carrick, Carol, and Donald Carrick. *A Clearing in the Forest*. Dial, 1970.

Rylant, Cynthia. *Miss Maggie*. Illustrated by Thomas Di Grazia. Dutton, 1983.

San Souci, Daniel. *North Country Night*. Doubleday, 1990.

COLLECTION DEVELOPMENT

Explore what might really happen when humans and bears meet. Include *Deep in the Forest* in displays, booklists, text sets, thematic units, and programs on encounters between bears and humans.

RELATED MATERIALS

Dalgliesh, Alice. *The Bears on Hemlock Mountain*. Illustrated by Helen Sewell. Macmillan, 1990. (Reprint)

Gage, Wilson. *Cully Cully and the Bear*. Illustrated by James Stevenson. Greenwillow, 1983.

McCloskey, Robert. *Blueberries for Sal*. Viking, 1948.

Naylor, Phyllis Reynolds. *Old Sadie and the Christmas Bear*. Illustrated by Patricia M. Newton. Atheneum, 1984.

Schwartz, Alvin. *Fat Man in a Fur Coat*. Illustrated by David Christiana. Farrar, Straus & Giroux, 1984.

Van Woerkom, Dorothy. *Becky and the Bear*. Illustrated by Margot Tomes. Putnam, 1975.

Ward, Lynd. *The Biggest Bear*. Houghton Mifflin, 1952.

MAKING A DISPLAY

Use *Deep in the Forest* as the center of a display featuring books about woodland animals during the fall. Use a dark brown or tan backdrop. Have children cut leaves from construction paper in tans, oranges, and yellows. Pin some of the leaves to the backdrop and scatter others about the display area. Open *Deep in the Forest* so that the front and back covers are both displayed. On the cover, the curious bear cub is peeking around the tree. He might be enlarged, drawn, cut out, and positioned as if peeking around the books.

RELATED MATERIALS

Bartoli, Jennifer. *Snow on Bear's Nose*. Illustrated by Takeo Ishida. Whitman, 1972.

Bird, E. J. *How Do Bears Sleep?* Carolrhoda, 1989.

Dabcovich, Lydia. *Sleepy Bear*. Dutton, 1982.

Freedman, Russell. *When Winter Comes*. Illustrated by Pamela Johnson. Dutton, 1981.

Miller, Edna. *Mousekin's Woodland Sleepers*. Prentice-Hall, 1970.

Tejima, Keizaburo. *Bear's Autumn*. Translated by Susan Matsui. Green Tiger, 1986.

In the Classroom (or In the Library)

DRAMATICS

Have students work individually or in pairs to write dialogue for a chance meeting between Goldilocks and the little bear from *Deep in the Forest*. After editing and revising the dialogue, have students pair up and practice the dialogue to present in front of the class. Simple props such as a blond wig and a bear mask might be used.

LANGUAGE ARTS I

Share *Deep in the Forest* with a group and have them discuss the similarities and differences between this story and the familiar tale "Goldilocks and the Three Bears." Both stories have curious main characters, although the characters and settings are different.

Invite students to write their own stories using a modern-day setting, a curious character, and a different environment. Examples might include:

- A curious possum in a condominium
- A curious monkey in a farmhouse
- A curious goat in a summer camp cabin
- A curious raccoon in a university dormitory
- A curious lamb in a farmhouse
- A curious kangaroo in a suburban house

LANGUAGE ARTS II

Deep in the Forest is set in an early American time period with a pioneer family who live in a log cabin in the woods. After sharing the book, have students imagine that they are one of the human characters in the book. They can write a letter to one of their friends or relatives living in the East about what they have experienced with the curious bear cub. Students should use good letter-writing form and address an envelope for their letter. After letters are completed, discuss mail delivery in early America. Develop a delivery system in the classroom so that each student receives another student's letter to read and answer.

RELATED MATERIALS

Brighton, Catherine. *Dearest Grandmama*. Doubleday, 1991.

LANGUAGE ARTS III

Make flannel board pieces for both *Deep in the Forest* and "Goldilocks and the Three Bears." After sharing both stories, invite students to retell one of the stories using the flannel board and flannel board pieces.

LITERATURE SHARING

The number *three* is important in many stories; there may be three characters, three episodes, and so forth. Have each student read three books with the number *three* in the title and then compare the books in chart form regarding the characters, setting, type of story, plot, and theme. A bulletin board can be made of the charts, and students can make an oral presentation to the class or to a small group about their stories and what they have learned.

RELATED MATERIALS

Bollinger, Max. *Three Little Bears*. Illustrated by Jozef Wilkon. Adama, 1987.

Croll, Carolyn. *The Three Brothers*. Putnam, 1991.

Galdone, Paul. *The Three Bears*. Clarion, 1985.

_____. *The Three Billy-Goats Gruff*. Clarion, 1981.

_____. *Three Little Pigs*. Clarion, 1979.

_____. *The Three Sillies*. Clarion, 1981.

Jeffers, Susan. *Three Jovial Huntsmen*. Macmillan, 1989.

Martin, C. L. G. *Three Brave Women*. Illustrated by Peter Elwell. Macmillan, 1991.

Suteyev, V. *Three Kittens*. Illustrated by Giulio Maestro. Crown, 1988.

Three Blind Mice. Illustrated by Lorinda Cauley. Putnam, 1991.

Zemach, Margot. *The Three Wishes: An Old Story*. Farrar, Straus & Giroux, 1986.

Ward, Lynd

The Silver Pony: A Story in Pictures
Houghton Mifflin, 1973.
ISBN 0-395-14753-0; LC 72-005402

ABOUT THE AUTHOR AND HIS BOOKS

Lynd Ward was born on June 26, 1905, in Chicago, Illinois. He received a B.S. degree from the Teachers College at Columbia University and then attended the National Academy for Graphic Arts in Leipsig, Germany. He was the director of the graphic arts division of the Federal Art Project during the Depression years of 1937-1939.

Lynd Ward has authored six wordless novels for adults using woodcuts. He has exhibited his wood engravings in numerous national art shows, and his prints are in permanent exhibits at many museums, including the Library of Congress, the Metropolitan Museum of Art, and the Smithsonian Institution. He has illustrated more than 80 books using wood engravings, lithography, ink, and oils. He has won numerous awards for his work, including the 1948 Library of Congress Award for wood engraving and the 1953 Caldecott Medal for *The Biggest Bear*.

Lynd Ward and his wife live in New Jersey. They have two grown daughters.

Selected Books by the Author

The Biggest Bear. Houghton Mifflin, 1952.

Nic of the Woods. Houghton Mifflin, 1965.

Selected Books Illustrated by the Author

America's Paul Revere by Esther Forbes. Houghton Mifflin, 1990.

Brady by Jean Fritz. Puffin, 1987. (Reprint)

Cat Who Went to Heaven by Elizabeth Coatsworth. Macmillan, 1930.

Early Thunder by Jean Fritz. Coward, 1967.

Fog Magic by Julia Sauer. Puffin, 1986. (Reprint)

Johnny Tremain by Esther Forbes. Houghton Mifflin, 1943.

The Little Red Lighthouse and the Great Gray Bridge by Hildegarde Swift. Harcourt Brace Jovanovich, 1942.

Selected Media from the Author's Books

The Biggest Bear. Sound filmstrip. Weston Woods, 1968.

The Silver Pony. 16mm film/video. Churchill Films, 1981.

ABOUT THE SILVER PONY

The Silver Pony is a novel-length wordless picture book, with all of the subtleties, subplots, symbolism, and complexities of a longer work of text-narrated fiction. This book can be read on many different levels. The plot revolves around a lonely midwestern farm boy who escapes from his limited world and has adventures in the larger world when he befriends a winged silver horse that no one else can see.

The winged horse takes the boy on four flights to the four directions pointed out by the weathervane on the top of the barn. During each flight the young rider sees another lonely child about his own age, and he interacts in some way with that child. In the far north, he shares an apple with an Eskimo boy who is ice fishing. Flying south, he provides a rowboat to a young African-American boy caught in a flood so the boy can rescue others. As he flies to the east, the boy carries an armload of sunflowers which he shares with a African-American girl on an inner-city rooftop and with another girl who lives in a lighthouse surrounded by the sea. In the west, the winged horse flies by a Navajo family, and the rider is able to rescue a lamb for its young herder. The fifth flight, however, takes the boy and horse into outer space, where rockets threaten them, and the boy falls off the horse and down through the night. He is found lying on the grass by his parents, who immediately call the doctor. The boy lies silently mourning the loss of his winged friend until his parents give him a real pony that looks very similar to his larger nighttime companion.

The artwork in the 80 pictures has a sculptural quality, especially in the faces and figures. The illustrations feature a wide tonal range of textured gray and white providing dramatic emphasis through the use of light and shadow.

In the Library (or In the Classroom)

COLLECTION DEVELOPMENT

Many children have imagined fantastic rides on either real or toy horses. Include *The Silver Pony* in displays, booklists, text sets, thematic units, and programs about such fantastic flights.

RELATED MATERIALS

Bauer, Marion D. *Touch the Moon*. Illustrated by Alix Berenzy. Clarion, 1987.

Byars, Betsy. *The Winged Colt of Casa Mia*. Illustrated by Richard Cuffari. Viking, 1973.

Dennis, Wesley. *Flip*. Viking, 1941.

Green, Timothy. *Mystery of Navajo Moon*. Northland, 1991.

McPhail, David. *Mistletoe*. Dutton, 1978.

Osborne, Mary Pope. *Moonhorse*. Illustrated by S. M. Saelig. Knopf, 1991.

Raney, Ken. *Stick Horse*. Medlicott Press, 1991.

Turska, Krystyna. *Pegasus*. Watts, 1970.

MAKING A DISPLAY

Many people collect model horses, and these horses can be used in a display featuring *The Silver Pony* and other books in which a horse is a special companion for the main character. Sprinkle silver stars on a dark background and hang a copy of the poem "The White Stallion" by Guy Owen or "The White Horse" by D. H. Lawrence; place *The Silver Pony* nearby. Use white fabric or silver foil to cover the display area, and position the horse models around the other books.

RELATED MATERIALS

Bulla, Clyde Robert. *Dexter*. Illustrated by Glo Coalson. Crowell, 1973.

Cohen, Peter Zachary. *Morena*. Illustrated by Haris Petie. Atheneum, 1970.

Hall, Lynn. *Mrs. Portree's Pony*. Scribner, 1986.

Henry, Marguerite. *King of the Wind*. Illustrated by Wesley Dennis. Rand McNally, 1948.

Lewis, C. S. *The Horse and His Boy*. Illustrated by Pauline Baynes. Macmillan, 1954.

Smith, Marya. *Winter-Broken*. Arcade, 1990.

Wallace, Bill. *Beauty*. Holiday House, 1988.

RELATED NONFICTION MATERIALS

Knock at a Star: A Child's Introduction to Poetry. Selected by X. J. Kennedy and Dorothy Kennedy. Little, Brown, 1982. ("The White Stallion"; "The White Horse")

BOOKTALK

Use *The Silver Pony* to introduce a booktalk on the theme of rescues. After describing the general plot, share the illustrations in which the boy and his flying horse help the boy and raccoon escape from the flood (p. 126) and in which they rescue the lamb (pp. 83-84). The boy also flies past a girl who lives in a lighthouse, just as Alex lives in a lighthouse in *Lighthouse Island*. In this book, Alex has to rescue his goat, Tagalong, from the rising tide.

Pets seem to get into trouble and need rescuing by their humans in many books. In *Silver*, Rachel rescues her sled dog puppy from a wolf. In *Travelers by Night*, two children, Charlie and Belle, kidnap an elephant in order to rescue her from the slaughterhouse, just as the two boys in *The Daring Rescue of Marlon the Swimming Pig* kidnap a pig to save it from being slaughtered.

Sometimes it is the animal that is the rescuer. The brown and white dog named Phil became famous for rescuing a lost child in Piatt County, Illinois, during the 1850s. This story can be found in the book *Go Find Hanka!*

RELATED MATERIALS

Alcock, Vivien. *Travelers by Night*. Delacorte, 1983.

Asch, Frank. *Pearl's Promise*. Delacorte, 1984.

Coatsworth, Elizabeth. *Lighthouse Island*. Illustrated by Symeon Shimin. Norton, 1968.

Crosby, Alexander. *Go Find Hanka!* Illustrated by Glen Rounds. Golden Gate Junior Books, 1970.

Gannett, Ruth Stiles. *My Father's Dragon*. Random House, 1986. (Reprint)

McInerney, Judith Whitelock. *Judge Benjamin: The Superdog Rescue*. Illustrated by Leslie Morrill. Holiday House, 1984.

Saunders, Susan. *The Daring Rescue of Marlon the Swimming Pig*. Illustrated by Gail Owens. Random House, 1987.

Steiner, Barbara. *Oliver Dibbs to the Rescue!* Illustrated by Eileen Christelow. Four Winds/Macmillan, 1985.

Whelan, Gloria. *Silver*. Illustrated by Stephen Marchesi. Random House, 1988.

BOOKSHARING AND WRITING PROGRAM

The loneliness and isolation that the boy feels in *The Silver Pony* is due to his living on a farm, away from other children. The flat landscape and distance between farms are often noted in books about farms in the Midwest. Develop a bulletin board and center the quote from the second paragraph of the first chapter of *The Wizard of Oz* where Dorothy talks about her Kansas farm. Leave plenty of space so that participants can find quotes to copy about farm life in the books that they look through, or invite them to write their own. Participants can read *The Silver Pony* and write a description of the farm shown in this book to include on the display board.

RELATED MATERIALS

Baum, L. Frank. *The Wizard of Oz*. Illustrated by Michael Hague. Holt, 1982. (Reprint)

Conrad, Pam. *Prairie Songs*. Illustrated by Darryl S. Zudeck. Harper & Row, 1985.

Fisher, Laura. *Never Try Nathaniel*. Holt, Rinehart & Winston, 1968.

Lawlor, Laurie. *Addie Across the Prairie*. Illustrated by Gail Owens. Whitman, 1986.

Mason, Miriam. *The Middle Sister*. Illustrated by Grace Paull. Macmillan, 1947.

Pellowski, Anne. *Willow Wind Farm: Betsy's Story*. Illustrated by Wendy Watson. Philomel, 1981.

Siebert, Diane. *Heartland*. Illustrated by Wendell Minor. Crowell, 1989.

Wyman, Andrea. *Red Sky at Morning*. Holiday House, 1991.

LITERATURE SHARING

Writers and illustrators both author their works by giving existence to their ideas through either textual or visual means. Lynd Ward has been prolific as an illustrator and has provided visual interpretations of many well-known books. Provide a display of books about illustrators as well as books they have illustrated and written. Compare the works of different illustrators for style and artistic technique. Try to imagine a book illustrated by Robert Lawson, redone by Dr. Seuss or Bill Peet—how would it change? Discuss the way that illustration and text work together to develop a story. As participants look at books about illustrators, have them design a book about Lynd Ward that can be kept in the library.

RELATED MATERIALS

Blegvad, Erik. *Self Portrait: Erik Blegvad*. Addison-Wesley, 1979.

Dr. Seuss from Then to Now. Random House, 1986.

Feelings, Tom. *Black Pilgrimage*. Lothrop, Lee & Shepard, 1972.

Hyman, Trina Schart. *Self Portrait: Trina Schart Hyman*. Harper & Row, 1981.

Lawson, Robert. *Robert Lawson, Illustrator*. Little, Brown, 1972.

Peet, Bill. *Bill Peet: An Autobiography*. Houghton Mifflin, 1989.

Zemach, Margot. *Self Portrait: Margot Zemach*. Addison-Wesley, 1978.

In the Classroom (or In the Library)

TEXT SET AND THEME UNIT

Weathervanes were an early weather instrument. They show the direction of the wind, which is one of the most important clues to forecasting weather. In earlier times, almost every house and barn in America had a weathervane. The earliest weathervanes were wind flags—strips of lightweight cloth attached to the top of a pole—which would indicate the direction of the wind. Later, large arrow forms were used. The feather part of the arrow was large enough to catch the wind, and the arrow would point in the direction that the wind was coming from; the letters N-E-W-S were used to indicate the direction.

Weathervanes became an art form with the arrow replaced by figures carved from wood or hammered out of metal. The rooster shape was a favorite because the large tail easily caught the wind; this form was often called a weathercock. The weathercock in the *The Silver Pony* points in the direction of each night's flight. Use the pictures of this weathercock to introduce weathervanes. Tell the folk story "The Half Chick," in which a chick refuses aid to a clogged stream, a dying fire, and the wind, and is later turned into a weathercock on a steeple.

The poem "The Pedaling Man" tells about a weathervane with a pedaling man who pedals in each direction into the weather. Use this poem as an introduction to having students make simple weathervanes. Directions can be found in *Evening Gray, Morning Red* and in Steven Caney's *Kid's America*.

Weathervanes are found in several fiction titles. In *Dorrie and the Haunted House*, Dorrie saves other witches from being turned into weathervanes. In *The Pentagon Spy*, the Hardy Boys search for valuable antique weathervanes. Another mystery is *The Case of the Wandering Weathervanes: A McGurk Mystery*.

RELATED MATERIALS

Arbuthnot, May Hill. *The Arbuthnot Anthology of Children's Literature*. Scott, Foresman, 1961. ("The Half Chick," pp. 264-66)

Coombs, Patricia. *Dorrie and the Haunted House*. Lothrop, Lee & Shepard, 1970.

Dixon, Franklin. *The Pentagon Spy*. Illustrated by Leslie Morrill. Wanderer Books, 1980.

Hildick, E. W. *The Case of the Wandering Weathervanes: A McGurk Mystery*. Illustrated by Denise Brunkus. Macmillan, 1988.

Tresselt, Alvin. *Bonnie Bess — The Weather Vane Horse*. Illustrated by Erik Blegvad. Parents Magazine Press, 1970.

Uttley, Alison. *The Weather Cock and Other Tales*. Illustrated by Nancy Innes. Faber & Faber, 1991.

RELATED NONFICTION MATERIALS

Caney, Steven. *Kid's America*. Workman, 1978.

Fitzgerald, Ken. *Weathervanes and Whirligigs*. C. N. Potter/Crown, 1967.

Gladstone, M. J. *A Carrot for a Nose: The Form of Folk Sculpture on America's City Streets and Country Roads*. Scribner, 1974. (pp. 11-18)

Hillman, Anthony. *Carving Early American Weathervanes: 16 Decorative Projects*. Dover, 1986.

Hoban, Russell. *The Pedaling Man and Other Poems*. Norton, 1968.

Schoonmaker, David. *Whirligigs and Weathervanes*. Sterling, 1991.

Wolff, Barbara. *Evening Gray, Morning Red: A Ready-to-Read Handbook of American Weather Wisdom*. Macmillan, 1976.

LANGUAGE ARTS

As the silver pony takes the boy flying through the night, the boy meets several other children that he could later correspond with. As a class, make a list of the children — the Eskimo boy, the boy in the flood, the girl on the rooftop, the girl at the lighthouse, and the Navajo boy. Have students work in pairs to write letters to each other pretending that one is the boy on the silver pony and the other is one of the children he meets. Introduce good letter-writing techniques. This could be a one-time assignment, or students could write back and forth for several weeks using a classroom mailbox.

RELATED NONFICTION MATERIALS

Joslin, Sesyle. *Dear Dragon ... and Other Useful Letter Forms for Young Ladies and Gentlemen Engaged in Everyday Correspondence*. Harcourt, Brace & World, 1962.

Leedy, Loreen. *Messages in the Mailbox: How to Write a Letter*. Holiday House, 1991.

Lincoln, Wanda, and Murray Suid. *For the Love of Letter Writing*. Monday Morning Press, 1983.

Mischel, Florence. *How to Write a Letter*. Rev. ed. Illustrated by Anne Canevari Green. Watts, 1988.

Oana, Katherine. *How to Write Notes*. Illustrated by Patti Carson and Janet Dellosa. Carson-Dellosa, 1984.

Tchudi, Susan, and Stephen Tchudi. *The Young Writer's Handbook*. Scribner, 1984.

LITERATURE SHARING

The Silver Pony is a unique wordless picture book due to its length and the fact that it is divided into seven chapters. This book provides the opportunity to examine how information in one chapter is used in developing the following chapters. Before reading the book in its entirety, divide the class into seven groups and assign one chapter to each group. As the group members read their chapter, have them take notes on characterization, scene, plot, and so forth. When all groups have had time to carefully examine their chapters, have the class tell the story of the silver pony, beginning with the first chapter and going to the last chapter. Then invite discussion about how much information readers were able to gather from reading only their chapter and how it helped to hear about the previous chapters in developing the story.

SOCIAL STUDIES AND LIBRARY RESEARCH I

As the young boy flies aboard the silver pony, he sees four very different regions of the United States—the far North, the deep South, the East Coast, and the Southwest. Divide the class into four groups to explore the differences the boy would find if he were able to stay with one of the children in each region for a week. Each group should select the state they think the boy would be visiting as well as the ethnic background of the child he would be visiting. Using library resources, each group can determine the following:

- What would the climate be like? What type of clothing would be appropriate in that climate?

- What is the geography of the area? What forms of transportation would be appropriate?

- What type of houses do people live in? Why?

- What types of work do people do?

- What foods would be eaten?

- What type of music, games, and leisure activities might be found?

- What stories or folklore are found in that area?

The classroom might be divided into four sections so that each group can display its findings. For the final presentation, each group could bring foods specific to its area to share with the rest of the class.

RELATED MATERIALS

Aylesworth, Thomas. *Kids' World Almanac of the United States*. Pharos Books, 1990.

Aylesworth, Thomas, and Virginia Aylesworth. *The Southwest (Texas, New Mexico, Colorado)*. Chelsea House, 1988.

Fifty Nifty States. Good Apple, 1990.

National Geographic Picture Atlas of Our Fifty States. National Geographic Society, 1988.

SOCIAL STUDIES AND LIBRARY RESEARCH II

Although the silver pony flew the boy only around America, he could have flown him anywhere in the world. Divide the class into four parts (north, south, east, west). Using a world map or globe, have students pretend that they are going to ride the silver pony from their own city to another city in the world. Each student can follow his or her own direction and select a different city to study. Using library resources, students can discover the following information:

- What language do people speak in that city?

- What is the climate like?

- What is the geography like?

- What country is the city in?

- What foods do people eat?

- What is the folklore of the country? (Find folktales to bring to class.)

- Other interesting information, such as sights to see, arts/crafts specific to the area, and so forth.

Students can make travel guides to their cities, or books of information. Students can share their books with the class, region by region.

RELATED MATERIALS

Lands and Peoples, 6 vols. Grolier, 1991.

The Marshall Cavendish New Illustrated Encyclopedia of the World and Its People, 19 vols. Marshall Cavendish, 1986.

Wright, Cliff

When the World Sleeps
Ideals Children's Books, 1989.
ISBN 0-8249-8443-9

ABOUT THE AUTHOR AND HIS BOOKS

Cliff Wright lives in Newhaven, England. He studied illustration at the Brighton College of Art and graduated in 1986. He has published greeting cards and a series of wildlife illustrations for the Royal Society for the Prevention of Cruelty to Animals. *When the World Sleeps* is Wright's first picture book. It was a runner-up for the Mother Goose Award.

Selected Book by the Author

Crumbs! Ideals Children's Books, 1990.

ABOUT WHEN THE WORLD SLEEPS

When a young boy wakes at night to look out his window at the full moon, he is shocked to see the moon tumble out of the sky and roll down a nearby hill. He puts his coat and boots on over his pajamas and goes out into the night to investigate, taking his dog and a flashlight. Small panels show the various night animals he finds, and the clues that lead him to the fallen moon.

In the full-page picture of the boy's discovery, the moon is seen with a drooping mustache and a sad, crater-pocked face. The boy laboriously rolls the moon back up the hill, but only succeeds in rolling it over the top and down the other side. It takes a little magical assistance from a tree to throw the moon back into the sky where it belongs. In the smiling light of the restored moon, animals dance with the boy before he and his dog return home to bed.

The watercolor illustration is appropriately luminous and shadowy, and it is presented in panels in various sizes and positions, with some unpaneled sequences showing such activity as the boy pulling off his boots and taking off his coat. The dreamlike quality of the woods at night is nicely contrasted with realistic detail, such as the muddy footprints of the dog on the boy's bed after they return from their adventure. The strong plot gives the book interest and appeal to a wide range of readers, even though the main character is a young boy.

In the Library (or In the Classroom)

LITERATURE SHARING

With a group of children, discuss what might happen if the moon were to come down from the sky. Compare ideas and share stories. Tell the scary story of *The Buried Moon*, and then share *When the World Sleeps*. Invite participants to compare the two stories, then to look at other books in which "the moon comes down," or is perceived to have fallen from the sky.

RELATED MATERIALS

Christiana, David. *Drawer in a Drawer*. Farrar, Straus & Giroux, 1990.

Demarest, Chris. *The Lunatic Adventure of Kitman and Willy*. Simon & Schuster, 1988.

Hodges, Margaret. *The Buried Moon*. Illustrated by Jamichael Henterly. Little, Brown, 1990.

Levitin, Sonia. *Who Owns the Moon?* Illustrated by John Larrecq. Parnassus, 1973.

Preston, Edna Mitchell. *Squawk to the Moon, Little Goose*. Illustrated by Barbara Cooney. Viking, 1974.

Ungerer, Toni. *Moon Man*. Harper, 1967.

Willard, Nancy. *The Nightgown of the Sullen Moon*. Illustrated by David McPhail. Harcourt, 1983.

MAKING A DISPLAY

When the boy in this story cannot roll the moon back into the sky, unexpected help comes from a tree that comes to life and catapults the moon to its rightful place. Develop a display of books that have trees that come to life in some way.

Use two armlike tree limbs and position them as if they are holding *When the World Sleeps*, which is displayed open to the double-page illustration in which the tree throws the moon back to its accustomed place in the sky. A related book display invites speculation about trees that come to life, or appear to come to life, and their characters.

RELATED MATERIALS

Bang, Molly. "The Mad Priest," in *The Buried Moon and Other Stories*. Scribner, 1977.

Baum, L. Frank. "Attacked by the Fighting Trees," in *The Wizard of Oz*. Illustrated by Michael Hague. Holt, Rinehart & Winston, 1982.

Brown, Roberta. *The Walking Trees and Other Scary Stories*. August House, 1991.

Heller, Nicholas. *The Tooth Tree*. Greenwillow, 1991.

Kraus, Robert, and Mischa Richter. *Rumple Nose-Dimple and the Three Horrible Snaps*. Simon & Schuster, 1969.

Mahy, Margaret. "Chocolate Pudding," in *The Girl with the Green Ear*. Illustrated by Shirley Hughes. Knopf, 1992.

Martin, Bill, Jr., and John Archambault. *The Ghost-Eye Tree*. Illustrated by Ted Rand. Holt, 1985.

Tolkien, J. R. R. "Treebeard," in *The Two Towers*. Houghton Mifflin, 1965.

Updike, David. *An Autumn Tale*. Illustrated by Robert Parker. Pippin, 1988.

STORYHOUR

Begin a storyhour by chanting or singing the old rhyme "I see the moon and the moon sees me." Tell the story of *The Moon Jumpers* while showing the double-page illustrations in the book; at the end of this story, the characters go inside to bed. The Man in the Moon knows when it is time for bed in the nursery rhyme "The Man in the Moon looked out of the moon." After chanting this rhyme, lead participants to the idea that after we are in bed, something wonderful might happen—even things that no one else will believe. Share the book *Lemon Moon*, which ends with a wordless sequence. Introduce *When the World Sleeps* with the rhyme "The Man in the Moon came down too soon..." (in other versions, "The Man in the Moon came tumbling down..."). In the book *When the World Sleeps*, the reader looks at one person's idea of what might happen if the Man in the Moon came down. Audiences enjoy helping you tell the story. A display of moon-related night adventures can accompany the program.

RELATED MATERIALS

Averill, Esther. *Jenny's Moonlight Adventure.* Harper, 1949.

Chorao, Kay. *Lemon Moon.* Holiday House, 1983.

Horwitz, Elinor Lander. *When the Sky Is Like Lace.* Illustrated by Barbara Cooney. Lippincott, 1975.

Poppel, Hans, and Ilona Bodden. *When the Moon Shines Brightly on the House.* Barron's, 1984.

Random House Book of Mother Goose. Selected and illustrated by Arnold Lobel. Random House, 1986. ("I See the Moon...")

The Real Mother Goose. Illustrated by Blanche Fisher Wright. Rand McNally, 1916. ("The Man in the Moon Looked Out of the Moon")

Ring o' Roses. Illustrated by L. Leslie Brooke. Warne, 1987. ("The Man in the Moon Came Tumbling Down")

Udry, Janice May. *The Moon Jumpers.* Illustrated by Maurice Sendak. Harper & Row, 1959.

COLLECTION DEVELOPMENT

Include *When the World Sleeps* in displays, booklists, text sets, thematic units, and programs about moon picture books.

RELATED MATERIALS

Alexander, Martha. *Maggie's Moon.* Dial, 1982.

Asch, Frank. *Moon Bear.* Scribner, 1978.

Baylor, Byrd. *Moon Song.* Illustrated by Ronald Himler. Scribner, 1982.

Brown, Margaret Wise. *Wait Till the Moon Is Full.* Illustrated by Garth Williams. Harper, 1948.

Dayrell, Elphinstone. *Why the Sun and the Moon Live in the Sky.* Illustrated by Blair Lent. Houghton Mifflin, 1990. (Reprint)

Griffith, Helen. *Alex Remembers.* Illustrated by Donald Carrick. Greenwillow, 1983.

Sleator, William. *The Angry Moon.* Illustrated by Blair Lent. Little, Brown, 1970.

Watson, Clyde. *Midnight Moon.* Illustrated by Susanna Natti. Collins & World, 1979.

WRITING INTEREST CENTER

Set up a display with copies of *When the World Sleeps* against a blue background. Stick shiny stars to the background and letter the lines from the opening of the book: "One night, when the world was asleep, something magical happened. No one knew of it, except...."

Use the same lines at the top of blank pages of paper, which can be put in a box at the center; place pencils nearby. Invite children to make up their own account of a magical nighttime adventure. Put their pages into a dark blue looseleaf notebook for others to read.

In the Classroom (or In the Library)

PROBLEM SOLVING

Have a class discussion. What is the problem in this story? How did the boy try to solve the problem? How did the problem get resolved? Invite students to suggest other possible solutions for the problem of the moon getting back to the sky.

Have students spend a few minutes thinking up imaginary problems. On the top of a sheet of paper have each student write out an imaginative problem to be solved, beginning: "The Problem.... Students then exchange papers and the next person writes down several possible ways to solve the problem using one sentence per solution: Ways to Solve the Problem.... Students exchange papers again, and the third person reads the problem and the possible solutions, then writes a complete paragraph on how the problem was solved, using one of the solutions or a different one that he or she has thought of.

When the writing is finished, have students exchange papers to read aloud — the problem, possible solutions, and how the problem was resolved.

SCIENCE AND LIBRARY RESEARCH I

The boy is very concerned about returning the moon to its place in the sky in *When the World Sleeps*. Where in the sky is the moon situated? Why is the moon important? This book shows a full moon, but the moon seems to change its size — why? Does the moon really have a face?

Invite the class to learn all they can about the moon by gathering class materials to study. Have students discuss and list the types of materials they might include (nonfiction books, reference sources, magazine articles, videos, filmstrips). Have small groups of students form research teams and formulate an inquiry question that they want to explore about the moon. List questions on the chalkboard with the names of the researchers to avoid duplication. The teams can share their research with one another as they learn about the moon.

COOKING AND ART

The moon in *When the World Sleeps*, with his large nose, sad eyes, and mustache, has an unusual face. Other picture books about the moon portray different types of faces. Read the poem "The Moon's the North Wind's Cookie" by Rachel Lindsay as an introduction to making moon-face cookies. As a class, bake large round cookies using a rolled dough recipe and cutting the cookies out with a 3-by-4-inch cutter. Students can draw moon-face patterns while the cookies are cooling. Prepare frosting in several colors for students to use to decorate their cookies; provide decorator tubes, toothpicks, and blunt knives.

RELATED MATERIALS

The Moon's the North Wind's Cooky: Night Poems. Selected and illustrated by Susan Russo. Lothrop, Lee & Shepard, 1979.

LANGUAGE ARTS

Read aloud a variety of poems about the moon and have students listen for the different ways one can write poetry using one topic. Copy the poems onto large sheets of paper to display around th classroom, and have books of poetry about the moon available for students to read. After students have read *When the World Sleeps*, have them write their own moon poems based on the story, using any style. Students can copy their poems neatly onto large sheets of paper to display.

RELATED MATERIALS

Bring Me All of Your Dreams. Selected by Nancy Larrick. M. Evans, 1980. ("Full Moon" by Walter de la Mare; "Who Knows If the Moon's" by e. e. cummings).

Field, Eugene. *Wynken, Blynken & Nod*. Illustrated by Susan Jeffers. Dutton, 1982.

Livingston, Myra Cohn. *The Moon and a Star: And Other Poems*. Harcourt, Brace & World, 1965. ("The Moon and a Star")

The Man in the Moon as He Sails the Sky and Other Moon Verse. Collected and illustrated by Ann Schweninger. Dodd, Mead, 1979.

Mizamura, Kazue. *Flower Moon Snow: A Book of Haiku*. Crowell, 1977.

Songs the Sandman Sings. Compiled by Gwendolyn Reed. Atheneum, 1969.

Still as a Star: A Book of Nighttime Poems. Selected by Lee Bennett Hopkins. Little, Brown, 1989.

SCIENCE AND LIBRARY RESEARCH II

When the boy and his dog go outside at night to help the moon, they encounter a number of animals who enjoy the night and are busy while the rest of the world sleeps. Have students look through the book carefully to find the animals, then make a class list. Discuss these animals and other animals that enjoy the nighttime. What night life might be found in different habitats (country, woods, seashore, city, desert, and so forth)?

Have each student choose an animal to learn about using library resources. Where does the animal live? What does it do during the daytime? What does it eat? Students can make a simple booklet to put their information in, with an illustration of their animal on the cover. Booklets can be displayed on a bulletin board covered with dark paper and labeled "Nature's Night Life."

RELATED MATERIALS

Banks, Merry. *Animals of the Night*. Illustrated by Ronald Himler. Scribner, 1990.

Burton, Robert. *Nature's Night Life*. Blandford Press, 1982.

Dragonwagon, Crescent. *Half a Moon and One Whole Star*. Illustrated by Jerry Pinkney. Macmillan, 1986.

Fisher, Aileen. *In the Middle of the Night*. Crowell, 1965.

Lindbergh, Reeve. *Midnight Farm*. Illustrated by Susan Jeffers. Dial, 1987.

Peters, Sharon. *Animals at Night*. Illustrated by Paul Harvey. Troll, 1983.

Rylant, Cynthia. *Night in the Country*. Illustrated by Mary Szilagyi. Bradbury, 1986.

San Souci, Daniel. *North Country Night*. Doubleday, 1990.

Stolz, Mary. *Night of Ghosts and Hermits: Nocturnal Life on the Seashore*. Illustrated by Susan Gallagher. Harcourt Brace Jovanovich, 1985.

Taylor, Kim. *Hidden by Darkness*. Delacorte, 1990.

The Other Bone

Harper & Row, 1984.
ISBN 0-06-026870-0; 0-06-026871-9 (lib); LC 83-47706

ABOUT THE AUTHOR AND HIS BOOKS

Ed Young was born on November 28, 1931, in Tientsin, China, and he spent his childhood in Shanghai. He attended the City College of San Francisco, the University of Illinois, and the Art Center College of Design, Los Angeles, where he received a degree in 1957. He did graduate study at the Pratt Institute in 1958-1959. He has been an instructor of visual communication and in tai chi chuan, a Chinese exercise he learned from an old Chinese master. He has also been director of the Shr Jung School in New York's Chinatown. Ed Young has illustrated over 30 books for young people. *The Emperor and the Kite* was a Caldecott Honor Book for 1968. *Chinese Mother Goose Rhymes* was on the 1969 Horn Book honor list. *Lon Po Po: A Red Riding Hood Story from China* won the 1990 Caldecott Award.

Selected Books by the Author

High on a Hill: A Book of Chinese Riddles. Collins, 1980.

Lon Po Po: A Red Riding Hood Story from China. Philomel, 1989.

The Rooster's Horns: A Chinese Puppet Play to Make and Perform. Collins, 1978. (Unicef Storycraft Book Series)

The Terrible Nung Gwama: A Chinese Folktale. Collins, 1978. (Unicef Storycraft Book Series)

Up a Tree. Harper & Row, 1983.

Selected Books Illustrated by the Author

Ai-Ling, Louie. *Yeh-Shen: A Cinderella Story from China*. Philomel, 1982.

Cats Are Cats: Poems Compiled by Nancy Larrick. Philomel, 1988.

Dawood, N. J. *Tales from the Arabian Nights*. Doubleday, 1978.

Frost, Robert. *Birches*. Holt, 1988.

Martin, Rafe. *Foolish Rabbit's Big Mistake*. Putnam, 1985.

Radin, Ruth Yaffe. *High in the Mountains*. Macmillan, 1989.

Root, Phyllis. *Moon Tiger*. Holt, Rinehart & Winston, 1985.

Scioscia, Mary. *Bicycle Rider*. Harper & Row, 1983.

Wolkstein, Diane. *8,000 Stones: A Chinese Folktale*. Doubleday, 1972.

Ziner, Feenie. *Cricket Boy*. Doubleday, 1977.

ABOUT THE OTHER BONE

In this book, tone and style are established on the title page, where the artist's name is cleverly written in the shape of a dog, enclosed in a small oriental artist's frame. The minimal background and gray sketches show the influence of oriental techniques in retelling this Aesop fable.

A flop-eared, long-tailed, short-haired hound is dreaming of a bone. A dream sequence shows the dog in overlapping action as she takes the dream bone and rolls over and over in ecstasy. The dog wakes, surprised that it was only a dream, then scratches, sniffs, and follows her nose to a garbage can. The dog knocks the can over and snatches a real bone from the cascade of trash. As she proudly carries the bone in her mouth, she sees her reflection in a pool of water. Thinking it is another dog, she snaps at the reflection and drops the bone into the water. Although she falls into the water, she can't retrieve the bone.

The dog is shown reacting in human ways—she is surprised at awakening from a dream and horrified at having dropped her bone in the water—yet the sketches are very naturalistic. A plain green line on cream-colored paper frames each sketch. With the minimal use of background, nothing appears that does not directly further the story. When the dog is first seen sleeping, isolated on the empty page, the reader does not know if the animal is outside or inside, nor in what part of the world this tale unfolds. Thus, all is concentrated on the substance of the story, reflecting the moral "beware lest you lose the substance by grasping at the shadow" (from *The Fables of Aesop*, retold by Joseph Jacobs). This moral is foreshadowed in the early dream sequence. Although some versions of this fable emphasize the greediness of the dog, in this version the character seems simply to be acting in a doglike manner.

In the Library (or In the Classroom)

PROGRAM

This story is adapted from an Aesop fable, "The Dog and the Shadow." Fables are a rich source for storytelling programs. Incorporate *The Other Bone* in either a single program or a series of programs featuring animal fables. Combine the techniques of storytelling, booktalking, and film/filmstrip or video viewing in the program. *The Other Bone* can be booktalked without using the illustrations, which are difficult to see from a distance.

RELATED BOOKSHARING MATERIALS

Aesop. *The Lion and the Mouse*. Illustrated by Ed Young. Doubleday, 1979.

Brown, Marcia. *Once a Mouse: A Fable Cut in Wood*. Scribner, 1961.

La Fontaine, Jean de. *The Lion and the Rat*. Illustrated by Brian Wildsmith. Watts, 1963.

McFarland, John. *Exploding Frog and Other Fables from Aesop*. Illustrated by James Marshall. Little, Brown, 1981.

RELATED STORYTELLING MATERIALS

Anno, Mitsumasa. *Anno's Aesop*. Orchard, 1989.

Hague, Michael, editor. *Aesop's Fables*. Holt, 1985.

Lobel, Arnold. *Fables*. Harper, 1980.

RELATED NONPRINT MATERIALS

An Aesop Anthology. Six sound filmstrips. American School Publishers.

Aesop's Fables. Video. SVE.

Aesop's Famous Fables. Filmstrips. SVE.

Lobel, Arnold. *Fables I*. Video/sound filmstrip; *Fables II*. Sound filmstrip. American School Publishers.

STORYHOUR

The dog in this fable is used to convey a message to the reader. Other authors have also used dogs in this way. After telling some short fables that have dogs as main characters, invite children to select books about dogs to read. Help them vocalize the "moral" or "message" they find in each book.

RELATED MATERIALS

Asch, Frank. *The Last Puppy*. Prentice-Hall, 1980.

Bonsall, Crosby. *Amazing the Incredible Super Dog*. Harper, 1986.

Flack, Marjorie. *Angus and the Cat*. Doubleday, 1989.

Gackenbach, Dick. *Bag Full of Pups*. Ticknor & Fields, 1983.

_____. *Claude and Pepper*. Clarion, 1979.

_____. *Claude the Dog*. Ticknor & Fields, 1984.

Peet, Bill. *The Whingdingdilly*. Houghton Mifflin, 1970.

Wagner, Jenny. *John Brown, Rose and the Midnight Cat*. Illustrated by Ron Brooks. Penguin, 1980.

Wildsmith, Brian. *Give a Dog a Bone*. Pantheon, 1985.

PROGRAM

Ed Young has illustrated many folktales. Use these tales in a program introducing him as an author and illustrator. After sharing information about his life, tell some of the stories that he has illustrated and share the illustrations. End the program with *The Other Bone*, showing the children how Ed Young wrote his name on the title page. You can enlarge this author's mark on a photocopier and make it into a bookmark for each child; include on the bookmark titles of books by Ed Young. Have paper and pencils available so that children can make animals of their own names.

RELATED MATERIALS

Ai-Ling, Louie. *Yeh-Shen: A Cinderella Story from China*. Illustrated by Ed Young. Philomel, 1982.

The Lion and the Mouse: An Aesop Fable. Illustrated by Ed Young. Doubleday, 1979.

Wyndham, Robert. *The Chinese Mother Goose Rhymes*. Illustrated by Ed Young. World, 1968.

Yolen, Jane. *The Emperor and the Kite*. Illustrated by Ed Young. World, 1967.

_____. *The Girl Who Loved the Wind*. Illustrated by Ed Young. Crowell, 1972.

Young, Ed. *Lon Po Po: A Red Riding Hood Story from China*. Philomel, 1989.

_____. *The Rooster's Horns: A Chinese Puppet Play to Make and Perform*. Collins, 1978. (Unicef Storycraft Book Series)

_____. *The Terrible Nung Gwama: A Chinese Folktale*. Collins, 1978. (Unicef Storycraft Book Series)

_____. *Up a Tree*. Harper & Row, 1983.

STORYHOUR

This fable begins as the dog dreams about a bone. After you have shared and discussed the fable with a small group, share the wordless picture book *Bobo's Dream*, which is also about a dog and his daydream. Compare and contrast the dreams of the two dogs and the action that follows.

RELATED MATERIALS

Alexander, Martha. *Bobo's Dream*. Dial, 1970.

Griffith, Helen V. *Plunk's Dreams*. Illustrated by Susan Lamb. Greenwillow, 1990.

MAKING A DISPLAY

When the dog sees her reflection in still water, she believes she is seeing another dog with a bone. Set up a display to draw attention to this and other books about reflections. Use a green background to pick up the green line frame in the book. Open the book to the page on which the dog leans over looking at herself and drops the bone. Obtain a large bone such as a cow bone (or use a large rawhide bone from a pet store) and position it under the displayed book. Lay a mirror under the bone so that viewers can see two bones. Pose a question for the viewer: "Which is the real bone?" Place multiple copies of the book and related materials nearby for checkout.

RELATED MATERIALS

Davies, Kay, and Wendy Oldfield. *My Mirror*. Photographs by Fiona Pragoff. Doubleday, 1990.

Gore, Sheila. *My Shadow*. Photographs by Fiona Pragoff. Doubleday, 1990.

Hoban, Tana. *Shadows and Reflections*. Greenwillow, 1990.

Webb, Angela. *Talkabout Reflections*. Photographs by Chris Fairclough. Watts, 1988.

In the Classroom (or In the Library)

LANGUAGE ARTS I

Ed Young has illustrated two wordless moral tales. Share *The Other Bone* and *Up a Tree* with small groups of students. Compare and contrast the characters and settings. Discuss the moral of each tale. Have students paraphrase the moral of each tale in written form. When all students have completed their written work, have class members share their writings with the class. Discuss the similarities and differences in the students' work.

RELATED MATERIALS

Young, Ed. *Up a Tree*. Harper & Row, 1983.

LIBRARY RESEARCH

The dog in this fable dreams about a bone, finds a bone, and is ready to get in a fight to get another bone. Have a class discussion on dogs and bones: Why do dogs like bones? Why do they bury their bones? How do they know where they buried their bones? Can a dog be given any type of bone to chew? On the chalkboard list the questions and note the various responses to each question. Have students work in groups to see if they can locate accurate answers to the questions. They need to be able to cite references to library resources for their answers. When all groups have completed their research, ask one question at a time and have the groups report in turn on their findings for that question. Are group answers the same or different from the answers originally discussed? Do all groups have the same answers?

LANGUAGE ARTS II

As the dog dreams about finding and chewing a bone, she becomes very active in her dream. After sharing the story, go back to those pictures and have students think about watching their own pets when they appear to be dreaming. Have they noticed their animals move or make sounds when they were asleep as though they were actively taking part in a dream? What could their pet be dreaming of? Have students write about their pets and a dream that their pet might have. They need to indicate the type of pet and the pet's name and might include an illustration of the pet as it sleeps and dreams. Create a bulletin board of "Pet Dreams."

LANGUAGE ARTS III

The dog in this fable loses her bone because she thinks she sees another dog with a bone. She doesn't realize that she is seeing her own reflection. How does this story compare to the saying, "Don't judge a book by its cover"? Encourage students to discuss situations where they have misjudged a person or a situation based on appearances, or situations that could occur. When we see a person who is dressed in dirty, old, torn clothes, is he or she necessarily a bum? Could that person be a physician or dentist who has been working on her or his car?

LITERATURE STUDY

Fables are brief narratives that take abstract ideas and attempt to make those ideas concrete so they will be understood and remembered. The main character in most fables is an animal or inanimate object that behaves like a human and has one dominant trait. The single action of the narrative points to an obvious moral lesson. There are four major groups of fables. Aesop's fables are known to the English-speaking world, and the fables of La Fontaine are known to the French. The Panchatantra and the Jatakas are two collections from India.

Students in grades 4-6 can learn to appreciate the humor and wisdom of fables as they become aware that the lessons apply to all humans. Have students examine fable collections and picture books that illustrate a single fable. Have each student select one fable to tell to the class, omitting the moral. How close does the class come to supplying the moral?

Appendix A
Author Birthdates

This chart can be used to develop monthly author studies or to celebrate an author's birthday. Birthdates were not available for all of the authors included in this book.

January
18 — Raymond Briggs

February
 5 — David Wiesner
20 — Tana Hoban

March
11 — Ezra Jack Keats
17 — Sara
20 — Mitsumasa Anno

April
 1 — Peter Collington
 8 — Susan Bonners

June
 6 — Peter Spier
 7 — John S. Goodall
18 — Pat Hutchins
25 — Eric Carle
26 — Lynd Ward

July
 1 — Emily McCully
30 — Pat Schories

August
15 — Brinton Turkle

September
 4 — Craig Brown
 7 — Alexandra Day
15 — Tomie dePaola
23 — Jan Ormerod

October
 8 — Janice Skivington

November
 2 — Jeannie Baker
28 — Ed Young

December
30 — Mercer Mayer

Appendix B
Author Geography

Wordless picture books are an international genre easily translated from country to country. This chart is organized by country and includes where the authors were born and where they currently live. Specific cities are included if known.

Australia
Jeannie Baker — current home
Jan Ormerod — born in Bunbury

Belgium
Claude Dubois — born in Liège; current home

China
Ed Young — born in Tientsin

Denmark
Henrik Drescher — birthplace

England
Jeannie Baker — birthplace
Raymond Briggs — born in London; current home in Sussex
Nick Butterworth — current home in Suffolk
Peter Collington — born in Northcotes
Philippe Dupasquier — current home
John S. Goodall — born in Heacham in Norfolk; current home in Tisbury, Wiltshire
Alastair Graham — current home in Warwickshire
Pat Hutchins — born in Yorkshire; current home in London
Jan Ormerod — current home in Cambridge
Cliff Wright — current home in Newhaven

France
Tana Hoban — current home in Paris
Sara — born in Nantes; current home in Paris

Italy
Ermanno Cristini — birthplace; current home in Varese
Mario Mariotti — birthplace; current home in Florence
Luigi Puricelli — birthplace; current home in Varese

Japan
Mitsumasa Anno — born in Tsuwano; current home in Tokyo

The Netherlands
Peter Spier — born in Amsterdam

Switzerland
Philippe Dupasquier — birthplace

United States
Arkansas
Mercer Mayer — born in Little Rock

California
Alexandra Day — current home in San Diego

Colorado
Craig Brown — current home in Colorado Springs
Pat Skivington — birthplace

Connecticut
Tomie dePaola — born in Meriden
Mercer Mayer — current home in Bridgeport

Illinois
Susan Bonners — born in Chicago
Emily McCully — born in Galesburg
Pat Skivington — current home in Wheaton
Lynd Ward — born in Chicago

Iowa
Craig Brown — born in Tama

Maryland
Robin Michal Koontz—born in Wheaton

Massachusetts
Eric Carle—current home in Northhampton

Montana
Lark Carrier—birthplace

New Hampshire
Tomie dePaola—current home in New London

New Jersey
Lynd Ward—current home
David Wiesner—born in Bridgewater

New York
Eric Carle—born in Syracuse
Henrik Drescher—current home in New York
  City

Ezra Jack Keats—born in Brooklyn
Emily McCully—current home in Brooklyn
Pat Schories—current home in Cold Springs
Peter Spier—current home in Shoreham
Brinton Turkle—current home in New York City
David Wiesner—current home in Brooklyn
Ed Young—current home in New York City

Ohio
Pat Schories—birthplace
Brinton Turkle—born in Alliance

Oregon
Kathleen Bullock—current home in Ashland
Robin Michal Koontz—current home in Noti

Pennsylvania
Tana Hoban—born in Philadelphia

Rhode Island
Susan Bonners—current home in Providence

Appendix C
Addresses for Nonprint Resources

American School Publishers
Macmillan/McGraw-Hill
155 North Wacker Drive, P.O. Box 4520
Chicago, IL 60680-4520

Churchill Media
A Division of Churchill Films, Inc.
12210 Nebraska Avenue
Los Angeles, CA 90025

Encyclopedia Britannica Educational Corporation
425 North Michigan Avenue
Chicago, IL 60611

Great Plains National Instructional Television Library
University of Nebraska — Lincoln
P.O. Box 80669
Lincoln, NE 68501-0669

Guidance Associates
Communications Park
Box 3000
Mt. Kisko, NY 10549

JTG of Nashville (for Caldecott Puzzles)
1024-C 18th Avenue South
Nashville, TN 37212

Kidstamps
P.O. Box 18699
Cleveland Heights, OH 44118

Learning Corporation of America
4640 Lankershim Boulevard
Suite 600
North Hollywood, CA 91602

Listening Library
One Park Avenue
Old Greenwich, CT 06870-1272

Live Oak Media
P.O. Box 34
Ancramdale, NY 12503

National Film Board of Canada Film Library
c/o Karol Media
22 Riverview Drive
Wayne, NJ 07470-3190

Random House/McGraw-Hill
McGraw-Hill Educational Resources
Box 408
Hightstown, NJ 08520

Society for Visual Education, Inc. (SVE)
1345 Diversey Parkway
Chicago, IL 60614

Texture Films
1600 Broadway
New York, NY 10019

Troll Associates
100 Corporate Drive
Mahwah, NJ 07498-0025

View-Master Video
102 Mineola Boulevard
Mineola, NY 11501

Walt Disney Educational Media
108 Wilmot Road
Deerfield, IL 60015

Weston Woods Studio
389 Newtown Turnpike
Weston, CT 06883-1199

WJ Fantasy
955 Connecticut Avenue
Bridgeport, CT 06607

Photograph Credits from Section 1

Individual Author Studies

Photograph of Mitsumasa Anno courtesy of Mitsumasa Anno and reproduced with his permission.

Photograph of Alexandra Day by Erin Spencer, reproduced with permission of Alexandra Day.

Photograph of Tomie dePaola by Jon Gilbert Fox, copyright Jon Gilbert Fox. Reproduced with permission of Tomie dePaola.

Photograph of John S. Goodall courtesy of John S. Goodall and reproduced with his permission.

Photograph of Tana Hoban courtesy of Tana Hoban and reproduced with her permission.

Photograph of Mario Mariotti courtesy of Mario Mariotti and reproduced with his permission.

Photograph of Mercer Mayer courtesy of Mercer Mayer and reproduced with his permission.

Photograph of Emily Arnold McCully courtesy of Emily Arnold McCully and reproduced with her permission.

Photograph of Peter Spier courtesy of Peter Spier and reproduced with his permission.

Photograph of David Wiesner courtesy of David Wiesner and reproduced with his permission.

About the Authors

KATHARYN TUTEN-PUCKETT

Katharyn Tuten-Puckett holds the degree of Education Specialist in Language Education from Indiana University. She also has a master's in reading education from Boise State University (Idaho) and a master's in library science from California State University, San Jose. Katharyn has a wide range of experience in schools and libraries. She has worked as an elementary school library-media specialist in California and Idaho, taught high school English and developmental reading in Idaho, and taught graduate and undergraduate classes in children's literature and library science at Boise State University, Indiana State University, and Indiana University. Katharyn is currently library coordinator for the public school system in the Commonwealth of the Northern Mariana Islands.

VIRGINIA H. RICHEY

Virginia H. Richey holds the degree of Master of Library Science from Indiana University. She also has a bachelor of arts degree from Centre College of Kentucky. Virginia has worked in public libraries since 1969 in Louisville, Kentucky, and Bloomington, Indiana. She has worked for 17 years in children's services and is currently head of the Children's Department at Monroe County Public Library. She has taught graduate classes in children's literature and library services for children part-time for 14 years. She is active in the Indiana Library Federation, the local chapter of the International Reading Association, and is a founding member of the Bloomington Storyteller's Guild.

Katharyn and Virginia have coauthored several articles on early literacy and wordless picture books as well as *Wordless/Almost Wordless Picture Books: A Guide*, published by Libraries Unlimited in spring 1992.